HOW TO JUG A HARE

Sarah Rainey is a features writer for *The Telegraph*. She writes on a range of issues, from popular culture to history, fashion, health, politics, gender and the royal family – but, mostly, she writes about her favourite subject: food.

Her foodie achievements including making a cake for *The Great British Bake Off*'s Mary Berry and Paul Hollywood, attempting the *Masterchef* invention test and whipping up 339 traybakes in a single weekend.

Originally from Northern Ireland, Sarah studied Law and lived in Madrid before settling in a small flat in south-east London with her fiancé, a collection of withered tomato plants and an overflowing larder. She throws more dinner parties than she can afford and is inspired by her Cordon Bleu trained, chef extraordinaire mother.

Bee Wilson writes 'The Kitchen Thinker' food column for *The Sunday Telegraph*'s *Stella* magazine, for which she has been named food journalist of the year three times by the Guild of Food Writers. She also contributes book reviews to *The Sunday Telegraph* and other newspapers, and is the author of four books on the history of food.

HOW TO JUG A HARE

The Telegraph
BOOK *of* *the* KITCHEN

Edited by Sarah Rainey
Foreword by Bee Wilson

Aurum
Press

First published in Great Britain
2015 by Aurum Press Ltd
74—77 White Lion Street
Islington
London N1 9PF
www.aurumpress.co.uk

ISBN 978 1 78131 423 4
ebook ISBN 978 1 78131 466 1

1 3 5 7 9 10 8 6 4 2
2015 2017 2019 2018 2016

Typeset in Fournier by SX Composing DTP, Rayleigh, Essex
Printed and bound by CPI Group (UK) Ltd, Croydon, CR0 4YY

Contents

PART TWO: SUMMER

Foreword

Bee Wilson

Fanny Cradock had strong views on fruit, as she did on so much else. On 23 June 1970, the colourful TV cook's 'Bon Viveur' column in the *Daily Telegraph* – co-written with husband Johnnie – was headlined 'Simply, Strawberries'. Berries were best unadorned, Cradock proclaimed, assuming, that is, that certain – rather fierce – rules were obeyed. Where a modern recipe writer might worry about how to buy a variety of strawberries that were sweet enough, and not bland or mushy, Cradock was more concerned with the cream and the sugar. 'Let us serve them with cream and sugar, but let the cream be farm fresh and not that absolutely tasteless shop stuff which has to be tiddled up (otherwise all it provides is density) and let the sugar be that pale, beige, sand-textured...sugar which anyone can get if they *try*.'

The person reading this feels admonished. Note to self: try harder when buying cream and sugar.

But Cradock's strawberry column – which also includes an enticing recipe for choux buns filled with homemade strawberry ice cream – epitomises the particular pleasure and power of newspaper food writing, which is quite unlike that of a cookbook. In essence this hasn't changed much from 1970 to today and can be summed up in a single word: timing. Cookbooks may very well include strawberry recipes but the author has no idea when – if ever – anyone will try them. By contrast, Fanny Cradock knew that, this being two days after midsummer, *Telegraph* readers would already have strawberries on their mind, and be primed for guidance on the matter of cream and sugar. For those unfortunates who had only shop cream and bog-standard caster sugar in the house, she helpfully suggested using them to make an orange sauce, remarking that oranges and strawberries had a 'great affinity'.

Many aspects of the *Telegraph* food pages have been transformed over the years, as the book in your hands vividly reminds us. There is not so much talk these days of 'housewives' and the problems they face at the fishmonger, a subject of debate in 1937. Quinoa, lime and coriander feature far more often than in the past; and jugged hare, less so. Nor do you see articles on 'fare for convalescents', a subject from 1915, when the First World War made the question of feeding the wounded and the sick a pressing concern. That year, the paper's food correspondent warned that new potatoes could be 'disastrous' to a convalescent, but looked favourably on calves' brains and feet and 'sheep's tongues cooked fresh, and tripe'. Another article, from 1925, recommends a 'marvellous' new food called Marmite as 'specially useful in cases of influenza and severe chill' and even beneficial to 'those troubled with sleeplessness'.

One thing that hasn't changed, however, is the unique power that newspapers have for keeping readers company in the kitchen. Unlike with a cookbook, which doesn't hear you when you scream at it – I am forever getting annoyed with recipes that miss out ingredients, or stipulate the wrong-sized cake tin – a newspaper offers the chance to become part of the cooking conversation. Just this week, I had a letter from a reader complaining that I was an idiot for thinking it was possible to make Yorkshire pudding with oil when, obviously, only beef dripping would do. Since the early days, *Telegraph* readers have also contributed their own recipes.

These readers' teatime recipes appeared in October, when 'the return to the fireside gives new importance to teatime entertaining', as the food editor put it. The great advantage of writing – almost – in real time is the ability to respond to the changes in the food calendar as they happen, whether it's the yearly transition from summer to autumn or larger changes in dietary habits. In 1980, Marika Hanbury-Tenison, the *Sunday Telegraph* cook for many years, said: 'People always ask me how I manage to think up something to say week after week.' I regularly get asked the same question about my 'Kitchen Thinker' column in *Stella*, and my answer would echo Tenison's, who said: 'My problem is that I have too much to say...every single day I make some discovery working in my kitchen that I feel must be shared.'

One of the areas that food has changed most dramatically over the paper's history is in technology. As kitchens modernised, the paper's food writers have tried to make sense of such puzzling new developments as the fridge, the three-tiered steamer and the microwave. Such a 'revolutionary new way of cooking does have its mysteries', warned Ann Chubb in 1983, before recommending some terracotta-coloured plastic dishes and a cooking course at the 'microwave cookery school' in London.

The newspaper medium encourages a taking of the temperature of where we stand on certain matters: a standard setting for such questions as the ethics of veal, the virtues (or otherwise) of low-fat cooking and a decision as to whether ready-made marzipan is ever acceptable. In 1982, in a column on Simnel cake, Denis Curtis was more tactful than Fanny Cradock had been on the question of 'shop cream', but still made his preference for home-made marzipan quite clear. 'You can buy very good pure almond paste ready made,' he began, 'but for this cake pound 1 lb sweet almonds till quite smooth with a little rose water. Mix in ½lb icing sugar and as much beaten egg as will bind it.'

The food pages have also been the ideal place to explore changing tastes in cuisine. Again, it's about timing, as certain ingredients – and indeed whole countries – pass in and out of favour. In 1931, X. M. Boulestin was urging *Telegraph* readers to eat the 'natural' and 'balanced' diet of the French, for the sake of health as well as pleasure (before giving a recipe for chicken and foie gras in pastry). The current *Telegraph* food sections feature extraordinary recipes from globe-trotting chefs, especially from Diana Henry and Stevie Parle, who plunder the world for the most intense flavours, from Scandinavia to Korea. Their writing continues in the tradition of Claudia Roden, who introduced readers to all manner of 'foreign food'.

It's a big leap to choose to buy a whole book of recipes from Turkey, say (though if you change your mind, try Ghillie Başan), but newspaper food writing gives you none of that heavy feeling of 'I really ought to cook this, and this, and this' that sometimes descends when perusing one of the latest cookery 'bibles'. You open a newspaper in a different, more casual frame of mind. Recipes appear as a bonus, or a gift. No obligation.

You are free to tear out and keep the things that catch your eye and discard the rest.

Newspapers have a curious ability to be both ephemeral and permanent. Although they belong to a particular moment, the torn-out recipes that you keep are often referred back to for years, if not decades. Most good cooks I know have a store of dog-eared treasures from weekend supplements, either stuffed in the end pages of a cookbook or — if they are organised — laminated and filed away. I've noticed that the most cherished are those that relate most strongly to the passing of the seasons: a stash of damson recipes for the autumn, say, or hearty puddings for the winter. The *Telegraph* recipes I have clipped the most — by a long way — are Christmas ones: Tamasin Day-Lewis's mincemeat, Rowley Leigh's bread sauce, Diana Henry's perfect crunchy roast potatoes. Christmas seems to arrive sooner every year. There is always the turkey to roast — or an alternative feast to dream up — the pudding to make, the sprouts to cook in such a way that the festive mood is not dented. It is now that food writers can offer just what you are looking for. It's timing, again. I'd never have dared to brine my turkey in a bucket had I not read Elisabeth Luard describing it in the *Sunday Telegraph* magazine at the very moment I was fretting about serving up dry meat to my in-laws. Since then, I've abandoned the brining method, but that's another story. Luard was there for me when it counted.

What the following pages contain is not just a collection of period comedy food — though there is always vintage amusement to be had reading about the likes of spam and fake eggs. It is a series of writers — some famous such as Elizabeth David or Fanny Cradock, many anonymous like 'Home Cook', the food writer for the *Daily Telegraph and Morning Post,* as it was then called — trying to help their readers to eat and cook better at that particular moment in their own kitchens.

Many summers have passed since the one in 1970 when Fanny wrote about strawberries. It's become easier to buy beige sugar (yes!) and harder to buy farm-fresh cream (no!). The strawberry season has extended from a few brief weeks in the summer to nine months of the year. Many *Telegraph* readers have migrated online and view their recipes cleanly on a screen, rather than with inky fingers on the page. But some things remain: you may still arrive home with a punnet of strawberries one hot day and find, to your delight, that someone has written something in the paper telling you exactly what to do with them.

Introduction

'The kitchen is the great laboratory of the household and much of the "weal and woe", as far as regards bodily health, depends on the nature of the preparations concocted within its walls.'

Isabella Beeton, *Mrs Beeton's Book of Household Management* (1861)

The kitchen, as the saying goes, is the heart of the home. Here is a place of family, of cooking side by side, dining together and sharing the washing-up. Here is a place of alchemy and transformations. Here, too, is a place of nostalgia, of childhood favourites and long-gone grandparents, and recipes passed down through generations. A place of toil and devotion, of care and patience, of solace and escape, of frustration and joy. Most important of all, here is a place of passion, where emotions can run higher than in any other room in the house.

In Italy, there is a popular proverb: 'Even a small kitchen makes a house big'. Whatever place the kitchen occupies in your home, it will no doubt be a significant one. As the beating heart – or Mrs Beeton's 'great laboratory' – of every household up and down the country, it is the kitchen's role to nourish the family; to keep us healthy, happy and well-fed every day of our lives.

Since its very first edition in 1855, the *Daily Telegraph* has recognised the importance of the kitchen – and everything associated with it – to its readers. Food writing, cookery tips, recipes, restaurant reviews, interviews with chefs; all have been an integral part of the newspaper ever since. Over nearly 160 years, its kitchen content has grown, too, into the heart of the *Telegraph*. It has employed some of the country's greatest cookery writers, delighting readers with their avant-garde serving suggestions and delicious dinner party ideas; it has visited some of the finest restaurants in the world, tasting exotic delicacies most of us could only dream of; and it has, day after day, celebrated every aspect of food, from the mundane to the majestic, the calm to the chaotic, the simple to the sublime.

It will come as no surprise, then, to know that the *Telegraph*'s archives are quite comprehensively well stuffed when it comes to all things kitchen. Delving into 160 years' worth of food writing would be, I feared, when this project was first suggested, a mammoth task. In the mere five years I have been at the newspaper – the recent ones spent moonlighting as the *Telegraph*'s 'baking correspondent' – I have been overwhelmed by both the writers' and the readers' fascination with food. Most days, there is at least one full broadsheet page dealing with everything edible – be this the latest trends in kitchenware or a shortage of some vegetable or another, or the latest happenings on *The Great British Bake Off*. And that's just the daily paper. At the weekend, the *Telegraph*'s obsession really comes to the fore – with magazines and supplements brimming with recipes from cherished columnists, reviews of the latest restaurants and page after page of mouthwatering words about our favourite subject: food, glorious food.

Well stuffed, it turned out, was a gross underestimation. The *Telegraph*'s archives are positively groaning with kitchen-related material. Right from the very beginning, through two world wars, rationing, shortages, strikes, technological advances, inventions, imports, exports and changing tastes, one constant has remained: *Telegraph* readers' insatiable appetite for food writing in every shape and form. I started my quest, in the spring of 2014, armed with little else but curiosity and a list of forty-three topics which I hoped might guide me to some of the most interesting archive material. I finished it umpteen months later – my weekends spent at the office photocopier, hands blackened with newspaper print, squinting through faded pages from a century ago for a glimmer of something useful – sharing utterly in their gluttony. It was a long, laborious journey, but a wonderful one.

Before I take you on that journey, here are some of the things I learnt along the way. First: the *Telegraph* has, since its inception, had a bizarre yet unwavering passion for pancakes. No Shrove Tuesday has passed without a recipe appearing for drop scones, crêpes or American-style treats with maple syrup – and over the years I counted no fewer than 178 pancake-related items in the newspaper. Bourguignon, too, has enjoyed a plethora of coverage through the decades – and not just beef: *Oeufs à la Bourguignonne* was a favourite of *Telegraph* food columnist and national treasure Fanny Cradock (more of whom later) and *Fondue Bourguignonne* has appeared many times in these pages.

Meat is another favourite; when I asked to see the archive material indexed under this topic, I wasn't prepared for the seventeen bulging files that arrived in a box so heavy I could barely lift it. It was, however, worth it: there were insightful parallels with the recent horse meat debacle in the great 'kangaroo scandal' of 1981, when knackers' yards were raided for cheap meat, which was then sold at a mark-up by dodgy butchers. I learned, too, how to jug a hare, how to cook reindeer, how to make a pie keep its crust, and why goat meat was used during the Second World War, according to a rationing announcement in 1942. The construction of the 18ft Denby Dale pie of 1964 was another highlight, as was the lament on the decline of the once great British classic: 'bangers and mash'.

The *Telegraph*'s long, appreciative association with the kitchen can be traced right back to its beginnings. Between the years 1855 and 1899, the newspaper was, however, primarily focused on crime reporting – and so food content was relegated to a footnote in news stories, with updates on market prices, shortages and the ebb and flow of local and international eateries. It wasn't until 9 April 1899, with the advent of 'A Page for Women', that food writing became a component of the paper in its own right. 'A Sunday Lunch – by A Careful Cook' was the first incarnation of a *Telegraph* recipe: comprising *Consommé* à la Royale, *Poulet Portugais* and Chocolate Mousse. 'Greatly, I fear, to the disgust of our domestics, the practice of dining late on Sundays is ever on the increase,' wrote the anonymous columnist, 'but if things are properly arranged ... there is really no scope for complaint.'

For the next eighty-seven years, the Women's Page continued, in various guises and with variable regularity – and it was here that the *Telegraph*'s kitchen content was born, flourished, and eventually began to migrate to other parts of the newspaper. The offerings were rich and diverse: from daily advice to musings on the merits of French cooking;

reviews of recipe books and restaurants, to tips for wedding catering; letters from readers and reports from food conventions to celebrations of meals and ingredients: breakfast, blackberries, cheese, jam-making, haggis and Marmite, to name but a few.

Much of the writing was anonymous, penned by 'A Careful Cook' or the '*Daily Telegraph* Home Cook', but from around 1920 onwards, food writers began to include their names. They were, of course, all female, with the notable exception of London-based French chef and restaurateur Xavier Marcel Boulestin, a major influence on Elizabeth David (more of whom, too, later), who was persuaded to write a seminal 'Lesson in French Cookery' for the Women's Page on 4 February 1931. 'We never hear in France all these sermons on vitamins, calories and the like, because the French people of all classes eat as a matter of course this or that food which they grow or buy,' he chastised. 'They do this instinctively, like a cat, who, feeling out of sorts, eats a blade of grass in the garden. Teaching dietetic values is a poor inducement to eat, and it is treating a pleasant and normal function as if it were an acquired habit or a disease.'

This attitude was to set the tone for the Women's Page for the foreseeable future. For although many column inches were, inevitably, devoted to diets and slimming techniques – 'Soups for Slimming', 'Willpower Dieting', 'A Diet for Mrs Average' – the emphasis tended far more towards the celebration of food; and not its avoidance. Elsie Wetherell was one of the first named kitchen experts in the *Telegraph*, from the early 1920s to early 1930s, publishing home-baking recipes – 'Teatime Dainties' and 'Favourite Puddings' – beloved of housewives nationwide. In later years, her role was filled by other notable names: Claire Butler, Winifred Carr, and the Women's Page editor, Evelyn Garrett.

Readers would write, avidly, to the editor of this page, to express grievances, submit recipes and request agony-aunt style guidance on matters of the kitchen. Such letters – marked 'Cookery' and posted to *The* Daily Telegraph *Office, 135 Fleet Street, EC4* – provide cheering insights into the daily lives of housewives, such as the following one on 10 August 1905, entitled 'Thriftless Wives'. 'It is essential that the kitchen should be bright and clean,' writes Mrs Bertha B, of London SW. 'An airy, cheerful room, with smokeless fires, no unnecessary corners, no pipes all over the walls, nor fixed cupboards to harbour dirt and hidden things... Given these conditions, what is to prevent the courageous

Englishwoman donning an apron and rolling up her sleeves . . . There are many wholesome and cheap dishes which give very little trouble to make. To learn young the secrets and mysteries of "cuisine" is the best way. Let not Englishmen grumble over much if their wives cook badly, but think how they have been spared the risk of overeating and red noses.'

During the two world wars, the *Telegraph*'s food coverage, as expected, abated – to be replaced with news of rationing, prices and availability of fresh fruit, vegetables, bread and meat. The Women's Page remained, irregularly, providing advice on cooking fare for convalescents; home tests to see if milk had been watered down or coffee 'faked'; preserving tips; recipes using all manner of substitutes; and practical advice for feeding a family in times of need. In 1941, the *Telegraph* published *Good Fare*, a book of nutritious wartime recipes designed to help readers use up their home-grown food, make meat go a long way and cook with cheap, unfamiliar cuts. In 1944, *Good Eating* followed, collating readers' recipes for wartime dishes: omelettes made with dried eggs, mock fish pie made from artichokes, marrow compote, meat mayonnaise and bramble jelly.

As ever, the readers – and their hearty, industrious kitchens – were at the heart of the *Telegraph*'s dedication to cookery. 'It is to the home cooks rather than the food specialists and the scientists that we must now look for the most practical and pleasing solutions of new problems,' the foreword to *Good Eating*, written by the *Daily Telegraph* Home Cook, reads. 'Day by day they are conducting, quietly in their own kitchens, painstaking, purposeful research, producing the attractive fare that will constitute the basis of post-war cookery. In this way, they are mastering a new technique.'

Post-war, the *Telegraph*'s kitchen coverage was dominated by one person and her ferocious, no-nonsense personality: Fanny Cradock. Having published her first recipe book, *The Practical Cook*, in 1949, Fanny caught the eye of the *Telegraph*'s Women's Page editor, who asked her to come on board – not as a cookery writer, as the newspaper already had one of those – but as a travelling reviewer, along with her husband, Johnnie. As Fanny later wrote, the conversation went as follows: 'It's simply a series I think might hold up for six weeks,' said Evelyn Garrett. 'We'd pay expenses, of course. I want you to find out if there is anything left that is worthwhile in the inns of England.' 'What sort of anything?' asked Fanny. 'A warm welcome, honest fare, integrity, Fanny, if it still survives,' was the reply.

Fanny proposed the name 'Bon Viveur' for the couple's column – and what began as a tentative experiment blossomed into a five-year voyage of discovery for Fanny and her put-upon husband. It was so widely read that, on one occasion at the Royal Festival Hall, the Queen Mother confided to Fanny that she 'occasionally' read her articles and believed they were 'largely responsible' for raising standards of British catering. Fanny was so startled that she forgot to curtsey.

An indomitable character – she had been widowed at seventeen and slogged her way up the career ladder, washing-up in canteens and selling vacuum cleaners door to door – Fanny relished her eventual success. During the early 1950s, she and Johnnie (who occasionally wrote solo about wine for the newspaper) opined on everything from Yorkshire pudding to kippers, marmalade to double Gloucester, and she is credited with inspiring many readers to properly embrace home cooking. Her personality was too big to be contained in newsprint alone, and the *Telegraph* was soon staging nationwide roadshows, entitled 'Kitchen Magic', for her to showcase her talent and flair.

The archives swell with colourful, often controversial, Bon Viveur columns, each one encapsulating a fragment of that forceful Fanny Cradock appeal. Though she briefly left the *Telegraph*, between 1955 and 1959, Fanny returned to the fold and continued to write during her TV career until the early 1980s, churning out cookbooks, lamenting the 'dawn of couscous parties', 'carping about cabbage', and giving thanks for 'the best friends of a working woman – a three-tiered steamer and a casserole dish'. This volume would have been incomplete without a chapter on her witticisms.

It was thanks to Fanny and Johnnie that the *Telegraph* struck up a relationship with another of its great kitchen writers: the Hungarian-born critic Egon Ronay. His French restaurant Marquee, a former tea room near Harrods in London, had been praised by Bon Viveur and he appeared as an expert at one of the Cradocks' live shows. Win Frizell (nom de plume of Winifred Carr), reporting on the show for the Women's Page, recalled a tension between the two greats: 'He was a bit of a tart with her. One day, she was going on about making this stockpot. "Everything goes into it," she said, "scraps of meat, bones." And Egon piped up: "I'd hate to be a dog in Fanny's kitchen." She turned on him like a tiger and said: "I wouldn't have you in my kitchen."'

Despite their sparring, Ronay was taken on by the *Telegraph* in the late 1950s and wrote successfully for the paper for many years, including his 'Out and About' series and a hugely popular guide to feeding a family of four for elevenpence. While Fanny, who died in 1994, was very much a mouthpiece for housewives, Ronay's focus was on Britain's 'culinary scene', and some of his finest writing covered topics such as the Frenchification of London's restaurants, the rise of so-called 'eating clubs', and why every good dinner party requires hors d'oeuvres. In 1957, on the back of his *Telegraph* fame, he published *Egon Ronay's Guide to British Eateries*, which sold 30,000 copies and was a precursor to the modern AA Guide. Like Fanny, Ronay was a unique character: gregarious, always impeccably dressed, steadfastly refusing to reveal his age. Somewhat ironically, his favourite food was an undercooked omelette, topped with cheese sauce and browned under the grill.

Restaurant reviews and essays on eating out have been the backbone of the *Telegraph*'s food coverage over the years, and it was here, indeed, that many cookery writers cut their teeth. Gretel Beer, the celebrated cook and for a time the Women's Page editor of the newspaper, bemoaned the perplexing language of restaurant menus for diners in an article in September 1966. 'It seems strange,' she wrote, 'that when the laws concerning the labelling of packet and canned food are getting stricter, the "poetic licence" granted to restaurant owners appears to be unlimited.'

The great American chef, Robert Carrier, contributor to the food pages from 1967 onwards, also featured frequently in the paper as a restaurant reviewer and kitchen oracle. 'The right blend of simple food cooked to perfection and carefully matched to your guests is the secret of success,' he wrote in November 1977. 'No gimmicks needed.'

The *Telegraph*, on the other hand, had to keep up with the changing pace in the world of cookery. The arrival of newfangled kitchen equipment and technology was treated in these pages with a mixture of concern, confusion and practical advice. From the invention of the domestic refrigerator in the early 1900s, to the advent of home freezing in the 1960s and the befuddling arrival of the microwave the following decade, the *Telegraph*'s team of expert writers was ever on hand to advise readers on how to handle the latest home helper. 'So many people have asked me what I feel about microwave ovens that I felt it was time to get one in my kitchen,' wrote Marika Hanbury-Tenison, the feted cookery editor of the *Sunday Telegraph* from 1968 until her death in 1982. '"This oven," the demonstrator told me, "is so simple to use that I have just sold one to a blind person."' She, it must be noted, felt rather more at ease with it than Fanny, who wrote just one year later: 'We approached our new microwave oven with the trepidation of two people returning to a reactor station after a leak.'

No one was a more familiar and comforting guide through this strange new world than Elizabeth David, the doyenne of British cookery writers. As a contributor to the *Telegraph* in the 1960s and 1970s, David – who introduced a generation of home chefs to Mediterranean fare and ran a cooks' equipment shop in Pimlico, south London – explained simple, everyday techniques through stories from her own experiences. David paved the way for other notable names – the inestimable Mary Berry (who started her career, and was featured in the newspaper, as an Aga tester) and writer Alice Hope.

It was important, too, for the newspaper to keep up with transforming tastes in food. As wartime make-do meals made way for imports from foreign shores, dishes became ever more different from the simple fare featured on the Women's Page in 1899. British diners first developed a fondness for French food, then Italian, Spanish, American, South African, Australian, Turkish, Japanese, Chinese, Indian, Thai – and beyond. Material in the *Telegraph*'s archives charts our growing appetite for, and desire to emulate, delicacies from around the globe. The rise of fast food, takeaways and ready meals has also been chronicled, as has the recent resurgence of afternoon tea and the popularity of brunch.

As trends came and went, and food fads went in and out of fashion, so did the *Telegraph*'s cast of writers on the subject. Denis Curtis was the *Sunday Magazine*'s food writer from the late 1970s to the mid 1980s, and his 'Thought for Food' column – a potted personal story followed by a sliver of a seasonal recipe, which was made into a book in 1982 – gained him a loyal fanbase. Josceline Dimbleby (wife of broadcaster David and mother to Henry, founder of the Leon restaurant chain) was the Sunday paper's cookery correspondent for fifteen years; while Claudia Roden, the champion of Middle Eastern food, fulfilled the now-defunct (and much envied) role of 'foreign food correspondent'. Others who have graced the *Telegraph*'s pages include the cookery writer Tamasin Day-Lewis, chef and food campaigner Hugh Fearnley-Whittingstall, and part-MP/part-chef Clement Freud.

More recently still, however, in only the past few decades, our relationship with the kitchen has changed more dramatically than at any other point in history. Cooking has evolved from a mundane necessity to a national pastime. Food is no longer mere nourishment, but a global obsession. Television chefs, from Delia Smith to Jamie Oliver, are idolised like Hollywood superstars; recipe books sell in their millions worldwide; the British baking industry alone is worth £3.4 billion. Programmes such as *MasterChef* and *The Great British Bake Off* have turned the kitchen into a stage and its produce into a spectacle. And we simply can't get enough.

With such global wealth riding on food, its place in national newspapers has been elevated to reflect readers' demand. No longer buried away on the Women's Page, nor the exclusive preserve of housewives, nowadays cookery is the jewel in the *Telegraph*'s crown. Week after week, the newspaper partners with top chefs to publish recipe supplements; its online food section, complete with videos and how-to guides, is one of the website's most popular; and its cookery writers – Diana Henry, Bee Wilson, Stevie Parle, Xanthe Clay and Rose Prince, to name but a few – are known nationwide. The lowly kitchen, it seems, has become a powerhouse.

Yet, though much has changed, some things will always be the same – as my research revealed. You'll be glad to hear that we still love puddings, the spongier and more custard-topped, the better. We're still struggling to find the best dinner party menu – essentially the same article appears in both 1947 and 1997, neither of them providing a solution. We're still pondering the perfect Christmas pudding, wondering what to put in our children's lunch boxes, taking comfort in crumpets, struggling with sauces and dunking digestives in our tea. Familiarity in such perennial issues will no doubt pervade the *Telegraph*'s food archives for another 160 years – and beyond.

The journalist A. J. Liebling once said, in documenting the cuisine of Paris: 'The primary requisite for writing well about food is a good appetite.' It is also, I believe, the primary requisite for reading about food. And so, as you make your way through the pages to come, I hope you will enjoy this snapshot of kitchen history from the annals of the *Telegraph*, and do so feeling much the way I did as I compiled it: enlightened, educated, entertained – and, above all, very, very hungry.

Sarah Rainey,
Spring 2015

SPRING

A Dash of David

27 September 1960
101 YEARS ON – AND STILL
'MRS B' IS QUEEN OF THE COOKS
Alice Hope

Isabella Beeton little knew what she was starting when, 101 years ago, she and her husband Sam put an advertisement in the *Daily Telegraph* announcing their monthly magazine called *Household Management*. Isabella died when she was 28, but she has had as profound an influence on the British home as any politician.

And this influence is still present. Next month a new centenary edition of Mrs Beeton's *Household Management* will appear – 1,344 pages of it between a washable cover, which is something Isabella never dreamed of.

Although there have from time to time been abridged versions of 'Mrs B' this is the first time since 1950 that a complete volume, as extensive as the first, has appeared.

As for the original, there are few copies left now and even the publishers, Ward Lock, who have been associated with Mrs Beeton right from the beginning, have only one rather battered book. Their records and around a million books were all burned during the war on the night when fire ringed St Paul's.

It has taken 58 contributors five years to complete the new Mrs Beeton. The preserves section alone took two years; one year was necessary for the complete cycle of fruits, and another to see how the preserves kept.

As I myself have contributed a section on the home, I feel I can claim to have watched it grow.

Isabella's original book came out in 3d monthly parts until it was eventually published as one splendid volume, divided into 46 exhaustive chapters from 'The Mistress of the Household', to 'Legal Memoranda' and recipes for everything from The Common Hog to The Calf, The Sheep and The Lamb.

Through the years, Ward Lock have remained the publishers and for 90 years the printing has been done by the same firm, Butler and Tanner.

With millions of others I have always had an affectionate regard for Mrs Beeton. I suppose there are few homes in England where there has not been at some time or another a copy of the book in one or other of its various forms. So that when a crisis arises (like an unexpected brace of grouse) there is a universal call for Mrs Beeton.

When Isabella wrote her book she was coping with all the problems of family life as well as helping her husband in his business. Yet she wrote: 'Every head of a household should strive to be cheerful and never fail to show a deep interest in all that appertains to the well-being of those who claim the protection of her roof. Gentleness, not partial nor temporary, but universal and regular, should pervade her conduct.'

The new book has the same calm, soothing atmosphere. It says: 'Tact and inborn loyalty towards husband, children and staff are constantly required; it is a great mistake to discuss the shortcomings of any member of the household with friends and neighbours.'

The mammoth job of preparing Mrs Beeton has been carried out by a comely Lancashire woman, Mrs Irene Hirst, who is on the publishers' editorial staff. One of a family of nine, Mrs Hirst was born and brought up on her father's smallholding where they dealt with all the chickens, pigs and turkeys in the traditional way.

Many cooks have stirred the broth for the new book, among them Marguerite Patten and Louise Davies and a number of domestic science experts. There is a large section, too, on traditional foreign and Commonwealth recipes from Europe to India and China. Here are some facts about tea from the Chinese section:

Tea in China broadly falls into two categories, red or black tea and green tea. The first is dried over the fire, the second in the sun. One of the green teas is 'Dragon's Well' tea and that which is picked before the rain is best. This is appropriately labelled 'Before the Rain'.

The most expensive China tea is rarely exported. It grows high up on the rocks and monkeys are trained to pick the leaves. So it is called 'Cloud Mist Tea' or 'Monkey Pluck'.

As the Russians are in the news, here is a recipe (for six people) from the foreign section. It sounds just like Khruschev's favourite sweet on gala nights:

> *Vinnoy Krem* (Brandy Cream):
> 1pt double cream;
> 1 wineglass brandy;
> Juice of half a lemon;
> Nutmeg;
> ¼lb sponge fingers

Whip the cream, adding the brandy gradually and the lemon juice. Pile into individual glasses. Grate a little nutmeg on top and put into a refrigerator until ready to serve. Sugar may be beaten into the cream if desired. Serve with sponge fingers.

If this recipe reminds you of the old and totally untrue story of the Mrs Beeton who said 'Take 12 eggs', there is one on another page for Bubble and Squeak.

16 December 1978
A WAY WITH WORDS ON COOKERY
Elizabeth David

A cosy image of a cookery writer may well be of her whisking egg whites for an inspired soufflé in an immaculate kitchen. The reality is more likely to be of somebody stirring about four different mixes for a Christmas pudding in a midsummer heatwave.

Elizabeth David is a high priestess among cookery writers. Her books have been a delight. Say 'French Provincial Cooking', or (her earliest) 'A Book of Mediterranean Food' with woodcut illustrations by John Minton and you get an appreciative 'Aah...Elizabeth David' from women who care about cooking – and indeed from men too.

She is a rather grand lady now and would not dream of writing about cookery in any newspaper or magazine any more – no matter how august. Although some of her loveliest advice was gathered from years in Provence, she says with regret that food in France 'has deteriorated far beyond slightly'. In Britain, she supposed a style was developing but wondered why so many people were 'too ambitious, too pretentious, doing dreadful things to avocados, over-decorating food with tomatoes shaped like flowers, and cream piped on to everything'. Simplicity is her gospel – perfection too.

It would be unthinkable for Elizabeth David to be commercial – or to appear tossing pancakes in a television studio kitchen. She hates giving interviews but agreed to lunch if only to find out the name of the industrialist who I said had told me that he felt she had done more for Britain than many politicians.

Wearing a white woolly hat and a white blouse, Elizabeth David was sitting at her kitchen table sorting through strange old Mediterranean recipes wondering if shrimp and pumpkin soup would be good for a book of Christmas recipes – 'For 1979 you understand. These little books pay for ingredients. I want to get on with research for a book on old Italian cooking – pre-tomato-with-everything.'

You tend to imagine cookery writers as large and ebullient. Elizabeth David is a tiny, frail creature with brown eyes, rosy cheeks and a mouth which looks puckered from too much tasting. Her father was Conservative MP Rupert Gwynne and her grandfather was a Victorian Home Secretary, the first Viscount Ridley. Her mother (a spirited lady who knew nothing about cooking – the servants did it all) decided that her daughter Elizabeth had enough education just as she was about to sit for her school certificate. 'She thought I was getting too hockey-stickish and sent me off to France.' We should be thankful to Mrs Gwynne for steering her daughter towards a long, lyrical love affair with Provence.

Her house in Chelsea which she shares with her sister has a kitchen which bulges with cookery books, pine dressers supporting flame pumpkins, and waxy yellow quinces, baskets of walnuts and shelves of white porcelain pots.

'My job means I have to stay at home and cook a particular dish several times. My ideas are a mixture of old recipes and my own thoughts. Any elation about a recipe is often false, because the next time you do it, it could be quite wrong.'

In that clipped Mitford-type voice, Mrs David thought that culinary disasters were 'awfully depressing – and due to not paying attention'.

A purist about food, Mrs David rarely goes to restaurants. She goes to the Capital in Knightsbridge and simply for their consommé.

Her feeling for food began when she realised that 'if I was to have good food, I would have to cook it myself', she said with a hoarse chuckle.

After years in France, she went to the Middle East where she ran a reference library in Cairo. There was a shortage of ingredients, not to mention cooking pots, and a devoted but erratic Sudanese cook called Suleiman.

Gradually Elizabeth David and Suleiman concocted wonderful 'shining vegetable dishes – lentil or fresh tomato soups, salads with cool mint-flavoured yoghurt dressings and dishes of black beans with olive oil and lemon and hard boiled eggs'.

Her pet hates include – stock cubes, they are simply salt and colour, a complete con; *pommes frites*; avocados stuffed with prawns or crabmeat instead of being served with olive oil (no other will do) and lemon juice.

It would be totally wrong to give the impression that Mrs David is in any way patronising – but she does regret terribly the ill-treatment of quiches.

'Quiches, quiches everywhere. But they bear no relation to those lovely creamy tarts from Alsace and Lorraine. The pastry is unspeakable in what is laughingly called a quiche in this country.'

After the Middle East, Miss David went to Delhi and was married briefly to an Indian Army officer in 1946. It was an unhappy time – 'My husband was in Auchinleck's headquarters and we were not allowed outside Delhi. It was a sad time in India, everyone was terribly grumpy and knew it was the end.'

Post-war 'dustbin cookery' and pathetic cookery articles drove Mrs

David to submit a few suggestions to a friend of hers working on *Harper's Bazaar*. The then editor Miss Anne Scott James was delighted. That was the beginning of a reformation in cooking in England. Women worn by rationing and synthetic food learnt to abandon stodge and serve beautiful food like a tomato salad with chives or tarragon, a beautifully cooked trout and a bowl of apricots.

Mrs David thought one of the main arts of fine cooking was to learn to leave food well alone. Her recipe for salmon trout is so simple – when you have wrapped it in tinfoil with the minimum of fuss 'leave it severely alone for the whole cooking time'.

The restaurant chosen by her for lunch had a delectable Cuisine Minceur-ish menu.

'That whole new wave of cookery in France – the nouvelle cuisine without heavy sauces and flour – is really a revolt by top chefs against mediocre, second-rate cooking. There has been a steady deterioration in France over the past ten or 15 years – all steak and *pommes frites*.'

Her fish soup, the colour of cinnamon, was served with croutons and garlicky sauce. Totally absorbed, as professional as a jeweller examining a diamond or a gardener a rose, Mrs David bent her face to the soup, tasted and sniffed.

There is a likable imperiousness combined with a difference about Mrs David. Evelyn Waugh loved her writings. There is a touch of Sitwell hauteur about her – and the use of the word 'impertinent' to convey disapproval could be hers.

'Jesus Christ, what is that, it really is awfully ugly,' when a pale ice cream was served with a vivid raspberry sauce. The suggestion that it could be served in prettier ways was received impassively by the maître d'hôtel.

'Oh I should hate to run a restaurant, the boredom of it, the monotony,' Mrs David said pronouncing the lunch excellent, though it had prevented her from going to Harrods for some rock salt.

Her main venture into business was the opening of a shop in Bourne Street, under her name, selling kitchen things.

But it ended acrimoniously – 'In 1973 I simply walked out of the shop. I dissociated myself with it completely as soon as they started selling things like ashtrays and tea-towels. Unfortunately my name is still there.'

There is Welsh blood in her veins and this is where she would like a country cottage. She no longer hankers for France – 'Too many sad things have happened there. I want a house in Wales with water.'

She will write academic works on cookery but is rather scathing about the word 'creative'. 'It really is a term flung around – just because you put something down on paper,' but was grudgingly pleased that she might have had some impact – 'it would be lovely if I have reached even a few people'.

Luckily for those of us who try to cook, Mrs David did not continue to be a librarian – or become an actress, which she would have loved. For her part it would make her feel her words have not been in vain if we vowed to treat tomatoes with respect and not add them to everything, use only olive oil and keep food simple.

23 May 1992

OBITUARY: ELIZABETH DAVID

Elizabeth David, the grande dame of the kitchen, who has died aged 78, wrote a remarkable sequence of books in which she transformed previous conceptions of cookery writing in Britain and America.

Her writing was distinguished by its ease and grace, its blend of profound scholarship with practical advice, and a rare ability to convey an unaffected delight in matters of the table.

Even today her books of the 1950s seem wonderfully evocative; to the reader still fettered by the constraints of 10 years of food rationing they provided a window on a larger and an almost magical world, shaping the attitudes and aspirations of a generation.

The publication in 1950 of Mrs David's first work, *A Book of Mediterranean Food* (revised 1988), was greeted with the joyous enthusiasm accorded to those who touch a tender nerve in the national consciousness. That the ingredients in her recipes – eggs, butter, fine seafood, meat, poultry and game, tomatoes, pimentos, almonds, figs, melons – were often difficult, or impossible, to obtain at the time, augmented rather than diminished her impact.

Her recipes for herb and garlic-scented stews, flavoured with olive oil and wine, sent ripples of nostalgic delight through austerity-ridden Britain.

Suddenly, through Mrs David's enlightened eye, beleaguered Britons were shown the sunshine at the end of the tunnel; how, with the gates of Europe once more open, they might eat and live.

Mrs David's cookery books have earned their place on kitchen shelves from the Outer Hebrides to Tasmania. They had immediate universal appeal, both as kitchen manuals that became thumbed and sauce-spattered with use, and for their incisive prose.

Of Sussex landed stock, she was born Elizabeth Gwynne on Boxing Day 1913. Her father, Rupert Gwynne, was a barrister, MP for Eastbourne and briefly a junior minister at the War Office; her mother, Stella, was the second daughter of the 1st Viscount Ridley, the late-Victorian Home Secretary.

Her early upbringing might have seemed to presage for Mrs David a conventional English upper-class life, but her time at the Sorbonne as a student of history and literature altered her destiny. In Paris during the 1930s she lived with a family 'of which every member appeared to be exceptionally food-conscious'.

When she returned to England, 'forgotten were the Sorbonne professors and the yards of Racine learnt by heart . . . what had stuck was the taste for a kind of food quite ideally unlike anything I had known before. Ever since I have been trying to catch up with those lost days when perhaps I should have been profitably employed watching Leontine in her kitchen'.

The food which she resolved to learn to recreate for herself was that 'which constitutes the core of genuine French cookery, but which to us seems so remarkable because it implies that excellent ingredients and high standards are taken for granted day by day, whereas in our own kitchens the best efforts tend to be made only for parties and special occasions'.

She brought a vivid intelligence and the habit of scholarship to her study of the literature of the table, and to her collection of recipes and cooking methods; and an informed judgment to her analysis of the resultant dishes.

During the Second World War she served with the Admiralty and the Ministry of Information. In 1944 she married Lt-Col I. A. ('Tony') David of the Indian Army (the union was dissolved in 1960).

Her life gave her the experience of keeping house in France, Italy, Greece, Egypt and India. She fixed her curiosity upon the dishes and culinary traditions of each country and upon their relation to a wider culture.

On her return to England after the war, she began to write articles and then, in 1950, published *A Book of Mediterranean Food*. Four more Mediterranean-based books appeared in the next decade.

She described *French Country Cooking* (1951, revised 1987), with characteristic self-effacement, as 'no more than an indication of the immense diversity and range of French regional cookery'.

It included a poignant chapter on stuffed cabbage dishes, 'to show what can be done with a cabbage apart from the one and only, and far too notorious, way common to railway dining-cars, boarding-schools and hospitals'. It could equally be 'an acceptable main-course dish, inexpensive, but abounding in the rich aromas of slow and careful preparation'.

Her pioneering *Italian Food* (1954), the fruit of a year's officially funded research in the kitchens of Italy from Sicily to Milan, was hailed by Evelyn Waugh as the book that had given him most enjoyment that year. It revolutionised attitudes to what had previously been regarded in Britain as nursery fare.

Summer Cooking (1955, revised 1988) was an eclectic and entertaining collection of seasonal dishes relying on fresh ingredients and fresh herbs.

And then, in 1960, Mrs David published her undoubted masterpiece, *French Provincial Cooking*, a book that may be read as literature, as a work of reference, and as a splendid and representative collection of recipes.

Readers were plunged, through the passion and skill of her writing, deep into the sights and scents of the markets and kitchens of rural France.

As the novelist Angela Carter observed: 'Elizabeth David's books are full of the essence of place.' They also penetrate to the essence of good food.

Britain's young post-war housewives found the delicious traditional dishes of the French bourgeoisie entirely to their taste.

Mrs David, galvanised into action by unpalatable English provincial catering, then turned her attention to the culinary habits of her native land. Having suffered a stroke, and temporarily lost her sense of taste (happily later regained, although she came to find the smell of her beloved onions offensive), she decided, by way of a restorative, to open a kitchen shop in Pimlico in 1965.

This immensely influential establishment was stocked with the handsome fish-kettles, earthenware cooking-pots, copper saucepans and those indispensable little kitchen gadgets which French housewives accept as their birthright but which were so hard to obtain in London. Soon Mrs David's disciples were opening kitchen shops all over the Anglophone world.

Then followed the first of what was intended to be a trilogy entitled *English Cookery, Ancient and Modern*. In the first volume, *Spices, Salt and Aromatics in the English Kitchen* (1970), Mrs David explored the influence of Empire on the English store-cupboard, and revived recipes for home-pickled meats such as brawn, brisket and spiced beef, potted shrimps and fish pastes.

The book's publication fuelled a national revival of interest in traditional English dishes, the influence of which is still being felt today. *English Bread and Yeast Cookery* followed in 1977.

An essentially private person, Mrs David never wrote an autobiography, although much of her life and philosophy can be found in her collected journalism, *An Omelette and a Glass of Wine* (1984). This became an immediate bestseller – a tribute to her phenomenal reputation in a decade when mass recognition comes easily only to television cooks.

These pieces, laced with Mrs David's laconic wit, include few recipes. They were chosen principally from her contributions to the *Sunday Times* from 1955 to 1960 (where Mrs David had a less than happy relationship with the late Ernestine Carter, for whose busy editorial shears she had harsh words), and from articles published during her 'joyous years' under Katharine Whitehorn at the *Spectator*.

Under Mrs David's benevolent patronage *Petits Propos Culinaires*, Alan Davidson's idiosyncratic culinary publication, was launched in 1979. It was under this magazine's auspices that, two years later, the first international Oxford Symposium on Food was held in St Antony's College.

She was appointed OBE in 1976, CBE in 1986 and elected a Fellow of the Royal Society of Literature in 1982. In 1977 she was appointed a Chevalier du Merite Agricole of France.

Her pen did not merely inspire a thousand cooks. It is largely to Mrs David that Britain owes its growing appreciation of good food.

'Whoever,' wrote her friend Norman Douglas, 'has helped us to a larger understanding is entitled to our gratitude for all time.' These words might serve as Elizabeth David's epitaph.

16 November 1980
AT HOME ON THE RANGE
Pearson Phillips

He was probably joking. With Clement Raphael Freud ('Clay' to friends), Member of Parliament for the Isle of Ely and former assistant soup chef at the Dorchester hotel, it is never easy to tell. But sitting over sausages and spinach soup in the kitchen of the house he bought in Fenland to establish a constituency base, he explained how he was saddled with a career as cook and all-round gastronome.

'It was my father's doing,' he said, using his famous lugubrious grunt and his sideways peer. 'He enjoyed his food. He saw the war as a threat to his gourmet habits. Was starvation imminent? He felt that a son strategically placed in the kitchens of the Dorchester would be good insurance. An aunt who was staying at the hotel had a word with the manager. There I was, at 16, an apprentice working under the soup chef; the celebrated Silvino Trompetto, later ruler of the Savoy kitchens.'

To anyone who has observed the globe-encircling Freud family network in action this story is all too credible. Clay's father was Ernst Freud, a gentle architect who removed himself from Nazi oppression in Austria before the Second World War and established a Freud bridgehead in Hampstead. Others of the family, including the great patriarch, Sigmund Freud, Clement Freud's celebrated grandfather, followed.

His basic beginning in the cooking business helped form Clement Freud's antagonism to the amateurish 'fripperies' of much fashionable *haute cuisine* (his training continued after the war at the Hotel Martinez, Cannes, several London restaurants and the Royal Court Theatre Club in Sloane Square, which he bought in 1952 aged 27). 'It so happened that I started my working life as a cook,' he wrote in the introduction to his only published cookery book, 'unlike the majority of cookery critics, who tended to hover around the perimeters of gastronomy'.

As can be gathered from that sentence, he has a scornful side to him which has made him a few enemies in the food world. His style in the kitchen is one of vigour and dash. He enjoys slapping things together at speed as though competing against the clock. It was typical of him to get into the *Guinness Book of Records* for making 105 omelettes in 26 minutes

25 seconds. He probably was not hurrying. His logic holds that it is better to produce a dish in 20 minutes which is 80 per cent as good as something which takes an hour and a half.

While other cookery writers might dwell on the lengthy pounding of leftover lobster pieces to make a *bisque*, he advises 'putting the pieces in a good strong cloth and bashing it against an outside wall'. Short of breadcrumbs? 'Use a rolling pin on some Weetabix.' He is, horrors, an advocate of a certain brand of ready-made bottled mayonnaise.

Since he became Liberal MP for Ely (winning a by-election in 1973 and steadily increasing his majority ever since), he has been trying to play down the cook, general all-round celebrity and his reputation for good living. 'When people look at me they see a man in a chef's hat, or that man with the bloodhound in the dog food television advertisement. They don't realise that I haven't done any of that for seven years.' He does not help his efforts to change his image by continuing as a director of the British Playboy Club company, squeezing in regular appearances on television and radio, and contributing a restaurant column to the *Financial Weekly* and one on food to *Punch*.

His wife of 30 years, actress Jill Raymond, says that getting into Parliament was the thing he had been waiting for all his life. 'He didn't regard it as just another challenge, like doing the Cresta Run, learning to fly or winning a horse race' (he once won £1,500 by beating Sir Hugh Fraser in a 1½ mile match at Haydock Park on his horse Wild Fair). 'He is a man with an incredible depth of compassion, who never says no to a cry for help.' It was certainly Freud who was the one Liberal MP to be conspicuous in standing by Jeremy Thorpe.

Answering cries for help as a conscientious constituency man (he is much praised as an indefatigable worker in Ely) does not leave him much time for cooking.

He believes that sleep after 6 a.m. is a waste of time and is usually out of his Wimpole Street flat to be at his House of Commons desk by seven, a sole Member among the cleaning staff and policemen. As Liberal spokesman on broadcasting he has been involving himself in the minutiae of the Fourth Channel. He seems to be in his seat more consistently than most MPs, and is a regular voice on radio's *Yesterday in Parliament*.

On Fridays and Saturdays he likes to be out at his constituency home, a small Georgian house with garden in the village of Mepal, near Ely.

In between meetings and 'surgeries' he bakes bread for his agent. On Saturdays he buys parsnips, carrots and celery from a farm shop in the nearby village of Wilburton to take back to London. 'Vital political maxim: always buy your veg in the constituency...'

In London on Saturday evenings he says that he usually plans to have dinner with his daughter Nicola (favourite restaurants: Lacy's in Whitfield Street, and the Mumtaz Indian Restaurant near Regent's Park). Nicola, 27, is the eldest of his five fairly individualistic children, the others being Ashley, 23 (studying at the Royal College of Art), Dominic, 20 (at Christ Church, Oxford), Emma, 17 (hoping for the stage and – to judge from recent performances, playing and singing at an Islington Wine Bar – not far off it), and Matthew, 15.

Nicola earned some early points with her father by leaving school to ride racehorses for £5 a week at a National Hunt stable.

Sunday, however, is the day when some of his old self emerges. 'It is the day when I do some serious cooking.' Sunday lunch at Wimpole Street (or at another country place at Walberswick on the Suffolk coast in holiday times) is what he calls 'a traditional family affair,' if anything about this family can be considered traditional. There is roast chicken, lamb or beef, accompanied by his voters' veg. There is white sauce. And there is *crème brulée*. He does it all.

Possibly the only concession to frivolity one could detect was in the horseradish sauce made from whipped cream. (Take ⅛ of a pint each of double cream and top of the milk; whisk until it thickens, and fold in a heaped tablespoon of freshly-grated horseradish, a good pinch of salt and a coffee spoon of lemon juice.)

The success of the occasion appears to hinge on the gravy. He says he makes 'the best gravy in Wimpole Street'. But as experienced gravy-makers will know, there is a problem attached to making such a claim. A properly cooked joint of beef, sealed with an initial blast of full heat, will keep its juices inside the meat. But the best gravy is made from the juices which run out into the roasting pan. That is the problem. How do you get juicy meat *and* good gravy?

Clement Freud has put his logic to work on this. His solution is to buy some odd bits and pieces of meat to put round the joint for the sole pur-pose of providing the gravy juice. 'Just put scraps, gristle, fat, the odd bone and some mince beside the joint and you will get all the juice you need. You only need add a glass of red wine, a touch of browning and a correction of seasoning. Then boil it up, loosen the meaty deposits and strain it into the gravy bowl.'

Grandfather Freud would probably have some theories about the great gravy ritual which possesses the Wimpole Street household on Sundays. Roast beef and rich gravy symbolise England. By mastering the gravy Clement Freud (so grandpa might say) is cementing himself into the English landscape; his family's adopted home.

Certainly his need to excel, his bumptious competitive urge, and his early desire to win approval and acceptance as a wit could be traced to his youthful experience of being dumped into a Hampstead prep school, hardly able to speak English, an oddity and a target for bullying and ragging.

During our visit to Mepal to take photographs of him in his constituency kitchen he announced, as if the thought had suddenly occurred to him, that 'we must have some dinner'. It was the kind of test by which he separates a good cook and hostess from a mere gastronomic fiddler. 'With a little training anyone can achieve a series of well-cooked courses. What separates The Woman from twitty ladies is an ability to cater for impromptu, unexpected snacks.'

There was a sudden opening and closing of refrigerator doors. A bowl was put into my hands and I was instructed to go down the garden and pluck spinach for soup. Potatoes were placed in his favourite new gadget, a saucepan which boils without the need for water. Sausages were put under the grill. Wine was opened. Salad was washed, spun and tossed. The spinach was crammed into that modern miracle the Magimix. All was movement, vigour, virtuosity and noise. As we sat down he looked at his watch. 'There you are, 20 minutes, including eight minutes for you to pick the spinach.'

Mr Trompetto of the Savoy would no doubt have been proud of us.

28 May 2005
A ROUX AWAKENING
Tamasin Day-Lewis

This year, the 29-year-old winner of the Roux Scholarship, Matthew Tomkinson, a junior sous chef at Ockenden Manor in West Sussex, has requested his prize should be spent 'cooking in the countryside somewhere in France'. This prestigious award for young chefs under the age of 30 sends each winner to a restaurant of their choice to work a 'stage'.

Michel Roux's first scholar, Andrew Fairlie, the Michelin-starred chef at Gleneagles in Scotland, who has been chosen to cook for the G8 Summit this summer, went to Michel Guérard's three-star Michelin restaurant, Les Prés d'Eugénie, in south-west France 22 years ago. Since then, four other Roux scholars have gone on to win Michelin stars. Roux's recent decision to send Tomkinson to Michel Guérard, too, makes perfect sense. 'It is modern without being classic and the ingredients are superb,' he says.

Michel Roux and his brother Albert have spent the past 40 years working to improve and inspire our food industry. Michel's Waterside Inn at Bray in Berkshire is the only restaurant in England to have won three Michelin stars successively for the past 20 years. His son, Alain, has moved gradually into his father's role over the last 10 years and at Le Gavroche in London, Albert has in turn been followed by his son, Michel junior.

In February, I was asked to be a judge for the scholarship, at the Waterside Inn, alongside both Michels and Alain Roux, and chefs Gary Rhodes, Rick Stein, Brian Turner and David Nicholls. Marks were given to the 30 young chefs who had entered with recipes for king crab. As Michel senior eddied around the room, attending to every detail, our marking discrepancies were seized on with curiosity and delight. Alain offered nul points to one competitor – justifying his tough stance with clear, disarming reasoning – before the marks were totted up and the semi-finalists unanimously agreed on. Ten went on to cook the king crab in London, the other eight in Birmingham.

When the Roux Scholarship was inaugurated in 1983, the Roux brothers employed more than 400 people and were the only chefs owning and running restaurants in England who had been awarded the title Meilleurs Ouvriers Pâtissiers de France. The task they faced was immense. 'Britain was a gastronomic desert,' says Michel, who started cooking at 14 and vividly remembers the horrors of eating out in London as a teenager. 'It was the dark ages,' he says.

Le Gavroche, which the brothers set up in 1967, was an overnight success, despite their qualms. 'We had never cooked in a restaurant and I wanted to go back home it was so frightening,' says Michel. 'I couldn't even speak English.' Firing them on was the ambition to have the best restaurant in England. 'It took five years, until 1972, when we opened Waterside,' he says. When the Michelin guide was first published, in 1974, both restaurants received their first star, and by 1985, both had gained three.

Recognition abroad was still a problem. 'No kitchen on the continent would employ our chefs because the British reputation was so poor,' says Michel. Determined to do something about it, he launched the competition in order to help young chefs get off to a flying start within the industry. 'The winners all say they wouldn't be where they are now without having won it,' he adds.

The finals took place last month at the Mandarin Oriental Hotel in London. Michel gave the six chefs an Escoffier recipe for navarin of lamb. The classic French dish was not pulled off perfectly by any of them, but Tomkinson, the winner, was the only one who cooked the meat to spoon tender and got all the baby vegetables right. 'If I ate it blind I would have known it had the true taste of a navarin,' says Michel.

Irrelevant as such competitions can seem to people outside the industry, each Roux Scholarship winner embarks on a career trajectory that, in the long term, can only raise food standards and improve our experience of eating out in this country. 'The scholarship opens the eyes of our young chefs and gives them confidence,' says Michel. 'In our own little way, we came to change the habits of the British and now we are doing it through the scholars. They have all gone on to greater things.'

17 April 1999
PROFILE: JAMIE OLIVER
James Delingpole

If Jamie Oliver weren't so charming, it would be hard not to hate him. He's young, good-looking, talented, cocky. And, at the age of 23, he has just been given his own cookery show on BBC2 by the team responsible for *Two Fat Ladies*.

'You do realise that you're soon going to find yourself mobbed in the streets by nubile girls hungry for your body?' I ask him over lunch at Passione, a chic Italian restaurant in London run by one of his mentors, Gennaro Contaldo. 'That designers will be begging you to wear their clothes? That you're going to become incredibly rich and famous?'

But, instead of smirking knowingly as I expect, Oliver looks at me with a mixture of horror and amazement. 'What do I know?' he says. 'I'm just a chef.'

For once, he is being unduly modest. Described by Thane Prince as a 'Boy Wonder' and 'the next hot tip for stardom', by BBC *Good Food* magazine as 'the hottest chef on the block' and by *GQ* as the 'Michael Owen of cookery', Oliver has been cooking since the age of eight and has worked under luminaries including Antonio Carluccio and the River Café team of Ruth Rogers and Rose Gray. 'I think it's in his blood to be a cook,' says Rose Gray. 'I feel sure that he will become one of the country's great chefs.'

So, apparently, does Optomen Television's Patricia Llewellyn. She turned the Fat Ladies, Jennifer Paterson and Clarissa Dickson Wright, into television culinary superstars and now she's hoping to do the same with Oliver in his new six-part series, *The Naked Chef*, which began on Wednesday.

Filmed in the style of a fly-on-the-wall documentary at Oliver's cramped rented flat in Clerkenwell, *The Naked Chef* is a good deal hipper and more streetwise than your average television cookery series. Its presenter looks like a rock star, talks with the strangled Mockney accent of a Rolling Stone and bashes out his recipes with a verve and carefree swagger a million miles from the measured precision of grown-ups such as Delia Smith. And, unlike the Two Fat Ladies, who tend to cook for village cricket teams, Inns of Court and noble houses, Oliver will be shown catering for a younger, groovier crowd: his sister's hen party; his fellow chefs; his newly reformed rock band, Scarlet Division ('I'm the drummer. It's the only proper exercise I get these days').

But *The Naked Chef* is not one of those gimmicky yoof programmes where students show you how to make dinner for six with a tin of Spam, three eggs and a jar of Nutella. Oliver really cares about good food. While part of his mission is to persuade the young that buttered taglierini with seared scallops, white wine, chilli and parsley is nearly as easy to prepare as baked beans on toast, another is to 'hit loyal foodies in their forties and fifties with beautiful-looking, gutsy, colourful food'.

His recipes are heavily biased towards Italian cooking, partly because he prefers its simplicity to the fussiness of classic French cuisine, partly because it reflects his training. The River Café, he admits, has been a huge influence. 'Ruthie and Rose are so clever it makes me mad.'

He believes his cookbook (published by Penguin to coincide with the series) is different from most in that it strips cooking down to its barest essentials. Even culinary amateurs, he insists, should be able to tackle his recipes without fear.

'Oh, really?' I say. And what about his homemade pasta? 'Look,' he replies, 'I've got this mate called Damian. He's this huge Maori rugby player and has never cooked in his life. I gave him the instructions and first time off he was making fantastic sheets of pasta. If you used to play with Play-Doh as a child, you're not going to have any problems making pasta.'

That's the charm of Oliver. He makes it sound so easy. But, then, he's had an awful lot of practice. At the age of eight, he was podding peas, peeling and chipping potatoes, and bothering the chefs at his father's pub restaurant in Clavering, near the Essex town of Saffron Walden ('£7.50 for two afternoons' work: think how many penny chews you could buy for that'); at 11, he could julienne vegetables like a pro; when he was 15, the head chef at the Starr, in Great Dunmow, put him in charge of a section; and, by the time he was 16, he had won a place at Westminster Catering College and could chop faster than his lecturers.

On his first day at college, he recalls, his classmates watched his technique with awe. And then foolishly tried to keep pace with him. By the end of the first week, his fellow students all had their fingers covered in blue plasters. So he was a bit of a cocky so-and-so, I suggest. 'Oh, I am cocky,' he agrees, 'but in the nicest of ways, I hope.'

Oliver fell into his career as a television chef by accident when a crew came to film Christmas at the River Café. 'When it came to the cutting-room stage, I ended up appearing in quite a lot of it.

'After that, the staff all started taking the mickey, ringing me up and pretending to be the BBC. So, when Optomen rang me up, I didn't believe them. My mates were chucking food at me and I was saying to the people on the phone: "Yeah, yeah, I know this is a wind-up."'

Only when the voice at the other end started using 'commercial telly, media-type words, such as "pilot"' did he realise that the job offer was for real.

He doesn't, he insists, stand to make a fat fortune from his television debut. He's being paid £2,000 an episode and, in the six months of filming, he could have made far more money working shifts – as he still does – in the River Café kitchens. Nor will he receive more than a tiny percentage from sales of *The Naked Chef* cookbook. 'It costs £18.99 and I get something like 70p per book.'

Not that he's bothered. It will provide publicity for the restaurant he plans to open within the next 18 months, somewhere near Cambridge. ('London's all very well but the language people use, the aggression! I'm a country boy at heart.') He'll do the cooking and his fiancée, Juliette, a former model who has worked as a waitress in the River Café, will take care of the front of house, he says.

'She can't get remotely excited about nipping down the market for some spinach and tomatoes,' he says. 'She's not interested in food in the slightest. It's probably why we've stayed together for six years.'

1 March 2010

OBITUARY: ROSE GRAY

It all began in the late 1980s when Ruth's husband, the architect Richard Rogers, moved his business headquarters to Thames Wharf in Hammersmith and realised that he and his staff had nowhere to eat. Ruth suggested to her friend Rose that they team up, and in 1987 the River Café was born.

In theory it should have been a disaster. Neither woman was a trained cook, and the restaurant was situated not on the river, but on a traffic-choked corner nearby. What made the difference was their determination to provide the kind of 'truthful' home cooking which they enjoyed eating on visits to Italy. As a result River Café expanded to become one of the most talked-about and fashionable restaurants in London.

Success, naturally, bred resentment. The restaurant was depicted as serving up 'Italian peasant food that no Italian peasant could ever afford', and labelled the 'New Labour' hang-out of choice (in happier days) of Blair, Mandelson, Brown and cronies. The proprietors were always anxious to dispel such 'myths', though they were forced to admit that on his first day at No 10 Tony Blair had been fortified by a picnic of River Café prosciutto, figs and melon.

Whatever the hype, the Gray-Rogers insistence on using only fresh, seasonal ingredients and cooking them simply but brilliantly found an appreciative audience which grew as they hosted their own television series, *The Italian Kitchen* (Channel 4, 1998), and published a series of bestselling cookbooks, each marking a particular epoch in the pair's cooking odyssey. Their crusade was taken up by a younger generation of cooks – including Hugh Fearnley-Whittingstall and Jamie Oliver, both graduates of the River Café kitchens. A. A. Gill, who described the establishment as 'the pot of gremolata at the end of the property boom-baby boom rainbow', was forced to admit that the proprietors' palates had 'the culinary equivalent of perfect pitch'. A Michelin star duly followed in 1998.

A striking-looking woman with a shock of white hair and what one critic described as 'the demeanour of a sexy convent headmistress', Rose Gray likened her relationship with Ruth Rogers to a marriage. Interviewers noted that they tended to talk over each other, laugh together, finish each other's sentences and admonish each other. In an affectionate account of his time at the River Café, however, Jamie Oliver credited Rose Gray as the *genius loci*: 'She seems to bring every last flavour out of things. It's about passion, basically.'

Clemency Anne Rose Swann was born in Bedford on 28 January 1939 in the most harrowing of circumstances. A few months before she was born her mother had returned home from a trip to London to find the marital home burned to the ground. Inside were the bodies of her first child, a seven-month-old baby girl, and the child's nanny. Her husband, a 26-year old flying officer in the RAF, died 24 hours later of burns incurred in trying to rescue them.

Rose grew up in other people's houses, her grandmother's and her aunt's, the solitary child of an unhappy mother, and as soon as possible she was packed off to a boarding school, which she hated. Talk of the family tragedy was taboo and it was only when she was in her sixties that Rose learned the truth, after discovering some old newspaper cuttings which had been hidden for years.

She was much happier at Guildford Art School, where she met Richard Rogers and his girlfriend (and first wife) Su. After graduation she moved to London to work as an art teacher at a girls' school and remained in touch with both of them as their marriage broke up and they both remarried.

In 1962 Rose married Michael Gray, a trainee film editor with whom she had three children. To make ends meet she and a friend went into business making self-assembly lampshades which sold to Habitat, Liberty and Heal's. She also set up a crêpe-making business (using proper French flour, naturally), catering for parties and nightclubs. By this time, though, her own marriage was breaking up.

Subsequently she married David MacIlwaine, a sculptor and artist with whom she had a son. Together they went into business importing and selling cast-iron stoves from the continent. When the business went bankrupt in the early 1980s they decided to sell their London home and move to Italy, where David could paint while Rose would try to write a cookbook. They rented a house near Lucca in Tuscany.

It was here that Rose began to take a serious interest in Italian cuisine, collecting recipes and learning about new ingredients. Progress on the book was interrupted, however, in 1985 when her husband had an exhibition in New York and she was invited over to work for a few months as a cook in a New York nightclub. It was the only professional cooking experience she had before Ruth Rogers contacted her about the River Café.

When it opened, Rose Gray was almost 50 and her children had grown up. She devoted herself to making the enterprise a success, sourcing ingredients, testing and adapting recipes and cultivating relationships with Italian suppliers. She paid huge attention to detail, from the design of the restaurant and staff uniforms to the characteristic uncluttered look of the River Café cookbooks.

The first of these, *River Café Cookbook One* (1995), sold nearly a million copies worldwide, and was succeeded by five other fast-selling books. Though there were complaints that some of the recipes were too complicated (the aptly named chocolate nemesis cake was notorious for its refusal to turn out like the one in the picture), the irony was that many of the recipes did not involve cooking at all, but were about assembling fresh ingredients in new and exciting ways.

Rose Gray was diagnosed with breast cancer in 2001. She underwent surgery, chemotherapy and radiotherapy and was clear for five years. When the cancer returned, she bore it with characteristic stoicism but last year, just as she was finishing *The River Café Classic Italian Cookbook*, she learned that it had reached her brain.

Rose Gray is survived by her husband and children.

Frumenty and Syllabubs

16 April 1899

A SUNDAY DINNER
A Careful Cook

Greatly, I fear, to the disgust of our domestic, the practice of dining late on Sundays is ever on the increase; but if things are properly arranged, so that the larger part of the extra work entailed by this is got through the day before, there is really little or no scope for complaint. In the subjoined menu I have endeavoured to give only such recipes as will lend themselves amiably to being prepared beforehand. Thus, the soup indicated, consommé à la royale, is simply a clear soup, with tiny squares of savoury custard and a few tarragon leaves floating in it; whilst the fish, coquilles of halibut and crab mayonnaise, a most delightful and uncommon plat, can also, to a certain extent, be prepared the preceding day. The sauce for the poulet Portugais can be got ready a day, or even two days, before it is required. Then the chaudfroid of small birds or game farcée, glazed and served round a croustade filled with macédoine tossed in a creamy 'dressing', can also be got ready, with the sole exception of the dressing. And the sweets, one hot, the other cold, can both be made and one cooked on Saturday. All these small details lessen the cook's labours in no inconsiderable degree, and therefore tend to keep that important personage in a good humour. By the way, à propos of cook, if possible, I would advise you to arrange for anything in the nature of a dinner party or small festivity so that it occurs on Mrs. Cook's 'Sunday in', as this does away with any cause for grumbling, and if good temper reigns in the kitchen you may take it as a foregone conclusion that the dinner will be a success, granted, of course, the fact that cook's powers are equal to the demands made upon them.

With regard to the flowers for the decoration of the Sunday dinner table it will be found a good plan to keep these in water to which has been added a teaspoonful of salt until just before they are needed, as this ensures freshness, and fresh flowers are not obtainable at the florist's, or even from the street vendors, except in the shape of exceedingly attenuated button-holes, on Sundays. By the way, the new specimen vases of crystal glass and copper scroll-work are to be recommended from a decorative point of view, as they are both beautiful and inexpensive. With half a dozen of these and a larger one, or a big copper bowl for a centrepiece, the task of decorating the dinner table should be a comparatively easy one, especially just now, when table centres of all descriptions have returned to popular favour and spring flowers are cheap.

With respect to a hors d'oeuvre, about the only thing I have omitted to mention when running through the above menu, you might try the following, since it is both delicious and uncommon: Drain a sufficient number of sardines (the large, not the small, variety) quite free from oil, then open them and remove the backbone. (This needs the greatest care, as otherwise the fish will break, and the appearance of the hors d'oeuvre be completely spoilt.) Having removed the bones, pour a little vinegar over, and leave for ten minutes. Next drain quite free from the latter, and dust with pepper. Chop a pennyworth of picked shrimps finely, and then pound them in a mortar, and a little bit of butter till they are of the consistency of a thick paste. Use this to stuff the sardines. Arrange in twos on small plates, grate a little hard-boiled yolk of egg over each, garnish with capers, and serve, with thin rolled brown bread and butter, handed separately. This is essentially a hors d'oeuvre, calculated to appeal to the masculine palate, and I have found it much appreciated.

To go on to the next item on our menu. The consommé à la Royale is only an ordinary clear soup. For the custard beat up the yolk and whites together of two large eggs; season them highly with pepper and salt, and add to them gradually half a pint of strong broth; the latter need not be clarified, but must be entirely free from even the most minute particle of fat; finally, add the well-beaten white of another egg, pour into a greased mould, and steam for half an hour; leave till cold; then turn out carefully; cut into slices about half an inch thick, and then these slices into tiny squares: allow a half a dozen of these to each soup plate, and about a dozen leaves of Tarragon. Note – the latter must be previously well washed and shaken till dry before the leaves are stripped from the stalks. For those who dislike the flavour it may be omitted altogether without the consommé suffering in the least degree.

The plat of fish is prepared as follows: Take a sufficiently large piece of halibut and boil it in the usual way in salted water, to which has also been added a little vinegar and a bouquet garni – viz., a sprig of parsley, a bay leaf, a bit of thyme and marjoram, and a blade of mace all tied together; as soon as it is done take out, and after draining carefully leave in the larder till cold; when cold, free the fish from skin, flake into rather large pieces, and reserve on a plate till needed; next take all the white meat from a large crab and chop it into neat squares; dust these with pepper and reserve them also; meanwhile prepare half a pint or more, according to the amount of fish and the number of persons to be catered for, of stiff mayonnaise sauce. Note – one egg will with careful whisking 'take up' half a pint of oil. When of the right consistency add a teaspoonful each of finely-minced parsley and chives, or, failing chives, shallot, a little French mustard – about a teaspoonful to be exact – and a few drops of Tabasco; toss the fish in this as lightly as possible; then use to fill the coquille shells.

By the way, if you do not possess these, they can be bought at any good china shop, at prices ranging from 6½d to 1s each. The 6½d size is, however, the best to choose, as the others are rather too large for ordinary purposes. Garnish the top with a prawn or two; scatter a little lobster coral, if obtainable, over, and serve. When once made, if not required immediately, the coquilles should be left on ice until needed.

The sauce for the poulet Portugais is made as follows: Scald, and then rub through a sieve a sufficient number of tomatoes to yield nearly a quart of pulp, rub a clean enamelled iron saucepan with a clove of garlic, and then pour in the tomato pulp; salt it to taste, and add to it a large teaspoonful of sifted sugar, a tablespoon of vinegar, a liberal dash of red pepper, and a wineglassful of either sherry or Marsala; make hot slowly at the side of the stove; meanwhile truss a large fowl as if for boiling; stuff it with a farce composed of breadcrumbs soaked in a little milk or cream, an ounce and a half of finely-minced lean ham, and four ounces of chopped mushrooms; add salt and pepper to taste, place an ounce of fresh butter in a clean enamelled stewpan, and directly it begins to fritter add the fowl, and fry till of light, bright brown all over; then take out and drain on clean kitchen paper till free from grease. While this has been going on, the Portugais sauce will have been getting hot; add the fowl to the saucepan containing it, cover tightly, and simmer gently till thoroughly cooked, taking care to remove all scum as fast as it arises; when done, dish up the fowl on a hot dish; add to the sauce another large glassful of either sherry or Marsala; let it boil up rapidly; reduce it a little, pour over the chicken, and serve accompanied by dressed macaroni, handed separately. The macaroni is prepared thus: Place an ounce of butter in a clean, deep stewpan, together with six ounces of grated Dutch cheese; shake the saucepan until the butter melts; then add half a pound of freshly-cooked macaroni or spaghetti, whichever is preferred; toss until the cheese is thoroughly melted; dust with pepper, and serve.

The chaudfroid of quails is prepared as follows: Stuff the birds with pâté de foie gras; then cook them slowly in a little melted glaze, and when done leave them in the latter till cold. Meanwhile, have ready a crisply-fried croustade, and see that no fat adheres to it; next, empty the contents of a 9d jar of macédoine on to a clean sieve, and let them drain till perfectly free from liquor; beat up the yolk of an egg with half a gill of vinegar, a dessertspoonful of cream, and the same quantity of oil; add pepper and salt to taste, a squeeze of lemon juice, and a dust of sifted sugar, toss the macédoine in this, and use it to fill the croustades; arrange the birds neatly at the base; garnish with olives and serve.

And for a pudding I would advise a mousse of chocolate served with a Curacao sauce for a hot, and a Chartreuse of fruit for a cold sweet. Space not serving, I cannot give the recipes for these, but I append the menu in order that you may see how well it appears in print.

Hors d'oeuvre
Sardines farcées aux crevettes
Consommé à la chiffonnade

Poulet Portugais. Macaroni au fromage
Chaudfroid de cailles. Macédoine des legumes
Mousse au chocolat. Chartreuse des fruits
Dessert
Café

26 April 1955
YORKSHIRE GIVES US GOOD ENGLISH FARE
Bon Viveur

The markets of England are flourishing once again. We had to go north to play town crier to the news we hoped to unfold on our first country foray.

It all began in Knightsbridge, at the London flat of Mr and Mrs Alastair and 'Bill' Fraser. They regaled us with a supper of pork tenderloins, farm butter, unsurpassed beef haslet, Scotch halibut and curd tarts. They had bought these good things in their Yorkshire home town – Doncaster – in a market evocative of France. So we joined them there later. Like a giant Victorian posy it sprawls across the centre of the town.

In the heart of the posy we found the 'petit marche' touch. Grandmas from outlying farms proffer, in gnarled fingers, butter pats, herb sprigs and little baskets of home-grown produce. Their grandchildren beside them clutched bunches of primroses. Ringing them round were mountains of white and brown new laid eggs (from 3s 3d dozen), aisles of red-and-cream meat carcasses, and acres of gleaming fish slabs.

Spreading out endlessly into the square is an outer frilling of open-air stalls from which we culled a prime harvest. There were potato cakes (6 for 7½d), cartwheel crumpets, parkin, potted beef and curd. There was 'Scarboro' Woof' (Scotch halibut, 1s 6d a lb), fat striped humbugs, aniseed bites, and raspberry balls which we bought for Bill's tiny son, Robert; giant pyramids of polished rosy apples and a cluster of 'Fairings', their coloured ribbons flying in the wind.

We bought string in decorated plaits (three generations have served at this stall), lemons at 2½d each, small pickling onions at 2½d a lb. We picked over bananas (9d a lb) to an encouraging 'Taste one, love', instead of the surly 'If you don't want the goods don't muck 'em about,' which is much more familiar to us. Finally, we sank exhausted into our seats in the elegant restaurant of the Earl of Doncaster for a well-served, well-presented 6s 6d luncheon.

With Scotch broth inside us, roast beef and melting Yorkshire pudding, followed by real apple pie, cheese and cream, we set out for Mr Sloan, the pork butcher. All beaming 20-stone of him paid glowing tribute to his merchandise. We sampled really tasty haslet (minced pork wrapped in curl, 4s a lb), while standing between huge blistered mounds of crackling-topped roast pork. 'I can't remember when pork was cheaper,' Mr Sloan confided in Bill.

So to add to our purchase of farm butter at 4s 2d a lb, we loaded up with hand-raised pork pies (2s 6d a lb), and a 30lb flitch of home-cured bacon to hang in our kitchen (2s a lb). Here too was pork tenderloin and home-made pork sausages (2s 4d a lb).

Dinner that night was an English celebration at the Danum Hotel, Doncaster, which is doing yeoman service under the youthful management of 26-year-old Mr Cash and his chef, Mr Brimblecombe. He makes a real dish of tripe and onions and a real Yorkshire hot-pot for the 5s 6d / 6s 6d three-course luncheon menu. Our 10s 6d dinner included prime roast turkey, cranberry sauce and a choice of two sweets which were unusual – puff-ball fritters with apricot sauce, and an orange cream with fresh cream. No wonder these Yorkshire folk are so friendly!

The same smiling welcome met us when Alastair drove us the following day to the little village of Castleford, where he always buys the Fraser beef. Mr Hirst, the butcher, sold us meat from carcasses which have 'never been off their farm from the day they were born till last Sunday'. He announced this as he sliced Alastair's steaks on the real butcher's block which has been in his family for generations.

'Talk to the young about meat,' Mr Hirst urged us, 'teach them the value of a good cheap cut, a bit of pickled brisket, stuffed breast of lamb, shin meat for casseroles and a round of beef for roasting. Tell them to live long like me on a rib of crop (fore-ribs) week-end joint. That's what I always take home for Sundays.'

Bill fed us with proper parkin, rich with ginger, and used the market curd for Yorkshire curd tarts, with eggs, cream, lemon juice and currants. She gave us the recipes for both.

She led us to Monk Friston Hall, the great house, lapped in trees in Monk Friston village, where M. Eugene Mabillard from the ever-delightful Peacock at Rowsley in Derbyshire, is at last providing a worth-while port of call only a mile off the Great North Road.

Here were soups made with vegetables from Doncaster Market (when not available from the Hall's enormous kitchen gardens), calves' liver of unsurpassed flavour from the Yorkshire butchers and pancakes and fritters. All of this makes 7s 6d an absurd price for a luncheon in a setting which suggests you might have to pay a guinea.

Lastly, we ran fine Yorkshire fare to ground at the Three Nuns restaurant on the Leeds–Huddersfield road. A six-course dinner for 10s 6d in a flower-bright setting as crisp as the pork crackling, as fresh as the Scotch halibut, as agreeable as the veal they use to make Schnitzels, confirms the Yorkshire insistence on good food and plenty of it.

There is only one sleeveless errand upon which this county's caterers are engaged. The rash of 'French' culinary endeavours is as much like the cuisine it apes as bottled salad cream resembles mayonnaise. Stick to your own good cooking, Yorkshire. You know and understand it. It is 'reet' good, but your French masses are PHONEY.

21 June 1951
GARLIC IN BAYSWATER
Doris Lessing

Novelist Doris Lessing, who writes this article, found success the hard way, from a stenographer's job in South Africa she came to rooms in Bayswater with few possessions beyond the manuscript of her first book, 'The Grass is Singing', which won her a name.

In addition to writing a second book, 'This Was the Old Chief's Country', and looking after her baby son, she did a secretarial job to help her pay her way.

I came to England a year ago prepared to suffer semi-starvation. What I suffered was not hunger. Every visitor must wonder helplessly why the British do not rebel against the tasteless stuff served up to them in some of the less expensive restaurants under the name of food. I had soon decided never to eat 'out'; and there was good reason why I should prefer to stay at home.

Ironically enough, my memories of this first year are of good eating. I chanced to live in a large house in Bayswater, owned by Italians who had a downstairs flat. All the other families in the house were English – an interesting contrast in national eating habits. Roast beef, good steaks, rich puddings – these are the English tradition, and the people in that house seemed mesmerised by it into complete apathy. The week's eating was geared to the Sunday dinner, with its roast and two veg – meat too tough to eat, roast potatoes, greens cooked in water. The whole meat ration sacrificed in a sentimental gesture towards the past.

Downstairs, no such inhibitions. Not that this Italian housewife did not grumble. Raising her hands and eyes to heaven: 'No eggs, no meat…expect us to cook with this? If you think you're going to get anything worth eating…' That ritual over, she settled down to cook. Her family ate like princes, though being working people, they bought no chickens, salmon, lobster or cream. What she saved on using the traditional cheap foods – potatoes, lentils, the pastes and rice – she used for good imported cheese and sausages. How did she do it?

Most important was the marketing. Vegetables were bought three times a week from the street market, a fortnightly visit paid to Soho for fresh pastes and olive oil, and a weekly visit to the butcher.

Next, the stock pot – she would not be without one. She used it for thick vegetable soups flavoured with herbs for sauces and stews. She never roasted meat, unless very lucky with the butcher. The ration was divided, used for risottos, sauces, stews. She cooked vegetables Continental fashion as main dishes: creamed spinach with cheese; braised leeks; cabbage and lettuce leaves were stuffed with savoury lentils, rice, or even rye bread moistened with stock and flavoured. She made delicate vegetable pies, of fine light crust, filled with chopped creamed cucumber perhaps, or cauliflower and cheese. She used olive oil for all frying, and kept as much butter as possible for cooking vegetables – nothing was ever cooked in water.

Nor did she despise tins, but – as she said – 'You've got to put the taste into it.' Her mushroom soup, for instance: A few mushroom stalks, half a bottle of sour milk, stock, and a tin of soup. With a good salad it made a substantial meal. A tin of tasteless stew, flavoured with garlic, onions, endive, with braised tomatoes and rice, became an epic dish.

Recipes? She used none, she was an inspired cook. It seemed her most wonderful meals were created out of a handful of vegetables, some scraps of meat and her fantasy.

Watching her, I became convinced that if the housewife would throw away her cookery books, her measures and most important of all her unattainable traditions of cooking based on fine materials, and simply use her imagination, England might yet, even with rationing, become a country fit for epicures. After all, even the basic ration would be a princely allowance for the working French housewife, whose soups and stews are only obtainable in England in expensive restaurants, under exotic names.

13 February 1934
REGIONAL COOKERY IS AN ART IN ITSELF
Florence White

Whether we are trying out a French, English, American, or Turkish recipe, or that of any other nation, it is important that we should prepare it in the best and most correct regional manner. Otherwise the dish or food preparation is not what it pretends to be.

How frequently Yorkshire pudding is slandered by the name being applied to a dish no Yorkshireman or woman would own! Someone once had the temerity to ask me for a recipe for a French Yorkshire pudding, which, of course, was the height of absurdity. You might as well ask for a recipe for English bouillabaisse.

Recently I have been told by an extremely intelligent man that certain business houses have found furmenty and syllabubs unpopular. The reason given in the case of furmenty or frumenty was in itself a proof that the recipe had not been correctly carried out; the objection to it was that the grains of wheat were too coarse or rough.

Now the characteristic of correctly prepared frumenty is that those wheat grains are cooked to a jelly. There is no roughness in frumenty when it is correctly prepared. Of course, if you want 'roughage' in your diet you can prepare frumenty in such a manner as to get it. It is the same with Scotch porridge; they can be prepared correctly and well or the reverse. The proof of a good dish lies in its recipe and preparation, both of which are tested by eating.

When rescuing syllabubs from oblivion I tried out several recipes before I discovered the correct one. And I defy anyone except those who dislike cream to dislike a solid syllabub correctly made. There is, however, an important point to remember, and that is that methods of preparation differ today from days of old. It is possible to make a syllabub by using an electric Mixa-beater, but you must learn to use your machine if you want to get the same texture you would have when using a Scotch whisk.

An important point is that gelatine is never used in making a correct solid syllabub. The use of gelatine for solidifying a syllabub is a modern act of culinary degeneration. All this is the result of historical, practical, literary, and direct research.

Not so very long ago a firm famous for its good cooking came a cropper over lambs' tails pie. It was not the fault of the cook or the manager or the organiser of the dinner, neither was it the fault of the butcher. It was the fault of the person who supplied the tails. He sent the tails out from the carcasses of lambs killed for the market. I was not present when they were served, but I knew what had happened when I was told they resembled a thin head of asparagus – and were bony.

The lambs' tails of which the pies are made are cut from the living lambs when they are about a month or two old, and when stewed are so tender that they are gelatinous. They are very delicious and a great delicacy only obtainable once a year, in the spring. I am not sure of the age when this simple operation takes place, but I have used the tails after they have been blanched, so I know what I am writing about.

I give a recipe for a correctly made Cornish pasty which is very good indeed, whereas an incorrect, badly made pasty is anathema.

Cornish Pasty as Made at St Ives

The following is the correct method of making a Cornish pasty. It must never be made with cooked meat and vegetables, and not a drop of water or stock of any kind must be added to the meat or other contents.

Ingredients

For the pastry take:
Flour ½lb;
Lard or dripping 3oz;
A pinch of salt;
Water to make a firm dough,
    about 1 gill (5 fl oz)

For the filling:
Uncooked beefsteak ½lb;
Uncooked calf's liver ¼lb;
Uncooked potatoes 2;
Onion, 1 large one;
Turnip, 1 medium-sized one;
Carrot, 1 large or 2 small ones;
Pepper and salt

Time: To bake 1 hour; at first in a good oven to raise the pastry, and then in a very moderate oven to cook the meat and vegetables.

Method

1. Roll out the dough fairly thin, cut in squares.
2. Chop the steak and liver finely, mix together and season.
3. Peel or scrape, and slice the potato, onion, turnip and carrot. Mix and season vegetables.
4. Put a layer of vegetables on half of each square of pastry and some of the chopped meat on top.
5. Brush edges of pastry with white of egg, fold the plain half over the meat and pinch edges well together.

It is important to close edges neatly and closely, so that no steam escapes. The contents cook in their own juices. The above amounts make two large or three medium-sized pasties.

16 September 1984

THE TASTE OF THE NORTH
Lady Maclean

The Scots have always been very proud of the hospitality they offer to visitors. Once it was deemed infamous in a man to have the door of his house shut lest 'the stranger should come and behold his contracted soul'.

In fact, hospitality was one of the Virtues emphasised in the Benedictine Rule of Iona in the 13th century, and it has been practised throughout the Highlands with enthusiasm and style ever since, to the delight – and often surprise – of newcomers.

But what makes the Scots such good hosts? Clearly it is the richness and variety of our natural resources, and the ingenious use we make of them. Our great rivers still run with sea trout and salmon, our sea lochs teem with lobsters and langoustines, and our hills provide Aberdeen Angus cattle, deer, grouse, ptarmigan and mountain hare.

What is more, the Scots know how to cook all of these delicacies. The kitchens of Mary of Lorraine and her daughter, Mary, Queen of Scots, left a legacy of delicately prepared but simple, tasty food which was nurtured by the civilised Stuarts and spread from court to castle up to the present day.

Breakfast at Beaufort, my childhood home, was ready when the gong sounded, and we arrived in the dining room to an appetising scene. There was always a white damask cloth on the long mahogany table, with plain wooden bowls lined with white napkins at intervals along it. The table would be piled high with freshly baked scones and a great bowl of hot-house fruit from the garden. On the sideboard would be four or five silver dishes with huge covers, under which were such breakfast favourites as Findon haddock à la crème, boned sea trout, or salmon fish cakes. Nearby was a great bowl of porridge and, on another table, cold dishes of York ham, potted venison, a mutton ham or kippered salmon.

A good hotel in Scotland will still serve some of these traditional dishes today. And you may be lucky enough to come across a Scottish cook who will know more about Highland breakfasts than any book will tell you. Try these recipes for brunch if not for breakfast.

Blaeberry Jam
Ingredients
Blaeberries;   *Sugar;*
Rhubarb;   *Water*

Method: Blaeberries grow in the acid, peaty soil of Highland woodlands and glens. Their small purple berries – similar to but much more tasty than blueberries – make delicious jam. Allow 1 lb of sugar to every 1 lb of blueberries, and 1 lb of thin rhubarb to every 7 lb of fruit. Wipe the rhubarb and cut it into 1-inch lengths. Put it into the preserving pan with the sugar and boil rapidly for 10 minutes, then add the blaeberries and simmer gently, skimming well, till the mixture reaches setting point. Test in the usual way. Pour into pots and seal.

White Girdle Scones

Ingredients

1 lb flour;

1 tsp bicarbonate of soda;

¾ tsp cream of tartar;

½ tsp salt, buttermilk or thick sour milk

Method: Sieve the flour, bicarbonate of soda, cream of tartar and salt into a basin. Add enough buttermilk or thick sour milk to make a very soft dough. Turn out on a floured board and divide into flour. Flatten each piece into a round scone about ½in. in thickness. Cut each in quarters, flour them, and place them on a hot girdle (you can substitute a large, heavy frying pan). Let them cook steadily till well risen and light brown underneath (about 5 minutes) then turn with a knife and cook on the other side for about the same length of time. When the edges are dry, the scones are ready. Serve freshly baked with butter.

Eggs in Black Butter

Ingredients

2 tbsp butter;

4 eggs;

Chopped parsley;

Juice of ½ lemon;

1 tbsp Worcester sauce;

4 rounds of thinly sliced bread

Method: Melt the butter in a small frying pan or omelette pan and heat it until it darkens to a very dark brown, without burning. Put in the Worcester Sauce and a squeeze of lemon juice. Fry the eggs very gently in this sauce, basting well. When set, trim into rounds with a pastry cutter. Drain. Fry the bread rounds in the remainder of the butter in the pan and serve with an egg on top of each round. Decorate with a pinch of finely chopped parsley and pour the rest of the sauce round the eggs.

Herrings in Oatmeal

Ingredients

12 really fresh plump herrings;   *2oz butter*

2oz pinhead (coarse) oatmeal;

Method: Scale and decapitate the herrings. Split and flatten them. Roll them in the pinhead oatmeal and sauté in butter for three minutes each side.

Findon Haddock à la Creme

Ingredients

5 large fillets yellow haddock   *1 pint cream;*

   (not frozen);   *Black pepper*

Method: Throw fillets into boiling water for about 3 or 4 minutes to remove a little of the salt. Drain and pick over them carefully, removing all skin, bones and hard pieces. Flake fish into a buttered ovenproof dish and cover completely with cream. Grate black pepper over the dish and cook in the oven for about 12 minutes then flash under the grill to brown the top, and serve.

15 December 1962

BRITAIN CHOOSES THE IDEAL MEAL
John Yudkin

Christmas in England...the palate conjures up turkey, mince pies and rich plum puddings. But ask the average Briton to name his ideal, money-no-object meal and what does he answer?

Tomato Soup

Sole

Rump Steak, Roast Potatoes, Peas, Sprouts

Fruit Salad and Ice Cream

Cheese and Biscuits, Coffee

Before the meal: Sherry. With the meal: Red and White Wine. With the coffee: Liqueurs.

(*This comes from a Gallup Poll conducted exclusively for The* Daily Telegraph Magazine.)

The Gallup Poll interviewed a representative cross-section of people throughout Great Britain. The question put to them was: 'If expense were no object and you could have absolutely anything you wanted, what would you choose for a perfect meal?' The menu above represents the consensus of the choices made for each course.

Gallup asked the same question 20 years ago – in the days of post-war austerity – and again in 1962. The most popular menus then were:

1947: Tomato Soup; Sole; Roast Chicken, Roast Potatoes, Peas, Sprouts; Trifle and Cream; Cheese and Biscuits; Coffee.

Before the meal: Sherry. With the meal: Wine, red and white. With the coffee: nothing.

1962: Tomato Soup; Sole; Roast Chicken, Roast Potatoes, Peas, Sprouts; Fruit Salad and Ice Cream; Cheese and Biscuits; Coffee.

Before the meal: Sherry. With the meal: Wine, red and white. With the coffee: Liqueurs.

Thus, in 20 years, there have been only three changes: roast chicken has given way to rump steak; trifle was overtaken by fruit salad in 1962; the cream to be served with the fruit salad has now been replaced by ice cream.

At first sight this suggests that the British are steadfast gastronomical conservatives. But in fact the changes in public appreciation of food are more far-reaching than a comparison of the menus would suggest. The top ranking dishes have not changed much over the years but they are having to meet increasing competition from many new competitors.

The higher standard of living, the wider availability of goods and the greater acquaintance with different customs and ways of living have produced a much more sophisticated approach to eating. The growth of foreign travel, the arrival in Britain of immigrant communities, the effect of television and the cinema, the impact of large-scale marketing and advertising are all contributory factors.

The most spectacular change since 1962 is in the popularity of rump steaks. They are now mentioned by 26 per cent of the population as their first choice for the main course. In 1962 only ten per cent made that choice.

While steaks have gone up, chickens have gone down, from 26 per cent in 1962 to 19 per cent today. Roast beef has maintained its popularity; it is still the favourite dish of the over 65s but other meats like pork and lamb have lost some support.

Public taste in vegetables is changing fast. Nevertheless, green peas remain the number one choice with a clear lead over the other vegetables. Mushrooms have greatly increased their appeal from 5 per cent in 1962 to 14 per cent today. Carrots, beans and salads are other items with increased popularity. But Brussels sprouts, having grown in popularity between 1947 and 1962, have now fallen back.

Roast is still the most popular choice of potatoes. The numbers preferring fried continue to increase, though 'chips with everything' is not yet true and a virtually new word, sauté, has entered the vocabulary, particularly the vocabulary of the young and the middle class. The advances made by potatoes served in these forms has been at the expense of mashed potatoes.

Fruit salad maintains the position it won in 1962 as the first choice of sweet. But now ice cream replaces cream as its accompaniment. Fresh fruit runs a close second to fruit salad.

Cooked puddings are now much more of a minority taste. Apple pie has kept most of its appeal, particularly with men, but the demand for rice pudding, except among the old, has halved. Fewer people now mention sponges, steamed and baked puddings, or such long established sweets as jam and syrup roll.

Britain is fast becoming a nation of cheese-eaters. In 1962 only 27 per cent wished to round off their meal with cheese and biscuits. The proportion is now 40 per cent.

The change in drinking habits is even more remarkable than the change in eating standards. One person in four – three times as many as in 1962 – would now choose to drink sherry before their meal. Indeed, only five years ago, as many as 73 per cent declined to have a drink before they started the meal. This number has now fallen to 29 per cent.

After sherry, some other type of wine and beer are the most popular drink before the meal. Beer, in fact, is preferred to sherry by men.

More people now like to drink during their meal. Forty per cent would like wine, compared to 29 per cent in 1962 and ten per cent in 1947. There has been a small decline in the number who like beer with their dinner, ten per cent now as against 13 per cent on both previous occasions. There are a number of men, particularly Scotsmen, who remain faithful to whisky as the drink to be had before, during and after the dinner.

A liqueur to end the meal is now the choice of one person in five – 21 per cent. This compares with half as many, 11 per cent in 1962 and an insignificant number 20 years ago.

Among non-alcoholic drinks, coffee has gone a long way to supplant tea as the Englishman's favourite after-dinner drink. It is preferred by more than four to one, 60 per cent for coffee compared to 14 per cent for tea.

Microdotty

6 July 1955
NO MORE BAD COOKS
Claire Butler

The reason? Not only are more and more cookers becoming automatic, but there is a move to make pots and pans do your thinking for you. Soon to be launched is a frying pan with a switch which you set to the heat required and leave to its own devices. I saw this at the recent British Electrical Power Convention at Brighton.

Here are new points I noticed. Ovens that light up automatically. A pinger which can be removed from the cooker and taken about the house so that wherever you may be, you are reminded that it is time to look in the oven. Another cooker which would be wonderful for those who get into trouble over the right heats. A red light goes on for hot, amber for moderate, blue for very moderate.

One oven has a time switch which can also be used to heat a plate warming drawer so that plates and dishes are warmed when the meal is ready to serve.

Revolutionary is one cooker's design. The oven and grill are at eye level above the hob. This makes cleaning easier and eliminates stooping. The grill is wide and can take a big sole or other fish full length. Using the grill as a boost, the oven can be heated up to 400°F in eight minutes.

This cooker also has space on the hob to put bottles or jars which are being used in cooking.

12 March 1994
COLD WAR RENEWED AFTER BIG DEFROST
Nicola Tyrer

Tidying my linen cupboard – surveying all those neat, lavender-scented piles – leaves me serene and fulfilled, like a 19th-century chatelaine. Defrosting the freezer leaves me feeling grumpy.

It's all sorts of things. The fact that nothing's properly labelled: you thaw what looks like stewed apple and it turns out to be fish soup. The freezer smell, which lingers on your fingers. Never believe those who say intense cold kills odour. What freezers do is blend the odours of whatever you have so that everything smells the same, from the raspberries to the duck to the fish fingers. It also leaves me feeling irritated with my husband, who, being a domestically inputting spouse, regards the freezer as being as much his domain as mine.

But, I have to confess, a substantial part of my spleen is due to shame. I know food that went to the Antarctic with Captain Scott was perfectly palatable half a century later, and that Russian archaeologists weary of Soviet sausages have voted frozen mammoth found in Siberia good enough to eat – but can I really justify having saved several portions of strawberry mousse from my wedding in 1978? After all, Marks & Spencer recommends you freeze its heat-and-eat dishes for no more than three months.

I am fiercely protective of the freezer. I like putting things into it – buying it presents – and I resist any attempts by others to remove things from it. What the freezer has done is to encourage the miser in me. In the old days, when there was a glut of runner beans you gave a basket to your neighbour. Now you stick them in the freezer.

I plead guilty to the charge of hoarding. More than once on finding sea bass at a giveaway price in a seaside fishmongers, I have taken two – one to eat, one to freeze, and bad luck to whoever was next in the queue.

But what happens to the frozen one? It stays in the freezer until it becomes too desiccated, too gnarled, to be remotely appetising and is then surreptitiously fed to the cats.

Revealing the contents of your fridge has become a smart parlour game with the famous. Alastair Little's humanity is boosted by the revelation that he owns a chilled bottle of ketchup. You could, I suppose, play a similar freezer game. But would London's hostesses really be more eager for my presence at their soirées if they knew that I found in mine the carcass of the 1989 Christmas goose, some pots of stock from, let us say, the Thatcher boom years, and a huge turbot caught in 1981 (an excellent year for fish) which, like the best wine, is still waiting for company grand enough to do it justice?

The problem with my freezer is that its contents represent a joint account and we are incompatible. Other couples row over children, money, the dog . . . We row over the freezer.

My husband does the weekly shop and it is he who buys the giant packs of frozen peas. All well and good, except that he and I have different ideas on purchasing. He, raised during the war, is a thrifty soul, intent on getting out of Tesco every week for less than £90. I, pampered postwar boom baby, choose quality whatever the price. And, before I am accused of not knowing my luck, let me explain what happened when my husband last defrosted the fridge.

This was three years ago at the height of the save-the-planet, green-or-bust movement. Muttering that the ice was so thick he could barely close the door, and implying that a real wife would have dealt with it long ago, he turned off the current and set about the ice with a carving knife. My suggestion that 'a hair dryer is gentle but effective' fell on deaf, impatient ears.

All too soon there was a loud hiss as the room slowly filled with fluorocarbons that were not merely toxic but unfashionable. As I shut the windows to protect what was left of the ozone layer, and he sullenly set off to buy a new fridge, we forged a silent pact. Defrosting is henceforth my responsibility.

Nonetheless, his imprint survives: in the slabs of Welsh lamb he bore home triumphantly shortly after Chernobyl – 'only 50p a pound'; in the ageing packets of frozen egg whites left over from countless mayonnaises – 'always wonderful for meringues'; in the mysterious ready-cooked dishes like Cumberland Pie; and above all in the infuriating unfastened packets of cheap mince, pies and fish fingers, whose contents remain stuck in the permafrost at the bottom of the freezer, like a colourful and surreal collage, the product of occupational therapy in an insane asylum.

The most depressing aspect of the voyage through one's rarely visited freezer is the brutal way it reveals the decline in one's standards. Descending through the gastronomic strata, like some archaeologist of the psyche, you come face to face with the person you once were.

When I bought my first freezer I was young, childless and an Elizabeth David zealot. I made my own stock, baked my own bread and would never have given houseroom to anything that wasn't grown, cooked or fished by me. I didn't know what a Cumberland Pie was. The high priestess of fresh food would turn in her grave at the frozen Mars bars, chicken nuggets and oven chips which haste, expediency and other people's fussy children have led me to fill it with today.

But I take comfort from the fact that in a world of change some things are reassuringly constant. After an afternoon spent grumpily defrosting, labelling and repacking, I scrubbed the freezer smell off my hands and sat back waiting for acknowledgement and praise. Minutes after my husband came in he went off in the direction of the freezer. Minutes later he reappeared: 'Who's been messing around with the freezer?' he snarled. 'I can't find anything.'

Like high-powered executive couples who have twin wash basins, we'll have to have His and Her freezers. Or we could be really brave and just get rid of it.

13 May 1949

MAKES LAZY COOKS

A bookseller and his wife at the B.I.F. were intrigued with one type of mixer. It makes Scotch broth in 10½ minutes, starting from raw vegetables. It mixes your eggs, cake, omelets.

'Does it make good cooks?' they asked.

'No, lazy ones,' was the reply. But it has brought £1,000 worth of orders a day from home and overseas buyers. Price £27 10s.

29 November 1993
PROFILE: MARY BERRY
Mick Brown

It was halfway through Mary Berry's Aga Workshop that I realised I was in heaven. Around me, 18 women were listening intently as she explained how to use the Aga to cook a Dover sole. Through the kitchen window, her rather large garden was cloaked in frost.

In another world altogether there was murder, strife, poverty, domestic mayhem and taxes. But here, all was peace and tranquillity, the intoxicating aroma of good cooking, quiet conversation, the discreet clink of wine glasses.

We were worshippers of the eternal verities of middle-class life, gathered around the altar.

Mrs Berry lives in a Queen Anne house in Buckinghamshire, in the heart of Aga country: big houses at the end of gravel drives, with ponds, and large dogs and estate cars with Game Conservancy stickers in the window.

The Volvos and Golfs were parked outside. There had been morning coffee, the distribution of recipe sheets; the getting-to-know you chat – 'are you a two-oven, or a four-oven?' Mrs Berry is a four-oven, but because most people are two, that's what she would be cooking on today.

She runs a variety of courses on Aga cooking. This was 'More Adventurous 2' – advice on pasta, lemon meringue pie, how to do something interesting with soy sauce, maple syrup and thyme. 'Agas,' she said soothingly, 'take the *thinking* out of cooking.'

As she spoke, Mrs Berry adopted the classic Aga user's pose, leaning *back* on the Aga, warming her bottom, with both hands resting on the rail – a gesture which on a normal gas or electric cooker would result in immediate self-immolation or third-degree burns.

I don't have an Aga. I can barely boil an egg. But even I could see the point.

The Aga was invented by the Swedish Nobel prizewinning physicist Dr Gustaf Dalen in 1922. But it wasn't until the seventies that it started making the journey into the heartland of British middle-class life. This was something to do with the faddish nostalgia for country house living, manifest in an eruption of pine dressers; 'strié' and 'nuage' effect wallpapers from Osborne & Little and Laura Ashley prints.

Anybody could fake the trimmings, but what was required was an authentic centrepiece: something practical, wholly in keeping with the spirit of the movement, but also deliciously expensive. The cheapest new Aga is £3,351.

As the kitchen became the centre of middle-class domestic life, as it had always been the centre of working-class life, so the Aga assumed the role of hearth and icon: the focal point around which all domestic life, its quiet pleasures, its anguished crises, revolved.

We come, of course, to Joanna Trollope, whose novels of the rural middle classes, and the passions that flow beneath the seemly veneer of bourgeois life, have earned the sobriquet 'Aga sagas'.

I turned to Trollope's *A Village Affair*. The Aga makes its first appearance on page 23. In Cecily's posh house 'at lunchtime they ate eggs and salad and homemade brown bread by the Aga, and Cecily always gave Alice wine…' Alice sits on the Aga, 'wrapped in a blanket feeling her salty hair dry into long whispering snakes down her back'. When Alice marries Cecily's son Martin she moves into a nice cottage and gets an Aga of her own.

Her friendship with the lesbian Clodagh simmers dangerously in the kitchen ('Clodagh put the plate of buttered bread on the table and then went over to the Aga and said something quietly to Alice who was making the tea…') and is consummated with their first lingering kiss. 'Clodagh went round the table to the two wooden armchairs by the Aga…'

You get the picture.

Trollope has expressed her distaste for the Aga-saga tag as 'a slightly contemptuous urban cliché for country life. It assumes Women's Institute, green wellingtons, Labrador, all those slightly patronising views of how most of England lives'.

One would dispute the 'most', but it is certainly how *some* of England lives, not least, it seems, Joanna Trollope, who is forever being photographed at her Gloucestershire home in her green wellingtons, with Labrador or Aga.

There is a knowing smile when you mention Trollope at the Aga Workshop. Mrs Berry acknowledged familiarity with the work – 'There's all sort of hairy tales that are told by the Aga,' she said lightly – but she was anxious to allay any suggestion that the Aga is a symbol of class. 'All sorts attend the Aga workshops,' she said. 'On one occasion I had a countess sitting next to a lady who had a stall in Watford market and they got on like a house on fire.'

On the day of my visit there was a magistrate, a part-time counsellor for Relate, a marketing consultant, a social worker. Mrs Berry never advertises. Every year she writes to people on her card-index telling them about new courses, and the same people keep coming.

I realised that in coming here we were actually being inducted into a particular way of life, what with Mary's references to going up to Scotland where the boys were at school and using up the sliced lemon 'left over from your gin and tonic the night before'. At one point she talked of living 'on an estate', and for a brief, hallucinatory moment I imagined somewhere with old sofas shedding their springs, burnt-out cars and children dealing crack on street corners. But that wasn't the kind of estate she was talking about.

Clare, Cherelyn, Jackie, Colette and Christine had come from Nottinghamshire: a two-day break from their families. All were in their thirties, smart in tweed skirts and crisp blouses.

They had met through the Young Farmers some time BA (Before Aga) and become friends. Then one bought an Aga, then another, and somehow they had all ended up with one.

They knew about Joanna Trollope but that was nothing to do with *them*. 'It's all about bored, upper middle-class people, isn't it? We're not like that. We're very busy people,' said Clare.

They didn't spend all morning around the Aga talking about their emotional problems. They were renovating a holiday cottage: helping with Riding for the Disabled, doing the school run, and leading busy country lives.

Nonetheless, the Aga was a topic of conversation – what kind you had, what you did on it. A sort of club. 'I don't think it would be quite the same talking about a Neff,' Christine said.

As they talked about their Agas, I noticed a tendency to lapse into ad-speak. This was particularly appropriate since the first man to promote Agas in the thirties was one David Ogilvy, who went on to found the Ogilvy and Mather advertising agency.

'At this time of the year it becomes a very good friend,' Cherelyn said.

'It's always welcoming, isn't it?' said Colette. 'We've had people come for the evening and never leave the kitchen. An Aga definitely becomes part of your life.'

The reluctant husband was a subtext of these conversations. When Jean, a magistrate, installed an Aga in her Chelsea townhouse she had been obliged to pay for it herself. It was, she thought, the 'woman's equivalent of buying a sports car'.

Cherelyn said she had had to make a bit of a case for hers. 'But I was helped by the fact that my parents had one, so my husband could see the benefits.'

Colette had had to prove that it would be useful. 'Jackie's Aga does hot water,' she said. 'Mine doesn't. We have a separate hot-water system. We had a Rayburn, but I wanted the Rayburn out and the Aga putting in, so I had to convince my husband it was a wise move.'

There is, said Jackie, 'a snob value in the difference between having a Rayburn and an Aga. I don't necessarily agree with it, but there is a social element there.'

'A Rayburn is cheaper,' said Clare.

'No, it's not cheaper,' said Christine.

'They *are* cheaper,' said Jackie, 'but they haven't quite the *impact* of an Aga.'

I turned to *A Village Affair* for guidance on this. Alice's fall from grace over her lesbian affair with Clodagh is complete when she walks out on her husband, and her Aga, and moves into a smaller cottage – virtually a hovel really. There she receives an unwelcome postcard which – lo and behold – she 'put in the Rayburn at once'. Say no more.

There are, as far as I can see, no Rayburn workshops. It wouldn't be the same.

Mrs Berry was taking the lemon meringue pie out of the oven. 'I hope,' she said, 'this is a really *spoiling* day.'

23 April 1978
MICRODOTTY
Marika Hanbury-Tenison

So many people have asked me what I feel about microwave ovens that I felt it was time to get one in my kitchen. I am basically an old-fashioned cook but in favour of anything that will make life easier in the kitchen, increase productivity and save the busy housewife time and money.

'This oven,' the demonstrator told me, 'is so simple to use that I have just sold one to a blind person. All you have to do is set the dial, press the knob, turn the dish once or twice during the cooking time and food is cooked in a fraction of the time it normally takes.'

Microwave ovens, which cost from about £180 to £500, cook by radio waves (not by radio-activity as some people fear) inside a sealed metal box. In my model the waves are cut off as soon as the oven door is opened.

These waves penetrate the food to a depth of 1½ inches, activating the molecules in the moisture content of the food and heating it from within so that, to my amazement, you can cook food in polythene containers without the polythene melting.

The smaller microwave ovens do not cope well with large dishes, joints of meat or family meals but they are magical when you need to defrost and reheat smaller quantities. But a major disadvantage of microwave cooking is the oven's inability to brown food. So I usually finish dishes off under a grill to make them attractive to look at.

Speed is the essence of the microwave oven and the results can be amazing. A cup of soup, for instance, will heat through in 1½ minutes and a one-portion casserole, meat pie or shepherd's pie in two minutes; or a 10oz steak straight from the freezer will defrost in three minutes.

Nine A.M. Party

10 October 1969
NINE A.M. PARTY
Clement Freud

The man on the telephone said he was sure I would remember him...how about that night he and I blew up the fish and chip shop in Buglawton at the end of the war? I told him that I remembered fish and Buglawton and especially chips and vaguely the end of the war – but to be perfectly honest I had no recollection of him.

He was undaunted. 'This,' he said, 'will surprise you: after I was demobilised I went to Australia and I saw you on the box and I said to my wife "when I go and visit the old country, I am going to look that chap up, and talk about those days." Do you remember the sergeant we called Walruss?'

I said not.

'How about lunch then, tomorrow?' We compromised on breakfast the day after and as a bonus issue he promised to bring three of his children who would be tickled to meet someone who knew Dad from way back.

'Say nine o'clock,' he said.

I said 'nine o'clock' before I realised that this was to be the time of the reunion (?) between me and the Australian family Robertsons.

To be cook-host at a breakfast party demands some thought and planning.

Orange Juice

1 tin orange juice;
1 fresh orange, pressed;
1 coffee cupful of water boiled for

three minutes with two
heaped tablespoons sugar;
6 lumps of ice

Liquidise and strain into glasses whose rims have been wiped with lemon and dried in caster sugar.

Cereal

Kellogg's Frosties. I stumbled on these when I found that the single packet of Frosties in the jumbo-breakfast-assortment disappeared as predictably as the All-Bran remained in the larder. Into a cereal bowl strew a thin layer of Frosties. A layer of fresh pear, peeled, cored and thinly sliced and then another layer of cereal. Sprinkle with demerara sugar and serve with very cold Jersey milk. Porridge – in the absence of minced Harris Tweed – is an alternative for addicts and Scotophiles.

Toast

This has to be made and eaten – in that order, preferably without much delay. An electric toaster on the dining table may be the answer. Otherwise rolls sprinkled with water and baked on a rack in a Mark 6 oven for a few minutes give the impression that you have just returned from the baker. Toast Melba is made by toasting thin cut slices of bread on both sides; remove the crust, slip a sharp knife between the two toasted sides and dry off the inner layers of bread under a not very hot grill. Butter should be unsalted and marmalade must be purchased with discrimination. There is a feeling that only cads or Frenchmen eat jam for breakfast. I agree.

Coffee

Use Nescafé Gold Blend, which is the best and most expensive instant brand. If you take cream and sugar in your coffee, use Nescafé, Maxwell House, Mace – or any other decent make. If you are among the one per cent of the population who can tell the difference between instant and fresh coffee, make fresh coffee – but don't talk about it; coffee snobs are even greater bores than wine snobs.

Then – and here is the master stroke – announce an interval during which the children can play in the garden, on the tenement staircase, or Ring-a-Roses in the throne room – and you return to the kitchen.

Eggs and Bacon
I scrambled eggs very slowly, turned them on to diamond shaped pieces of fried bread with accompanying rashers of crisp, streaky bacon.

My guests, I have to admit, were entertaining and appreciative. At home, said Robertson, all he had in the mornings was coffee, no cream, no sugar, no saucer.

I looked at him with new respect. Perhaps I really had known him.

30 January 1966
NO MORE *PETIT DÉJEUNER* – I WANT BREAKFAST
Jean Robertson

Gastronomically speaking, Britain's finest hour is between eight and nine in the morning. Or rather, it *was*. Breakfast has now become one of the casualties of our social revolution, written off as an expendable and rather fattening feast that some of us are too fragile to face and most of us too busy to bother with.

Women who, in addition to taking the brunt of the early morning *mêlée*, often have to get themselves ready for work have been quick to latch on to the Continental breakfast, bulked out if necessary with those packages of dried provender which (collectively) take the name of Ceres in vain.

But they would never have got away with abolishing the most comforting meal of the day had it not been for the war. The war and rationing broke the breakfast habit. And breakfast is a habit, a sound, healthy one, quite as important as lunch.

Though it is a life-giving gulp of coffee that most of us crave in the morning, what matters most for the body's well-being (and the temper's sweetness) is a rasher of bacon, a fillet of fish or an egg – in other words, protein.

By breakfast time most of us have not eaten for 10 to 14 hours (the majority of Britons have their last serious meal around 6.30 p.m. and few of us dine after 7 p.m.). So by lunch time the coffee-and-orange-juice brigade have been fasting for 17 hours.

One effect of fasting is a lowered blood sugar level, which means that in the morning, when physical and mental faculties should be at their best, the breakfastless among us are denying themselves the energy they need to function efficiently. They are also going to feel hungry and therefore tempted to nibble fattening buns and biscuits.

Breakfast does not have to be hot in order to be sustaining (though on these harsh, dark mornings the smell of hot food is the best way of getting sluggards downstairs), but it does have to be quickly prepared and familiar. Even the most adventurous eaters are rigid conformists at the breakfast table.

All the dishes suggested here, except porridge, can either be assembled in a few minutes in the morning or prepared the night before.

My favourite instant breakfast, which can if necessary be consumed on the run, is a clean-tasting combination of two breakfast favourites, egg and fresh orange juice. Allow one egg and one large orange for each person (though some people demand a double portion) and simply beat them together with a rotary beater until smooth and frothy.

If you own a blender you would of course use that. No sugar is needed, but the orange juice must be fresh. The squeezing can be done the night before provided the juice is stored in an air-tight jar.

Muesli

This was a word which as a child I often heard lisped rather nostalgically by a Swiss woman who lived with us. It was many years before I realised that the word was a breakfast food and not a term of endearment.

But I have, since discovering my mistake, been peculiarly fond of this robust combination of fresh fruit and oatmeal from Switzerland. It has, incidentally, remarkable staying power, which may explain its popularity at Gordonstoun.

For 6 people allow:

2oz medium oatmeal;   *½ gill yoghourt or thin cream;*
Water to cover (½–¾ gill);   *1½ tablespoons honey;*
Juice of 2 small lemons;   *6 apples*

Leave the oatmeal to soak in the water for 10 to 12 hours. Add lemon juice and then grated apples, stirring each in as it is grated so that the shavings do not go brown. Add yoghourt and honey and stir well. If it is not to be eaten at once, store in an air-tight box or jar.

Porridge

When translated the romantic and refreshing *muesli* goes under the unpalatable name of raw fruit porridge. Hot Scottish porridge, one of the finest breakfasts of them all, must be smooth, slightly salty and tasting as Harris tweed looks. If it is perfect it is magnificent. If it is just slightly less than perfect it is foul.

Porridge must be made with true oatmeal and served with cool, thin cream and salt. Gently trickle 2½oz coarse oatmeal into 1 pint fast boiling water, which you are stirring rhythmically with the *handle* of a wooden spoon.

Lower the heat and leave the mixture to cook for 10 minutes before adding ½ teaspoon of salt and covering. Continue cooking on a very gentle flame for another 25 minutes.

After reiterating the Gospel according to Robbie Burns in this manner, it may seem sacrilegious to mention canned porridge in the same breath. All the same, it is only fair to say that the porridge canned by Baxter (and sold at 1s 1d) has a remarkable and quite unexpected affinity with that made freshly with dry oatmeal – always provided it is served piping hot with cool cream and salt.

Oatmeal, incidentally, coats sprats just as well as it does herring and, for breakfast, sprats are so much easier to eat. Season the fish with salt and pepper, roll them in medium ground oatmeal and fry them for 5 to 6 minutes in butter.

Smoked Haddock

Kedgeree, with its undertones of the British raj and English country houses, is the stateliest way of eating smoked haddock. This does not, however, prevent it from being made the night before, covered, stored in the refrigerator and then heated up for breakfast in a hot oven with the aid of a little hot thin cream.

Two simpler ways of presenting smoked haddock for breakfast are:

1. Pile the cooked flakes on to a piece of hot buttered toast, season with black pepper and top with a generous knob of butter;
2. Top the cooked flakes with a soft boiled or poached egg (but remember, poaching is only possible when the egg is actually new-laid, not merely described as such).

Baked Eggs

Eggs are, of course, the main-stay of every serious breakfaster, providing as they do more pleasant and neatly packaged nourishment for less trouble than almost any food known to man.

Breakfast, when the palate demands simple food, is not the time to exploit their infinite variety, but one simple alternative to the repetitive fried-boiled-scrambled routine is oven-baked eggs.

Light the oven at Regulo 4 (350°F) and heat individual glass or porcelain *cocottes*. Put a little butter in the bottom, break in the egg, add a bit more butter and some seasoning and return to the oven for about 10 minutes.

Potato Cakes

A cheap and appetising dish on their own, they go well with a rasher of bacon.

1 lb floury potatoes (for about 10 cakes);
4oz plain flour;
2 teaspoons salt and freshly ground black pepper;
2 tablespoons melted butter

Boil the potatoes in salted water, drain thoroughly and quickly press them through a sieve. While they are still warm, sieve in flour and salt and black pepper, blending the mixture with the fingers. Add melted butter and, working very lightly, make the dough into a ball.

Sprinkle a board with flour and flatten the potato dough with palm of hand or floured rolling pin to a thickness of not more than ½ inch.

Cut out cakes 3 to 4 inches in diameter and set them to cook on a reasonably hot greased gridle or heavy frying pan. Allow about five minutes for each side – slightly longer if the mixture was put together the night before.

Fish Cakes
These are so much more appetising when they are tiny.

¾lb cod (poached in seasoned milk);	*2 heaped teaspoons butter;*
6oz baked potato (flesh only);	*2 eggs;*
4 anchovy fillets or anchovy sauce;	*breadcrumbs for coating.*

Pound the anchovies into the butter, flake the cod, scoop the baked potato out of its jacket and mix the three together. Season and bind with *one* of the eggs – beaten. Flour your hands before shaping the mixture into little cakes about 1½in in diameter.

Paint with the remaining egg (beaten), sprinkle with crisp white breadcrumbs (these can be bought by the pound) and leave till you are ready to cook them. Then melt fat and fry till golden, turning once. Drain and serve immediately.

11 August 1928
WHEN YOU HAVE NO MAID
Elizabeth Craig

Some hostesses make the fact that they have not a maid the excuse for not inviting guests to stay with them. I would not do so. For, given a certain amount of imagination and a tray wagon, it is very little trouble to cater for an extra guest or two.

To save trouble in the morning, serve the guest's breakfast in bed. This allows you to get on with the day's work without having to linger over breakfast, as you often have to do when there are guests present. If you have time the night before you can arrange the breakfast tray to simplify work in the morning, then when you are ready to breakfast yourself you can add finishing touches to the tray and take it up before sitting down to your meal.

Some morning trays are only equipped with a tea or coffee service. But it is better to have one of the larger sets which include eggcups, covered bacon-and-egg dish, toast-rack, and all the other little oddments required to serve a perfect breakfast. Otherwise you might feel it necessary to send up the bacon and eggs in a silver entrée dish, the butter in a silver butter dish, and the marmalade also framed in silver – whereas the whole secret of entertaining easily without a maid is to serve dainty food with as little labour as possible.

When entertaining at breakfast without a maid have the table set with a bright breakfast cloth, a bread-and-butter plate, and a knife and fork for bacon and eggs, and a butter-spreading knife for each. If grapefruit be served have it at each place with a pointed spoon on the side before announcing breakfast. Set everything in place before you sit down so that you haven't to rise in the middle of the meal and go to the kitchen. The guest can serve the bacon and eggs, you can pour out coffee or tea, and have a tray wagon close beside you so that you can move used dishes on to it, in order to keep the table tidy throughout the meal.

Better still, keep to the old-fashioned English way of having whatever hot dish is served arranged on a hot-plate on the sideboard along with plates, and let all help themselves.

When it comes to lunch or supper, arrange the table so as to save you trouble when the meal is in progress. If offering soup, have it served in individual bouillon cups when you sit down. Eliminate carving and serving as much as possible by making individual fish or meat creams or dishes en cocotte the savoury course. When a fish mayonnaise is on the menu arrange individual portions in the kitchen, and leave them in the refrigerator while the first course is being taken.

Salt Fish for Ash Wednesday

'CLOTILDE' ARRANGES A
LENTEN DINNER MENU
Clotilde

Some good Breton dishes:

Potage Purée de Haricots Blancs
Soles aux Fines Herbes et au Vin Blanc
Salsifis Frits
Oignons Farcis
Diplomate au Rhum

Potage Purée de Haricots Blancs

For 3 or 4 persons, put ¾ pint of haricot beans on the fire with enough cold water to cover them completely, and a small onion. When cooked take out the onion and rub the beans through a sieve, add a little milk, return them to the saucepan with a little butter and salt, heat, but do not boil, and serve with bread cut in dice and fried in butter.

Soles aux Fines Herbes et au Vin Blanc

Clean one or more soles according to size, remove the black skins and scrape the white skin. Place in a fire-proof baking dish a piece of butter as large as an egg. When it is melted add to it some finely chopped parsley and shallots, salt and pepper. Place your sole or soles on this and sprinkle more butter, parsley and shallots over them. Pour in a glass of white wine and dust with fine white breadcrumbs. Place some bits of butter on them. Bake until cooked and a fine colour. Serve in the dish in which it has been cooked.

Salsifis Frits
Scrub the salsify, but do not peel it; boil it until tender for about 30 to 35 minutes; peel it. Cut it in pieces to suit yourself. Make a batter with eggs, flour. Dip the salsify in this and fry. Serve dusted with salt and garnished with fried parsley.

Oignons Farcis
Peel some large onions and scoop out some of the middle of each to be filled with a savoury herb stuffing. For a Lenten dinner this is prepared with fried white breadcrumbs, powdered herbs, butter, chopped mushrooms, pepper, salt, and yolk of egg; for any other dinner sausage or other meat can be used. Place them in a buttered baking dish.

Now make a sauce with the onion that was scooped out, chopped finely, and fried in butter, add a little flour and vegetable stock, pepper and salt, finish with a teaspoonful of brandy. Pour this sauce over the onions, and bake them for one and a half hours in a good but moderate oven. Baste them frequently and serve them in the dish in which they have been baked.

Diplomate au Rhum
Butter a mould; take ½lb sponge fingers, split them, spread them with apricot jam; put the two halves together, place them in a dish and soak them in a syrup made of sugar, rum, and water. When soaked put them in the mould in layers with a few raisins, some minced candied peel and angelica between each layer. (Do not fill the mould too full, because this pudding swells in cooking.) Finish by pouring over it a good custard made with two eggs to every pint of milk, sweeten it very slightly. Cover with buttered paper and steam for about one and a half hours. Turn out and serve with or without a wine sauce.

23 February 1980
MAKING UP FOR LENT

To the Editor of the *Daily Telegraph*

Sir – Those of us who do not follow Dr Anthony Hall (20 February) in his Lenten abstinence can take comfort from the fact that 46 days after Easter his weight and girth will be restored to its present level.

E. J. R. Burrough,
Oxford

2 March 1978
MEETING THE MEATLESS DAYS, WITH SOME SAVOURY DISHES
Bon Viveur

Meatless days during Lent, or for the seemingly far longer period of punitive prices, need not be a penance. With over 400 egg recipes, as many cheese ones and close on a thousand for vegetables listed in *Larousse Gastronomique*, it should not be difficult to find something which appeals to everyone – except those of you who hate cheese and eggs.

We shall begin with a reminder that there is still, in Paris, a restaurant called Androuet just a step or two up the hill on the right hand side of the Gare St Lazare in the Rue Amsterdam where every one of the 22 hot specialities served daily is a cheese classic. Once, there were 450 dishes offered. Now the total has diminished considerably. We shall filch a dish from Androuet's repertoire.

Then there is Mrs Agnes Bertha Marshall, who invented a pell-mell cheese sauce which is sufficiently versatile to provide a Hot Cheese Flan, a filling for pastry canapés, and to dilute with extra milk as a sauce.

You can also use Mrs M's sauce undiluted for filling into baked savoury short paste flan cases, piling on to buttered toast, and serving with helpings of piperade; or just anchovy or tomato purée flavoured scrambled eggs.

Then, since we are devoting ourselves to the finest of cooks and chefs, let us filch from Ali-Baba his Symphonie d'Oeufs, and go back to Agnes

Bertha Marshall for something to keep potted up in the refrigerator spreading on toast rounds for supper.

The Recipes

Les Trois Trois
A soufflé omelette with a vegetable filling; poached eggs and a cheese fondue.

Method: Allow one poached egg apiece and 1 egg apiece for the soufflé omelette. Separate the yolks of the soufflé eggs from their whites. Whip the former with an equal number of tablespoons of cold water to egg yolks. Then whip the whites as stiffly as possible. Keep mixtures separate until moment of cooking.

Collect a large breakfast cupful of mixed, left-over cooked vegetables such as diced cooked carrots, diced cooked potatoes, a remnant of chopped white and green of cauliflower. Add to these a single slice of bread from a sandwich loaf diced small, crust and all, and fried until crisp in a very little hot dripping. Mix well together. Turn into a small saucepan, add 1 level tablespoon of tomato purée, salt and pepper to season, 1 generous tablespoon of top-of-the-milk, and 2½ fl oz thick white sauce made with stock not milk.

Fill a frying pan to a depth of ½in with boiling water, stir in, over a low heat, 1 tablespoon of wine vinegar and break in the eggs for poaching. If the water just heaves slightly, eggs will poach perfectly until white just begins setting around the edges. Flick some of the vinegary water over the eggs until white veils them. Draw to the side of the cooker and set omelette pan in its place. Melt enough butter or other fat in hot pan to coat the base. Fold egg yolk mixture into stiffly whipped whites, add a light salt and pepper seasoning.

Turn into pan over a low heat and leave for a few moments. As base begins to set, slide a spatula under to allow remaining fluid to flow beneath. When bubbles break on upper surface, put half vegetable filling over, with omelette still in pan, then fold it double and slide it out onto a heated dish. Lift out the poached eggs, drain and set on top of the omelette. Pour over remaining vegetable mixture and mask completely with the light fondue (see below). Serve at once with plenty of hot French bread, either plain or rubbed with garlic butter.

Light Cheese Fondue

Method: Put 6oz thinly sliced Cheshire cheese into a pan and cover with 6 fl oz of either dry cider or white wine. Allow to sit over an extremely low heat on an asbestos mat until contents become a goo with a wine or cider fringe. Bring them together by mixing 1 dessertspoonful of arrowroot (or ideally potato flavour) with a little more wine or water. Stir into the mixture in pan and keep stirring until mixture becomes thick and smooth. Use a wooden spoon throughout.

Symphonie D'oeufs Ali-Baba

Ingredients: 9 standard eggs; 1 tablespoon wine vinegar; 1 flat dessertspoon milled parsley heads; a little butter or other fat; 1 small raw, grated onion; 1 fl oz oil; salt; pepper; 2 medium tomatoes, vegetable mixture as given in Trois-Trois

Method: Hard boil, chill, shell and chop up 2 standard eggs. Prepare 4 of the eggs for a Belgian soufflé omelette (see previous recipe), adding parsley, salt and pepper when mixture is well blended just before cooking. Poach the remaining three eggs in boiling water and vinegar. Skin and cook the two tomatoes in a little fat with the raw onion until totally collapsed. Season with salt and black pepper. Make soufflé omelette over low heat to the point where bubbles break on upper surface. Spread tomato mixture over. Fold omelette in half, turn onto heated dish and serve with tomato or lemon sauce. Quantities given for four people.

Mrs Marshall's Cheese Crab

Method: Cut ½lb Gloucester or Cheshire cheese into extremely thin slices. Put into liquidiser or emulsifier with 1 teaspoon English mustard and 1 saltspoon French mustard, 1 teaspoon wine vinegar, a generous dash of freshly-ground black pepper, 1 tablespoon oil, 2 tablespoons thick cream and 1 small tin of Scandinavian appetit sild. Reduce contents to a spreading creamy mixture. Butter fresh, crust-less slices of toast, spread cheese crab on thickly. Brown under a fast grill and serve immediately.

Mrs Marshall's Cheese Sauce

Method: 1oz flour; 2oz grated hard cheese; 1¼oz butter or substitute; 2 raw egg yolks, pinch salt and pepper; 1½ gills cold milk, all flung into a small thick pan.

Stir over low heat to melt. Keep on stirring, relentlessly, until mixture becomes creamy and smooth, as it will. Use this to fill a short paste case for a cheesy flan. Add two tablespoons stiffly-whipped cream if you use it for piping. Dilute with extra milk, as needed, if using for saucing, for instance, in oeufs mollet.

Just boil eggs for mollet in fast boiling water for exactly 4 minutes. Tumble instantly into cold water. When quite cold, tap gently against side of sink, then turn on cold tap to yield a thin stream of water. Let water force itself between shell and inner skin to achieve these whole soft-boiled eggs perfectly every time.

4 April 1982
THOUGHT FOR FOOD: VICTORIAN SIMNEL CAKE
Denis Curtis

On Ash Wednesday Grandmama used to serve boiled salt codfish with triangles of boiled parsnip, and for 40 days we were made aware that Lent was upon us. I missed my rich puddings and cakes most. I was reminded of this when glancing through her recipe book: I found a dozen Lent cakes, some differing from the others by only a smidgin of grated nutmeg. We gained respite on the fourth Sunday in Lent, Mothering Sunday, when a rich Simnel cake was served (nowadays the practice of serving the cake has transferred to Eastertide). Grandmama's favourite cake was from an old Welsh recipe (her book contained many versions, including one from Shrewsbury and four from Bury St Edmunds). It clung to the past by being yeast leavened and having an almond layer baked in its centre; it also had a layer of almond icing on the top, in the modern manner.

Stir ½oz of fresh yeast into 5 fl oz of blood-warm milk together with 1tspn of flour and 1tspn of caster sugar. Leave until well-risen and frothy; about 1 hour. Meanwhile mix together 8oz plain flour and ¼ small nutmeg, grated, 1½ tspns cinnamon, 4oz caster sugar and into this rub 4oz butter. Now mix in 10oz currants and 3oz mixed chopped candied peel. Beat into the risen yeast mixture 3 well-beaten eggs and 2tblspns of brandy.

Combine the two mixtures, and mix well together. Leave in a warm place to rise for 2 hours. Spoon half the mixture into a well-buttered and lined 7in to 8in spring-sided cake tin. Cover with a round of almond paste (see below) and then pour in the rest of the cake mixture. Bake on the centre shelf of an oven pre-heated to 350°F (gas mark 4) and as soon as well-risen and slightly browned reduce the heat to 250°F (gas mark ½) and bake on for 2 hours, or until the cake shrinks from the sides of the tin and a skewer, inserted above the almond layer, comes out clean. Cool in the tin. Turn out, brush the top with apricot preserve and cover with a layer of almond paste. Place 11 marzipan balls (said to represent the 12 apostles, less Judas) around the edge; brush with white of egg and dust with caster sugar. Return to the oven at 300°F (gas mark 2) till slightly browned.

Almond paste: You can buy very good pure almond paste ready made, but for this cake pound 1 lb sweet almonds till quite smooth with a little rose-water. Mix in ½lb icing sugar and as much beaten egg white as will bind it.

Say Cheese, Please

22 April 1955
WE SEARCH FOR DOUBLE GLOUCESTERS
Bon Viveur

Car-prowling through the fresh green Gloucestershire lanes, we braked, just as you might do any week-end, outside a farmhouse of glowing Cotswold stone and under the sign 'Eggs laid while you wait'.

It need have been no more than agreeable that we 'waited' with the good-looking Potters in their log-scented study at Broad Campden; but when we spotted a farming weekly between a raft of 17th to 20th-century cook books and below a shelf of wine tomes, we quickly found we had stepped into a Happy Family of gourmets which even buys its meat from Mr Bragg, the local butcher.

So the Potters – Arthur, farmer, cook, antiques connoisseur and collector, and his wife Enid, mum and housewife to a lively family, interior decorator and managing director of a wholesale paper merchants – took charge of our marketing and restaurant selection.

Before we set off Arthur, wearing a weskit the Tailor of Gloucester would have been proud to own, gave us a lesson on the perfect way to dry roast the eight-week-old ducks he raises, plucks, dresses, wraps in vegetable parchment and cooks at 375° F, gas No. 5.

After packaging our mutually approved North Holland Blue unwashed warm chicken's eggs (not the regulation Packing Station washed eggs) we plunged into meat lore over Mr Bragg's barn door shop entrance. Our 6ft 4in cicerone selected his prime favourite lamb chops, not cutlets, and steaks from young bullock carcasses which had not yet grown all their teeth. 'That's where we country-folk score in our small licensed slaughterer butchers.' She smiled contentedly.

A genuine pork steak was cut under the critical eye from a nine score bacon pig – 'heavier, eh Mr Bragg, than the prime seven score bacon pig?' All the country folk around here know that over seven score the bacon fat exceeds the correct one-and-one-eighteenth inch thickness.

Then we were borne off to luncheon behind the giant copper kettle which shines in the entrance of the Noel Arms, Chipping Campden. Arthur chose robust stock-based family soup, a massive plate of home cured ham, home cooked tongue, home made pickles and chutneys and wound up with cream topped apricot pie (for 7s 6d).

Enid and we were excited about the light, pale 'pieces' coffee sugar which we agree has the best flavour of all especially (here we taught the Potters something) for gooey, crisp meringues. So, luncheon praised and ended, we bought 20 lb of it at 7½d a lb behind the bow-fronted windows of the old family grocer down the street. Now our blackcurrant jam will be really 'the tops' for next winter's coughs and colds.

We were excited too as we started our quest for Double Gloucester cheeses. We explored the Wednesday Gloucester market from end to end. No sign of it here, nor of farm butter like the beautiful pound we bought from a village shop (open on Sundays) in Halford over the Warwickshire border. We scoured the shops in Gloucester – found inferior butter, none of the local cheese and the statement: 'There hasn't been any since the war.' Temporarily defeated, we followed broad shouldered farm folk to a plain, satisfying dinner at the New County Hotel, Gloucester, where onion soup preceded oxtail, and a Welsh rarebit wound up an admirable English meal for 7s 6d.

Tewkesbury market failed us too, but we found the answer in the tiny hamlet of Stone where Miss Sybil Smith and her sister were busy in their cheese room with the last of the '54 Double Gloucesters; these included the two magnificent specimens Miss Sybil has made for the Queen when she comes to the county next month.

She served us with a pound (6s) as we stood ankle deep among kittens by the kitchen fire sipping Miss Sybil's crystal clear damson wine. If you place your small orders now you can have some of the '55 May to September Double Gloucester for Christmas, but the supply is limited.

Five by now (we had added a marmalade kitten, Mrs Gooseyplum of Gloucester, to our entourage), we celebrated at the Manor House Hotel at Moreton-in-the-Marsh. The deft waitresses are young, like the farm-supplied chickens, and there was the widest assortment ever of fresh salads.

Before we quit the county we went to the half-timbered Ship Hotel at Alveston for genuine pork sausage toad-in-the-hole in our three-course 5s 6d luncheon and just over the county border into Burford for tea at Huffkins where they make such featherweight currant bread.

This is a poor market country by comparison with the little shops and its catering successes seem to lie in food made and raised in home farms and kitchens, and sold in the smallest places.

*

We only report one failure; Mrs Gooseyplum took a powerful dislike to the Potters' family pet, Mrs Jemima Puddleduck, one goose who will never enter an oven door!

10 July 1970
SAY CHEESECAKE
Clement Freud

Cheesecake is a word I have never yet been given in a word association test. I suppose I would say sex, possibly breasts... even lips, which would be passed as normal – the whole point of word association being to flush out the mental hang-ups of a man who counters say, 'lawn' with 'pubescence'.

'That is very interesting,' says the shrink, 'lawn/pubescence'; and before you know where you are there is your signature at the foot of an agreement undertaking to indulge in four sessions a week at 12 guineas a throw.

Recently in a restaurant in Denham the head waiter asked if I would care for cheesecake and I said 'coffee' – which would just about be considered border-line. And the waiter said, 'You ought to try our cheesecake; it's rather a speciality.'

Now I have encountered this dish, usually in transport cafés where it snarls at prospective buyers from behind a glass case; it appears in delicatessen shops, sold by the slice – which is a denomination in which I prefer not to purchase – but as the waiter hovered I informed him that I would be very pleased to try his speciality.

It turned out to be so much better than I had expected and looked so ravishingly beautiful that I asked the good Swiss–German chef for the recipe. Having employed my new metric slide-rule to translate 36 eggs into numbers useful in small, planned families, I offer it to you as it was given. The dish is open to variations (you can stop when you have made the sponge cake and build a trifle), but it is a cook's confection; a logician's dream; everything that is done is done for a good reason – as you will see for yourself.

You begin by making a sponge: if you wish to save yourself this job there are grocers who sell sponge cakes; you will be a lesser human being if you take this shortcut, though it may make no great difference to the overall quality.

Take a whole egg; add to it two egg yolks and three ounces of caster sugar and blend into this mixture two stiffly beaten egg whites. To this light yellow froth contribute three ounces of sieved plain flour and when the mixture is well beaten, spread it in two ten-inch rounds, about one inch thick, on lightly buttered paper or foil on a baking sheet. The oven setting should be gas mark 3 (325°F) and the cooking time is likely to be 20 minutes. Use a knife to drive into the cake and remove sponge from oven only when the blade is clean on withdrawal. Thus do you produce the top and bottom of the cake, leaving, as the discerning reader will already have guessed, no more than the filling in the way of work outstanding.

A cheesecake when completed contains a solidly set off-white *crème*, nestling betwixt two sponge cake layers. It is important to mix this filling at warm summer day's kitchen temperature; let it set in a cool place prior to putting it *in situ*, and then chill it preparatory to consumption.

You need cream cheese, of good quality – such as Sainsbury's sell – or you can make it with milk gone sour, hung in a cloth for two days and the residue mixed with half its weight in whipped double cream. Of this take eight ounces. Add one whole egg, beaten; 1½ ounces of caster sugar from the airtight jar which your caster sugar occupies with a vanilla pod – beware of small bottles of essence – and to this mixture add the juice of half a lemon and that of half an orange. Blend well, add a quarter pint of double cream, lightly whipped, and an envelope of gelatine dissolved in a little warm sugar.

This then is the filling, give or take some pieces of crystallised fruit; chill it, sculpt it into place with a palette knife which, ever and anon, you dip into hot water so that a minimum of the mixture adheres to it . . . and when you have achieved the shape of a cake, put on the top layer and garnish with whipped cream cunningly piped, or dredge with icing sugar.

At raspberry time you may add a thin layer of raspberries, whole dry fruit insulated in whipped cream so that the pinkness is seen to be deliberate rather than giving the confection unpleasing indiscriminate specks of off-red.

As this is the milkshake season I felt it meet to inform readers that any milkshakes – coffee, chocolate, strawberry or raspberry – can become marvellously rich with the aid of a banana.

To a pint of milk, three tablespoons of sugar and four cubes of ice allow one banana and liquidise with whatever flavouring you like . . . and should it be a banana milkshake you are after, add another banana.

30 January 1929

DEVONSHIRE CREAM
By a Woman Chef

Devonshire cream need not be made in Devon or Cornwall.

Simply let the strained new milk stand in a wide-topped pan for twelve hours; then stand it over a pan of hot water on the fire or whatever means of heating used, until the milk is scalding hot and the cream on top is thick and looks somewhat crinkled; it must not boil.

Take off and leave another twelve hours or until cold. It may then be lifted off with a skimmer. The great aim is to keep the top thin crust as unbroken as possible because it looks so nice.

WHAT TO DO WITH CHEESE
Recipe from *Good Eating* (1944)
The *Daily Telegraph* Home Cook

A little cheese can do much in catering. As an ingredient in hot vegetable and other savoury dishes, it adds interest and nutritive value. There is also the bowl of grated cheese, which can turn soup, salad or savoury into a complete meal. Home-made oatcakes or potato cakes are a good accompaniment.

Put a bowl of grated cheese on the table for another simple meal – hot potatoes steamed or roasted in their jackets. This addition and plenty of pepper turns jacket potatoes into appetising savoury.

A Quick Savoury
2oz grated cheese;
1 reconstituted egg;
1 teacupful fine breadcrumbs;

Small teacupful milk, fresh or dried;
Pepper, salt;
Tiny piece of margarine

Beat up egg, add crumbs, melted margarine, cheese, seasoning and milk. Beat all together. Bake in moderate oven for 15 minutes.

N. S. Finchley

As A Spread
½lb cheese, grated;
¾oz margarine;
1 teaspoonful salt;

A little less than ¼ pint milk;
1oz cornflour or flour to thicken

Bring milk, margarine and salt to boil in saucepan and thicken with cornflour or flour. Add grated cheese (using up any dry pieces), cook over low heat, stirring all the time till contents of pan become smooth paste.

This takes about 8 minutes. While still hot pour soft creamy cheese into jam jar. Suitable for toasts, sandwiches, salad.

Mrs R. C. Wilson, Highwood House, Kingston Hill

Cheese Croquettes – Three Ways
(1) With potato:

1 cupful mashed potato;	*Seasoning;*
¼ to ½ cupful grated cheese;	*A little milk;*
1 dried egg (optional);	*Breadcrumbs;*
Shredded onion;	*Frying fat*
Dab of margarine;	

Make potato really smooth with a scrap of margarine, season, add shredded onion, dried egg in powder form and cheese. Beat well to make light. If too dry add a little milk. Form into flat thin cakes, coat in breadcrumbs (or brush over with milk) and fry golden brown in hot fat. Serve with salad, hot gravy or salad dressing.

(2) With macaroni or other paste:
Substitute 1 cupful cold cooked macaroni for potato and put through mincer. Add scraps of minced bacon or left-over meat. Proceed as before.

(3) With cauliflower, cabbage, carrot or swede:
Choose a green and a root vegetable. Use two cupfuls, one of each, in place of potato. Proceed as before. Serve with potato chips.

Pea Purée Pancakes

1 lb peas (fresh, dried or tinned);	*Dab of margarine;*
2oz grated cheese;	*Pancakes or fried croutons;*
1 dessertspoon chopped mint;	*Seasoning*
½ teaspoonful sugar;	

Cook peas till tender, adding sugar to water. Drain. Mash peas or rub through sieve, mix in mint, margarine and seasoning. Make two thick pancakes, using one dried or fresh egg. Turn on to hot dish with purée spread between as though for sandwich cake and serve with dish of grated cheese.

Another method is to serve pea purée very hot in bowls with grated cheese and fried croutons made either by cutting up slice of stale bread in small triangles and frying in boiling fat or dipping pieces in gravy and browning on greased tin in oven.

Mrs H. G. Goodall, The Wardenry, Farley, Salisbury

2 February 1946
NO MORE DRIED EGGS

To the Editor of the *Daily Telegraph*

Sir – 'There will be no further allocation of dried eggs!' Had an atomic bomb been hurled at the housewife it could not have had a much more devastating effect.

It is stated that it is hoped to increase the shell egg ration. Is there any likelihood that we shall get 12 shell eggs a month, the equivalent of one box of dried eggs, when we now, with luck, get one shell egg a month?

Yours truly,

(Mrs) B. Bell

To the Editor of the *Daily Telegraph*

Sir – Apparently we have enough dollars to buy America's films, but not enough to buy dried eggs.

The last stand-by is now wrenched from the English housewife.

Yours faithfully,

G. M. Bonham-Carter,

Guildford

Six Phases of the Carrot

10 February 2001
BRING BACK TRUE PARSLEY FROM DEATH AND OBLIVION
Germaine Greer

Ever since I first read *English Food* in 1977, I have revered the memory of the late great Jane Grigson. Her prose glowed with her pleasure when she described a traditional dish cooked properly (as distinct from Delia Smith, who is only enthusiastic about a traditional dish after she has 'improved' it). Grigson knew there was such a thing as 'getting it right' and would have shared my contempt for such abominations as pasta salad. I have made a winter ritual of brewing Assam tea and perching on my kitchen stool to read chapter and verse from Grigson's *Vegetable Book*, first published in 1978, but as I read, a cold draught occasionally blows across my mind. Grigson, the great Grigson, is now out of date. Much as I love and trust her I can no longer do as she bids me.

Under 'H' in Grigson's *Vegetable Book*, you will read of 'Hamburg Parsley or Parsley Root'. 'Hamburg Parsley,' Grigson writes, 'is a large-rooted variety of the familiar herb.' And what familiar herb might that be?

Parsley, of course (fool!). And what is 'parsley'? I was brought up with a huge disdain for parsley, which was principally known in those far-off days as the ingredient of a cornflour-based sauce that was used to conceal the hideousness of overcooked marrow or grey-fleshed fish. In the first restaurants I worked in, parsley was something the chef strewed in handfuls over plates of poorly presented food. Sometimes it was my job to make a mess more presentable by tucking two or three parsley flounces round the edges.

I have since learnt to value parsley greatly, first as one of the ingredients of maître d'hôtel butter, which can make anything edible, even a snail or a cultivated mushroom, and then as the perfume that presides over salsa verde and tabouleh. However, for both of these I would use freshly gathered young leaves of the flat-leaved variety; frilly parsley, however dark its green, seems to me to have very little scent at all.

Yet parsley ought to be pleated by nature, for nowadays its botanical name is *Petroselinum crispum*. The Greeks associated it with oblivion and death; though they crowned victorious athletes with parsley, it was never served at table. My Tuscan housekeeper used to say that parsley is slow to germinate because it has to go down to hell and pay its respects to the devil before it can come up; another tradition is to fool the seed that it is in hell by pouring boiling water in the seed-drill.

In England, the belief is that the uprooting of a parsley plant will be followed by disaster, so parsley is not thinned or transplanted. Charley, my old gardener, used to tell of a trivial accident in which he contrived to break both ankles, when he was riding his bike home after transplanting parsley.

Parsley originates in the Mediterranean, and its associations by the Greeks with death are justified because the herb as it grows on dry, sun-drenched mountain sides contains higher concentrations of the toxic oleoresin apiol, which has all kinds of applications, not least as an abortifacient.

The essential oil of parsley was called apiol because Linnaeus thought the herb a kind of celery and named it *Apium petroselinum*. Later taxonomists thought it a caraway and renamed it *Carum petroselinum*. Now we agree that it is a separate genus of two species, *P. crispum* and *P. segetum* or corn parsley.

Flat-leaved parsley, called by some disparagingly 'soup parsley', never had crisped leaves and seems more like a celery, and I wonder if it is in fact genetically identical. This would be less of a puzzle if common usage did not dub practically every smelly cut-leaved biennial umbellifer a 'parsley'.

Cow parsley is of the genus *Anthriscus*, as is chervil; the poisonous weed fool's parsley was also thought to be an *Anthriscus*; it is now separately identified as *Aethusa cynapium*; its other name, as you would expect, is dog parsley. Tempting as it is to imagine that parsnip is a parsley neep or root, the truth seems to be that it came by that name by a false etymology, when its Latin name *pastinaca* was so corrupted that it was forgotten.

Hamburg parsley was bred by Dutch horticulturalists in the 17th century because the root was the most valued part of the plant. It turned up regularly in English markets thereafter, but was rather less likely to be found when Grigson was writing in the 1970s. This year nurserymen are offering the seeds again, under the misleading name of *Petroselinum crispum* var. *tuberosum*, describing its root as 'rather like a parsnip but with a parsley flavour' while its flat, parsnippy leaves 'can be used as parsley'. It is time not to rewrite Grigson but to rehabilitate Hamburg parsley.

26 May 1923
SIX WAYS WITH ASPARAGUS
Elsie Wetherell

Asparagus, with its delicate flavour, is a general favourite, but although there are several attractive ways of serving it, in most households it is just plainly boiled, so I am giving some simple recipes that my readers may like to try. Care should be taken when buying to see that it is very fresh. If the heads are drooping and the ends of the stalks are brown, it is generally stale. It may be quite well kept a day or two in a jug of very cold water with the stalks downwards. Sprue, the last shoots of the asparagus plant, is excellent for cooking the following dishes, as it is much cheaper, but has the same delicious flavour. I will give recipes for cakes and small pastries by request in my next article.

Asparagus Soup

1 pint milk;	*Small bundle asparagus;*
1oz butter;	*Salt, pepper;*
1 onion;	*½ pint water*
1oz flour;	

Wash the asparagus, cut across the stalks in the middle, and boil in salted water until the tops are tender. Take them up and cut the green tops into small 'peas'. Put on one side and cover them up. Cut remainder of stalks into short lengths and simmer thirty minutes longer in the liquor. Strain through sieve, pressing lightly; then boil the liquor until reduced to half a pint. Put the onion to infuse in the milk, meanwhile standing pan with it in at side of stove. Then bring to boil and pour on to the flour, which has been mixed with the butter, in another saucepan, removing the onion. Add the liquor of the asparagus, and stir until it thickens lightly. Add the asparagus peas, season to taste with salt and pepper, and serve very hot.

Time, one hour. Sufficient for four or five persons. Probable cost, 2s 6d to 3s.

Asparagus Omelet

Beat four eggs in basin lightly. Add a tablespoonful of milk, season with salt and pepper, add also some asparagus heads previously boiled. Make one ounce of butter hot in omelet pan, let it get very hot, then pour in the eggs. When beginning to set stir it with a knife and keep as much as possible to centre of pan, not letting it spread out too thin. When ready the underneath part of the omelet should be a golden brown and the surface very soft. When sufficiently set slip one omelet from the pan on to a hot dish, letting it roll as you do so, so that it will assume a folded shape. Serve immediately.

Asparagus Salad

1 bundle asparagus;
3 tablespoons salad oil;
1 tablespoon vinegar;
Lettuce;

Salt and pepper;
1 teaspoon mustard;
1oz chopped parsley

Have the asparagus cooked in salted boiling water and let it get cold; then cut away any hard stalk, leaving the green part only. Have the lettuce washed and carefully dried. Arrange at the bottom of salad bowl, and pile the asparagus in centre. Mix with a wooden spoon in a basin the mustard, salt and pepper, oil, and vinegar, mixing very thoroughly. Add the chopped parsley, and pour over the salad just before serving.

Asparagus with Vinaigrette Sauce

Bundle of cooked asparagus;	*Salt and pepper;*
3 tablespoons salad oil;	*½ teaspoon made mustard;*
1 tablespoon tarragon vinegar;	*½ teaspoon chopped shallot;*
1 teaspoon each of parsley, tarragon, and chervil;	*1 teaspoon chopped capers*

Cook the asparagus in the usual way and leave until cold. If it can be put on ice so much the better. Arrange on dish when required. Mix all the other ingredients very thoroughly and send to table separately with the asparagus.

Asparagus au Gratin

3 hard-boiled yolks of eggs;	*Salt and pepper*
1oz breadcrumbs;	*Large bundle asparagus*
3oz butter;	*1 dessertspoon finely chopped parsley*

Cook the asparagus in the usual way. Butter an au gratin dish well, and put on it a layer of the asparagus. Rub yolks of eggs through sieve and mix with them one dessertspoon of finely chopped parsley. Sprinkle the asparagus with this and a seasoning of salt and pepper; then another layer of asparagus. Continue these layers until all is used. Then cook the 3oz of butter in a stewpan until a nut brown colour. Mix the breadcrumbs to it, and pour over the asparagus and serve at once.

Asparagus Soufflés

25 heads of asparagus;	*¼ pint milk;*
1oz flour;	*1 egg;*
1oz butter;	*Salt, pepper*

Cook the asparagus and cut up the green part into pea shapes. Have some small china cases buttered. Mix the flour and milk very smoothly, add the egg yolk lightly beaten, the butter, salt and pepper, and the asparagus. Stir over fire until quite thick and smooth, without allowing mixture to boil. Rub through a sieve and mix in the white of egg, which has been whisked to a very stiff froth. Half fill the little cases with this mixture and bake in a moderate oven for about 15 minutes. Serve immediately.

18 January 1962
CRISP SALADS TO CHEER
GLOOMY DAYS
Elizabeth David

In an effort to economise after last month's extravagances and also because dried pulses, pasta products, root vegetables and fat meats such as salt or fresh pork are suitable at this time of year for keeping out the cold, most of us eat a high proportion of starchy foods during these months of deepest winter. So we need also the contrast, the clean tastes, the crisp textures, not to mention the vitamin values, of raw vegetables, salads and fresh fruit.

I don't know how many readers feel as I do about this, but the colder and gloomier the weather, the greater my craving for salads and the olive oil which goes into their dressings.

My great standby winter salad is based on a mixture of Belgian *endives* (or chicory as most greengrocers call them) and oranges, in the proportion of two nice fat *endives* to one large orange.

As long as they are in season, I buy Valencia naval oranges. They are expensive, but seedless, full of juice and with a flavour which seems more orangey than any other sweet oranges.

The *endives*, root and outside leaves removed and the whole vegetable simply wiped with a soft cloth, is cut into chunks. Then it is mixed with the orange segments and a perfectly straightforward dressing of salt, freshly milled pepper, a dash of sugar, and three tablespoons of fruity olive oil plus a teaspoon or so of tarragon-flavoured wine or cider vinegar or lemon juice.

This is a salad which comes to no harm if mixed and dressed just before your meal; it goes well with or after almost any main course dish of meat, fish or poultry, and additions can be made according to fancy or what is available.

For example, try a few fine strips of raw red or green sweet pepper, freed of all seeds and core. Tinned ones are too soft and mushy.

A stick or two of raw celery cut into matchstick strips could be added, or three or four raw mushrooms, washed and sliced; or lots of parsley, washed and roughly chopped; or a little chopped watercress and the grated rind of a Seville orange.

A tablespoon or two of diced beetroot may be used – but this should be separately seasoned and mixed in only at the last minute. Half a peeled and sliced avocado pear, also separately seasoned with plenty of lemon juice and a little oil and, again, added to the basic mixture only just before serving, produces a delicious contrast in texture and flavour.

At mid-day, my winter salads often take the form of a very simple little hors-d'oeuvre, such as a bowl of freshly grated carrots, shredded celeriac, or a raw cabbage and sweet pepper salad with a rather sharp dressing flavoured with crushed juniper berries.

Whichever of these I have chosen will be supplemented by a small dish of sliced Italian *salame* and black olives, or perhaps a few anchovy fillets, or some tunny fish or stuffed vine leaves.

I might use smoked cod's roe pounded and stirred to a creamy consistency with a scrap of garlic, olive oil, water and lemon juice.

Some such little combination, followed by a hot fish, egg or cheese dish, or pork chops grilled or baked with herbs and oil makes, with fresh fruit to finish, a type of meal which I find is much appreciated by those who, while not actually on a slimming diet, are at least trying not to put *on* weight.

Céleri-rave Remoulade

To make this celeriac hors-d'oeuvre – a dish familiar to anyone who has eaten regularly in the smaller restaurants of Paris and the French provinces – you do really need that invaluable utensil known as a *mandoline*, *coupe-julienne*, or universal slicer (Selfridges are selling French ones for 11s 6d, the cheapest I have yet seen).

On the fluted blade of the *mandoline* shred the peeled celeriac into matchstick pieces. As you proceed, put them into a bowl of cold water acidulated with lemon juice or vinegar.

Bring a saucepan of water, also acidulated and salted, to the boil. Plunge the drained celeriac into it. Leave it until the water comes back to the boil again, no longer. Then drain it as dry as you can in a colander.

This brief blanching makes all the difference to a celeriac salad, for in its totally raw state many people find it hard to chew and digest. Also, after blanching it absorbs less dressing or mayonnaise.

When the celeriac has cooled mix it with a very stiff homemade mayonnaise very strongly flavoured with mustard. Pile the celeriac on to a shallow dish, sprinkle it with parsley, and serve it fairly quickly: if left to stand for any length of time it begins to look rather unattractive and messy.

An average sized celeriac weighing about 1 lb plus about a third of a pint of mayonnaise (two egg yolks) will make an ample hors-d'oeuvre for four.

Carottes Râpées

This is another French favourite all too seldom seen this side of the Channel. Trim and pare 1 lb good coloured carrots on the coarsest surface of your grater. Mix in a bowl with a grated shallot or small onion and season sparingly with olive oil, lemon juice, salt and a scrap of sugar.

This is a beautiful, cheap and delicious hors-d'oeuvre; don't mix it with any other vegetable.

Fennel

Bulbous root stems of the Florentine fennel are on the Soho market stalls and in the continental greengrocer shops now. In France fennel is served as an hors-d'oeuvre, finely sliced, raw, with salt and an oil and lemon dressing.

In Italy this *finocchi* often appears at the end of the meal, with the fruit. Either way, I love the clean, fresh, slightly aniseed flavour and the crisp consistency of this vegetable.

In a friend's house in Rome I once had an interesting salad of shredded fennel and fine slivers of Gruyère cheese, all highly seasoned with freshly milled black pepper plus the usual lemon juice and olive oil.

This was served at the end of a very simple meal composed of a classic saffron-flavoured Milanese risotto, followed by delicious little grilled red mullet.

The fennel and cheese mixture sounds perhaps outlandish, but when you come to think of it, it is not so very different from the combination of celery and cheese which is our own national invention.

12 January 1929
A GUIDE TO WEEK-END
FOOD SUPPLIES

Try a few fresh lichees in place of the customary lozenges if a sore throat threatens. They possess the rich flavour of the muscat grapes, and, like them, are a wonderful remedy for this complaint.

Unfortunately they are very rarely seen in this country, but just now it is possible to get them. There are famous singers who, immediately before going on the platform, eat a few lichees or muscats to clear the throat.

The dried lichees are better known in this country, but the fresh fruit are the choicest. They grow not only in China but in South Africa, where the present consignment comes from. They should be selected from the colour of the thin, nut-like outer shell; when this is a light brown the fruit is immature, but when it darkens the lichees are perfect for eating.

Another dish of Oriental character is provided just now by the diminutive Japanese artichokes, which look like a reproduction in miniature of the Jerusalem variety. They have to be 'topped and tailed' and lightly scraped with a brush. They are boiled and served with white sauce. Just now the food-shops are full of interesting fruits and vegetables, with which the English housewife is insufficiently familiar. It is curious how many women express the keenest interest in some of the newer things and only stop short at the idea of trying them!

This applies to the delightful Capo gooseberries which are in just now. Women point them out to one another, ask questions about them, and finally order a pound of apples!

Custard apples and passion fruit, however, are gaining steadily in popularity. A vegetable which is comparatively new to the English housewife but a very common dish on the Continent consists of flagolets – the French green haricot beans – soaked well, boiled gently, and served with a sauce.

Among choice fruits from warm countries which come to gladden the heart of English housewives in January are Tafilat dates. These Egyptian dates are specially selected from the finest grades, but the sugaring process is done in this country. They are soaked in hot water to open the pores, so that the sugar penetrates the skin and enhances the flavour. The process incidentally swells the fruit considerably.

Although it is still winter in the streets, spring has come into the shops. There are, amongst other things, new potatoes from Algeria, radishes from France, asparagus from English hothouses, and marrows from Madeira. All are proofs of the fact, now well recognised by the trade, that seasons will soon cease to be so far as food is concerned. Housewives will be able to get almost anything for the table at any time, as more and more advantage is taken by the shops of new transport and buying methods. The modern tendency to limit the restrictions of seasons is bringing about a steady and important development of the hothouse industry in this country, where many springtime vegetables are now being brought on.

A minor outcome of the severance of relations between this country and the Soviet is the absence of Russian cranberries from many West-end shops. 'There is a growing demand for cranberries,' it was stated at one store. 'Present-day housewives are using them more and more to make both sweet and savoury dishes "interesting". Yet we are not getting the best cranberries, which come from Russia, out of deference to the feelings of many of our customers who have suffered heavy financial losses there. Very good "second-best" cranberries come from America.'

The usual New Year shortage of fish is just over. It arises from the fact that thousands of Scotch fisher boats lie idle while thousands of Scotch fishermen hold their revels from Jan. 1 to 7. At shops where sales are large and there is, therefore, no problem of storage, the demand is growing for prepared fish, such as dressed crabs and cartons of shelled shrimps ready for sandwich-making. As many as 300 cartons are sold in a day by one store.

The flavour of Scotch beef and mutton is particularly good just now. This is because just before Christmas prize-winning animals come into the market. Farmers are beginning to breed smaller animals, in response to the modern demand for small joints and small ovens!

Average Prices in the Shops
Below will be found approximate retail rates for good quality food in Greater London. Seville oranges, for marmalade making, are being offered at a large store at 1s to 1s 6d a dozen, 4s to 5s 9d for 50, and 7s 6d to 11s 3d per 100, with preserving sugar 12 lb for 3s, or 27s 6d per cwt.

BEEF

	H.K		Ch'd			H.K		Ch'd	
	s	d	s	d		s	d	s	d
Aithbone	0	11	0	8½	Brisket	0	10½	0	6
*Topside	1	8	1	3	Sirloin	1	10	1	2
*Silverside	1	4	1	1	Wing ribs	1	10	1	2
Rump steak	2	7	1	8	Thin flank	0	7	0	4
Beef steak	1	8	1	4	Stewing meat	1	4	1	0
*Boneless									

MUTTON

LAMB

	H.K		Fzn			H.K		Fzn	
	s	d	s	d		s	d	s	d
Loins	1	10	0	11		1	10	1	3
Legs	1	7	1	2		1	8	1	4
Shoulders	1	5	1	0		1	10	1	2
Necks	1	6	0	10		1	7	1	1
Breasts	0	8	0	4		1	6	0	11

POULTRY AND GAME

	s	d	s	d		s	d	s	d
Surrey fowls ea	8	0	11	6	Turkeys lb	1	3	1	8
Country fowls	6	6	9	6	Geese	0	10	1	3
Capons	11	0	16	6	Rabbits	0	11	1	3
Aylesbury ducks	9	6	13	0	Teal ea	1	9	–	–
Quail	2	9	3	3	Pheasants	4	6	6	6
Plover	1	3	1	10	Partridges	2	3	6	0
Hares	3	0	5	6	Wild ducks	4	0	–	–

PORK

	s	d		s	d
Small legs	1	5	Loin, chest end	1	8
Hand, with foot	0	9	Spare rib	1	2
Bladebone	1	3	Chops	1	10
Pickles	1	0	Heads	0	4½

FRUIT AND VEGETABLES

		s	d	s	d
Apples –					
Dessert	ea	0	4	0	8
Cooking		0	4	0	5
English Bramleys		0	6	0	8
Dessert pears	ea	0	6	0	6
Custard apples		0	2	1	6
Bananas	doz	2	9	2	8
South African					
Peaches	ea	0	4	0	9
Plums		0	2	0	4
Apricots		0	1½	0	3
"	lb	1	3	–	–
Hothouse grapes –					
Black	lb	2	3	3	0
Finest		4	0	5	0
Muscat		9	0	12	0
Almeria grapes		0	10	1	3
Oranges –					
Jaffas	doz	1	6	2	6
Denia		0	9	2	0
Mandarins		1	0	2	0
Lemons		0	6	1	6
Kent cobnuts	lb	1	3	–	–
Brazil nuts		0	10	1	0
Pineapples	ea	3	0	6	6
Tunis dates	crtn	0	6	0	9
Tomatoes	lb	0	6	0	10
Cucumbers	ea	2	0	3	0

		s	d	s	d
Forced seakale	lb	1	3	1	6
" punnet		2	6	3	0
Mushrooms	lb	3	0	4	0
Rhubarb	bdl	0	8	0	3½
Marmalade					
Oranges	doz	1	0	1	3
Madeira beans	lb	1	3	1	6
Asparagus –					
French	bdle	10	6	20	0
English		6	0	14	0
Salsify		0	8	0	9
Belgian Chicory	lb	0	7	0	8
Lettuce	ea	0	5	–	–
Cauliflowers	ea	0	6	0	8
Savoys		0	3	0	5
Cabbages		0	3	0	4
Brussels sprouts	lb	0	2	0	2½
Scotch kale		0	2	–	–
Celery	bds	0	3	0	5
Onions	lb	0	2	0	2½
Parsnips		0	1½	–	–
New potatoes –					
Algerian		0	5	0	6
Azores		0	5	0	6
Guernsey		1	3	1	6
Old potatoes –					
16 lb and 12 lb		1	0	–	–

18 February 1989
TASTE RIGHT ON TIME
Lynda Brown

I have decided to start a 'Save our Seasons' campaign. Wandering round my local Sainsbury's last week, looking at asparagus from Peru and fresh tarragon from America, I couldn't help recalling the words of Marcel Boulestin, the 1930s cookery writer, whose books had the same kind of pioneering influence as Elizabeth David's have in our own time.

'Let us have things that are in season,' he wrote. 'What pleasure is there in eating out-of-season salad artificially grown? What taste in it? And what pleasure shall we have when it comes to us, in its time, as it were, a gift of nature, if we eat it all the year round?'

Which is not to say, 50 years on, that I do not appreciate the range and variety of fruit and vegetables now on offer, but just that I feel things have gone too far. Half the enjoyment of eating lies in its appropriateness, be it to match the mood, occasion or season. That is why strawberries taste best at Wimbledon and spring cabbage tastes best in spring.

Take, for example, fresh herbs. The first herbs to show through in the garden, and especially early this year, are sorrel, chives, mint, and chervil. Clean, lively, refreshing and astringent, they are just the thing to make you feel sprightly and spring-like. The fragrance of basil or tarragon, wonderful herbs, need sunshine and warmth and don't strike the right note till later.

In the 19th century, in my part of the world, green or 'saar grass' sauce, made like mint sauce but with strong vinegar, sugar and pounded sorrel, was a great favourite to serve with meat. Sorrel, the one herb that seems almost impossible to buy in this country, will grow on any patch of ground and the small arrow-shaped buckler leaf will put an ordinary salad into the designer league.

Mint (go for spearmint and apple mint), and lacy-leaved chervil with its faintly aniseed flavour, thrive in odd shady corners. Add tiny leaves of both to spring salads.

Chives are similarly easy, and a small clump begged from your neighbour will soon establish itself. These, too, are at their best now while the blades are young and tender.

Don't forget that later the pale mauve flowers make pretty additions to summer salads and have the same chive taste.

Lemon and Chervil Soup
(Serves 4)

600ml/1pt fine flavoured fish stock; *Juice of 1 large lemon beaten*
1 tbsp rice; *together with 2 eggs;*
1 tbsp finely chopped chervil

This is a perfect spring soup. Simmer rice in the fish stock in a covered pan until tender. Have the lemon and egg mixture ready in a bowl. Add a ladleful of stock, whisk together, then tip the mixture into the rest of the stock in the pan.

Keep whisking and cook until the mixture is very hot and thickens slightly, but on no account let it boil, or else it will curdle. Stir in chervil, and serve immediately, in hot soup bowls.

Noisettes of Lamb with Mint and Ruby Glaze

(Serves 4)

4 noisettes of lamb, taken from the For the glaze:
* fillet, approx. 2.5cm/1in thick;* *250ml/8 fl oz red wine;*
7g/¼oz clarified butter plus 1 dsp *1 sprig of mint;*
* vegetable oil for frying* *1½ tbsp redcurrant jelly;*
30g/1oz butter, cut into bits;
1 tsp finely chopped mint, plus extra
* for garnish*

1. Cook the lamb over a brisk heat in a non-stick pan in the butter and oil for approximately 2 minutes each side.
2. Remove and keep warm on four hot plates. Wipe out fat. Pour in wine, add sprig of mint and reduce by half. Turn down heat to low and stir in redcurrant jelly to taste. Remove mint and combine the sauce with butter, shaking the pan to amalgamate the sauce.
3. Stir in chopped mint and pour dark shiny sauce around each noisette. Decorate with mint leaves and serve with rice.

Sorrel Mayonnaise

Herb mayonnaises give a lift to the bought jars of the stuff we are now obliged to buy. The secret is to pound the herbs to a paste first, rather than simply chopping them. This results in a beautiful pale green speckled mayonnaise with real class.

Remove the midribs from a handful of sorrel, chop, then pound in a pestle and mortar to a dark green sludge. Stir in mayonnaise to taste. To use, let down with a little hot water, a tsp at a time, and use to coat hard-boiled eggs for egg mayonnaise; or mix with thick creamy yoghurt to make a delicate sauce for fish or vegetable terrines and mousses, and cold poached salmon.

Cheese and Chive Toastie

Toast bread on both sides and lay in a hot heatproof dish. Moisten with a little red wine, just enough to soak into the bread without making it too wet. Cover liberally with thin slices of a melting cheese such as Lancashire and grill until bubbling. Sprinkle generously with chives, cut into wedges and serve immediately.

This, incidentally, is a variation of the 18th-century recipe for English rabbit. To make the original version, omit chives.

SUMMER

Chuck Berries

12 June 1951
STRAWBERRIES AND CREAM
Claire Butler

This week is traditionally associated with the serving of salmon and strawberries. But until I enlightened him, the manager of London's newest exclusive restaurant – the South Bank's Regatta Roof – had not heard of Royal Ascot!

Both M. Wagner, who has never been in England before and came over to do this job, and the chef, are Swiss. Now they are catering for the V.I.P.s, including diplomats and visiting statesmen, who quite frequently dine in this attractive riverside room.

They agree that, in honour of Royal Ascot which starts today, salmon and strawberries should be on the menu. Here are some glamorous ways in which the chef, M. Spies, will serve the fruit.

1. Strawberry Regatta – Put servings of ice-cream in individual glasses, pour over each a little Grand Marnier. Arrange hulled strawberries round. Pour fresh cream over ice-cream, sprinkle on a little sugar.
2. Vacherin – Have a meringue base. Sieve some strawberries, cook with a little sugar till syrupy. Place on meringue, sprinkle a little kirsch over.

 105

3. Fruit Flan – Make a shortbread type of pastry. Leave ½ hour in refrigerator or in a cool place, then roll out ½-inch thick and line a flan ring with it, pressing it firmly against the sides. Remove surplus paste from top of ring. Prick bottom, cover with a round of greased paper and fill with rice or crusts. Bake on a baking sheet or tin in a very moderate oven (350°F, gas No. 3).

When cooked, remove paper and rice. When cold, fill with strawberries, pile over whipped cream.

M. Spies will cover his strawberries with a glaze made from sugar and sieved strawberries boiled together to a thick syrup, but many readers may not bother with this extra refinement.

An American Way

No one wants to spend long sunny hours in the preparation of meals. Here is a time-saving idea from an American friend for serving strawberries. You bake a quantity of sponge cakes (using your favourite recipe) in medium-sized patty tins, and scoop out centres ready for filling – in the U.S.A. these shells can be bought prepared. These little cakes will keep well in a tin and can be brought out when wanted. Here are a few suggestions for filling:

Strawberries topped with cream. Sliced bananas mixed with a little raspberry jam, and, for topping, chopped walnuts, custard or cream.

Strawberries with ice-cream, covered with meringue mixture, put into a hot oven a minute or two to set the meringue.

Sliced tinned pear or slices of fresh poached pear, covered with chocolate sauce.

A Baked Sweet

2oz butter, 2oz plain flour, 2oz sugar, ½ pint of milk, 2–3 eggs, ¼ pint of evaporated milk, vanilla essence.

Put butter into a small pan with the flour, stir over low heat for a minute or two without colouring, add milk gradually, cook a few minutes till mixture thickens, add sugar, remove from heat. Add well-beaten egg yolks, then evaporated milk and vanilla essence to taste. Whip egg whites stiffly, pour into custard mixture, blend together and pour into a square glass oven dish. Bake about 20 minutes, 400°F, gas No. 6.

When cooked, remove from oven, sprinkle with caster sugar, put under grill to melt sugar. When cold, cover top with strawberries and cream, if you want a specially delicious sweet.

Strawberry Sherbet

2 cupfuls crushed strawberries, a few whole ones, 1 cupful caster sugar, 1 cupful of cream, a little liqueur.

Stand crushed strawberries in a very cold place for 2 hours. Fold in whipped cream and sugar (saving a little for whole fruit), freeze fairly stiffly. Soak whole fruit in liqueur with sugar, put sherbet in glasses with a whole berry on each. Serve with sponge fingers or wafers.

5 April 1951
BANANAS AGAIN IN COOKERY
Claire Butler

First sign of bananas (now obtainable without green ration books) on English menus came from Brighton this week. Notable dish at a notable meal for Brighton's branch of the Wine and Food Society attended by the Society's president, M. André Simon and Mme. Simon at the Restaurant Lucien, was *Nonnettes de Poulet Petit Duc*. These chicken cutlets in cutlet frills, were served with fried bananas, potato straws and French peas.

Here is another continental dish which the housewife can do when she has enough eggs to allow one for each person.

Spanish Savoury

8oz rice, small onion, 4 eggs, 4 bananas cut in half lengthways, 3oz butter or margarine, salt and pepper.

Cook rice till tender, about 15 minutes. Melt 1oz margarine in pan and fry thinly sliced onion gently till soft and light brown, then fry the bananas. Drain the rice, add rest of the margarine, put over low heat to melt it and reheat rice. Stir in the fried onions. Put in the oven to keep warm while you fry the eggs. Put eggs on rice and the bananas round.

Savoury banana dishes are new to many British palates, but do you remember the excellent sweets one used to make? Here are variations:

Banana Pudding

4oz flour, 2 bananas, 2 eggs, 2oz margarine, 2oz sugar, 1 tablespoon water.

Beat margarine and sugar to a cream. Separate yolks and whites of eggs. Beat yolks lightly with water and add to margarine. Stir in flour, add thinly sliced bananas. Whisk egg whites stiffly and fold in lightly. Turn into a greased basin, cover; steam 1½ hours. Serve with jam sauce.

Baked with Nuts

Slice 4 bananas lengthways and put in a greased oven dish with a squeeze of lemon juice. Sprinkle with brown sugar and chopped walnuts, dot with butter. Bake at 350°F, gas No. 4, for 15–20 minutes until sugar and nuts are crisp.

Banana Cake

8oz S.R. flour, pinch of salt, ¼oz margarine, 6oz sugar, 2oz chopped nuts, 2 eggs, ½ cup evaporated milk, 1 cup of sliced bananas.

Beat margarine till soft, add sugar and cream together, beat in the sliced bananas and nuts, add well-beaten eggs one at a time. Sift flour and salt, add to creamed mixture alternately with the evaporated milk. Bake in two 9-inch sandwich tins in a moderate oven (350°F, gas No. 4) about 20–30 minutes. When cooked, spread chocolate icing between halves and on top.

Other Ways with the Fruit

For fritters, chop bananas and fry in batter. Use them as filling for pancakes. Make them into 'mushrooms' for a party, topping each banana with half a meringue spread with chocolate mock cream. Stand in chopped green jelly. For an open tart, slice bananas, cover with custard, sprinkle with desiccated coconut. They add variety to salads too.

9 April 1921
ORANGES AND LEMONS

Garden lovers are not always properly grateful to those whose talents and industry in past years have enriched our country by their attention to horticulture. We should never forget to acknowledge the accomplishments of our ancestors of the sixteenth century when we witness our gardens blushing with the beautiful flowers and luscious fruits, natives of more favoured climes. How faithfully Sir Walter Raleigh carried out the mandate of Queen Elizabeth who charged him 'to go forth to discover the plants of new countries!' There is apparently no account of orange trees being raised from pips and cultivated in England prior to these times, when seeds from fruits obtained by Sir Walter Raleigh were given to his nephew, Sir Francis Carew, who grew them upon his estate at Beddington, near Croydon, about 1380. The great Evelyn evidently paid a journey to see these trees, for he writes, fifty years later: 'I went to Beddington, that ancient seat of the Carews famous for the first orange gardens in England being now overgrown trees planted in the ground and secured in winter with a wooden tabernacle and stoves.' These trees lived for more than a century, when it is reported that they were killed during the great frost of 1739.

The early herbalist writers, Gerard and Parkinson, both give curious directions for the culture and preservation of these exotics from experience gained at Beddington. Special erections bearing the name of Orangeries began to be built in many notable gardens, and some of them stand today as embellishments in the grounds. Some of the best known were at the seats of Lord Burghley at Stamford, Lord Salisbury at Hatfield, Sir Hugh Platt at Bethnal Green. Queen Henrietta Maria at Wimbledon Park (this estate apparently covered the whole of Wimbledon, and at the sale in 1649 the orange and lemon trees standing in cases, or tubs as they would now be called, reached prices similar to that orchids fetch today). Evelyn evidently grew the fruit at Wrest Park, for he says in 1679 that he 'gave some friends who came to dine some China oranges off his own trees, as good as ever were eaten.' Sir Henry Capell also grew them at Kew. Pepys reports that he saw the first oranges in Lord Brook's garden at Hackney, some green, some half ripe, and some full ripe. 'I pulled one and ate it.' These old Orangeries have been described as pretentious in architecture and yet not beautiful, wanting in light and air more like a mausoleum than a home for trees condemned to a miserable existence within it. The Hampton Court trees are stated to be nearly 300 years old.

In the more genial southern parts of the country oranges are grown out of doors; when trained on walls they produce large handsome fruits.

Lemons are likewise treated, and are perhaps more hardy even, than oranges. This fruit is first referred to as being cultivated in the Botanic Gardens at Oxford in 1648.

While these fruits can never be grown as a commercial commodity here, the wonder is they are not more frequently seen in conservatories, either in the form of standards, bushes, or covering the walls, as the foliage always presents an ornamental picture if only for its glossy texture. The blossoms are attractive, and the fruits in all stages of development, both green and coloured, will often hang for two years. The culture is simple; all that is needed is a sweet and firm root bed, with a sufficiency of water at the roots and syringing of the foliage to keep it clean and healthy. In the summer specimens in tubs or pots may stand out of doors, along walks or on the terrace, to be brought again under cover before the inclemency of the winter months arrives.

The idea of growing an orange tree is often very much cherished by amateurs, and plants are occasionally raised from the fruits obtained from the shops. Although trees may be raised with such facility from pips, they must attain a fair size and strength before they will either flower or fruit, so that cultivators often get tired of waiting and ask why they will not fruit. While some seedlings will never do either, it is preferable that they should be grafted with kinds already in bearing and they may then be flowered in a moderately small state.

5 May 1906
SCARCITY OF APPLES

We are now in the height of the Australian apple season, and, as announced in these columns a little more than a month ago, the crop has fallen considerably short of the original estimates; indeed, the shortage is being felt throughout the country, for apples are distinctly on the dear side. The Colonials and importers may be deriving some little benefit from the high prices, but the retailers and general public are certainly suffering some inconvenience.

At the present wholesale rates of 11s to 16s per case, no apples can be calculated to cost the shopkeeper less than 4d to 5d a pound, whilst the choicer varieties work out at considerably more, so that the public must be content with a bottom price of 6d per pound for the unpretentious sorts, and anything from 8d upwards for handsome dessert fruit.

The Colonial apples of this season commenced somewhat disappointingly as to quality, but it is pleasing to report that each succeeding cargo has been an improvement on its predecessor, and the apples at present on the market are particularly fine, notably such choice dessert varieties as Cleopatras, New York pippins, Ribstons, and Jonathans. The nomenclature of apples varies in different parts of the country – traders in the North are unacquainted with the names by which Southerners know the various classes. In the South, the finest cooking apple is known as the Wellington, its Northern title being the Normanton Wonder, the Australian equivalent of which is the Dumelow seedling. This being the best-known and most-sought-for variety of cooking apple is never cheap, but a useful and inexpensive substitute will be found by those who try the rennet, a small apple with but little to recommend it in the way of appearance, yet for the economical housewife a welcome addition to the commissariat.

Beyond apples, oranges, and bananas, there are practically no fruits at the moment at anything approaching popular prices. Those who are disposed to pay for early arrivals may invest in gooseberries of very diminutive size as 1s–1s 6d per quart, or in specially-grown hothouse cherries, Circassians, at 8s per lb. English peaches, at 1s–4s each, green figs, at 4d–1s each, and grapes, from 2s 3d lb, must be classed as table luxuries for the few.

23 June 1970
SIMPLY, STRAWBERRIES
Bon Viveur

When it comes to fresh fruits in their season we refuse to fall over ourselves to devise dishes when the old-fashioned ones we enjoyed when we were children were so good.

Let us serve them with cream and sugar, but let the cream be farm fresh and not that absolutely tasteless shop stuff which has to be tiddled up (otherwise all it provides is density) and let the sugar be that pale, beige, sand-textured pieces sugar which anyone can get if they *try*. Otherwise use icing sugar and then there will be no grits.

Johnnie would like you to eat strawberries the way his grandfather taught him: fat strawberries were held by their stalks and dipped in the last few remaining drops of grandfather's claret or Burgundy before popping them into the mouth.

Then, if you have to buy shop cream, turn it into an Orange Sauce which not only gives it some flavour but recognises the fact that there is a great affinity between oranges and strawberries.

That is why a bowl of hulled strawberries moistened with orange juice and refrigerated under a liberal dusting of sifted icing sugar is also so delicious. Of course, it is considerably improved by a spoonful or two of orange curaçao.

But the whole thing will go by the board and curdle on your tongue if you go and sling cream on top of this mixture.

If you must have something 'made up' with strawberries, why not revert to either the good old-fashioned strawberry Choux Paste Buns which used to raise our nursery stock enormously every time these appeared for our parties; and more than once, we remember, some of the grown-ups popped in – a bit whiffy after their first drink of the evening – to utter a few bromides while eyeing any left-over strawberry buns and commenting casually: 'I wouldn't mind finishing that up Nanny, if you give me a plate.'

For the more sophisticated version, make a Paris-Brest aux Fraises, which is certainly elegant enough to put on the menu of a women's luncheon party – especially if your guests are dieting, because they will be so sugar-starved they will never be able to resist it.

For our last suggestion: that former delight of young and old Harrovians – Dringer.

We who remember and miss these things may as well make it for our young (they are very unlikely to get it elsewhere) and most certainly for ourselves when we go on summer picnics.

We make ours in a 4¼in diameter vacuum flask. First put in a layer of home-made ice-cream, cover with a layer of halved, smallish strawberries, cover thickly with real cream, repeat to the top of the flask.

3 May 1989
GIVE ME STRAWBERRIES THAT GO ROTTEN ANY DAY
Lesley Garner

What does a perfect supermarket strawberry have in common with a child's balloon? If you answer that they are both round and shiny and appealing and possibly red, you would not be wrong. But that is not the answer.

The balloons I have in mind were the gift of British Nuclear Fuels Limited to the Eskdale Show in the Lake District. As the children trailed the balloons across the grass, their mothers – filmed for a TV documentary – remarked drily that BNFL never gave them balloons before Chernobyl.

The strawberries, likewise, are not quite what they seem. They look perfect, but if you buy them and take them home it becomes clear that they have been denatured. They do not turn to mush when washed. They do not turn to mush at all. A week after a garden strawberry would have rotted they still wink at you from their box, glossy, firm and brazen. They have been irradiated to render them sterile and, like the balloons, they are the officially acceptable face of radioactivity.

We, the public, do not like the idea of doing something as unnatural as zapping food with gamma rays. One consumer poll found that nine out of 10 people would refuse to buy a product which had been labelled 'irradiated'.

And yet the Government appears to be disregarding our misgivings. Informed expectation is that it will respond to the recent working party report from the Ministries of Health and Agriculture and allow irradiation into Britain before the end of the parliamentary session. It is not hard to see why.

Both public and politicians are in a state of wary disenchantment with the current record of the British food industry. First we were alarmed by the salmonella crisis, which led to a mass suspicion of eggs and chickens. This was closely followed by the scare about listeria, another nasty organism which lurks in cook-chill foods.

Then those of us who congratulate ourselves smugly that we do not rely on pre-prepared foods got a nasty shock when the extent to which the most natural of products, like apples and potatoes, are contaminated with pesticides was revealed. These poisons cannot always be washed off. Suddenly the most innocuous apple becomes Snow White's poisoned fruit and I, the careful mother, am an involuntary Wicked Witch.

Irradiation comes to us as the panacea for all these ills, but by this time many wary, under-informed consumers have had enough. It does not help that this process is called irradiation. However safe we may be told it is, our hackles instinctively rise at the idea of letting rays of any kind into our systems. In South Africa they promote it as 'Radura – the symbol of quality'. But to disguise an unpopular process with a pretty marketing name is deeply cynical.

Besides, there are deeper objections than the choice of name. Irradiation is, by its very nature, a cover-up. If a product needs to be irradiated then there must already be something wrong with it. If there is something wrong with it then I would prefer not to buy it.

It reminds me of the recent Aids campaign where a beautiful HIV-positive girl was seen to look no different from a healthy one. Give us diseases which declare themselves with visible symptoms. Give us natural food which can turn brown and rot. As Richard Pugh of Tesco, one of the many retailers who is against irradiation, points out, one of the advantages of the natural process is that bad food goes off. Animals steer clear of contaminated food. Why deny us the same chance?

Once you get beyond instinct you get into darker and more serious arguments about irradiation's side-effects. One of its most vociferous opponents, the writer Geoffrey Cannon, is confident that the process is carcinogenic and points out that the small print of the report agrees that it is 'impossible to rule out the possibility'. The BMA refuses to give the unknown long-term effects any blessing, and is also concerned about vitamin loss. So who benefits?

One answer is the nuclear fuels industry, because, as Geoffrey Cannon points out, irradiation creates a market for nuclear power. Another answer is the less responsible end of the food industry, because this would rescue it from putting its own house in order. If there is a scientific whitewash for the dirt, why bother to keep clean in the first place? A third answer is the Government, because irradiation promises to clean up all its current problems with food contamination.

But nine out of ten of us have reservations which should not be ignored. Our part in this is not only to resist irradiation but also to question our own shopping habits. We must become less concerned with the cosmetic aspect and the convenience of our food if we want it to be wholesome. If we were not demanding perfect, blemish-free food in the first place there would not be an industry intent on embalming it for us.

Every fairy tale we have ever read, from the golden touch of King Midas to the Sorcerer's Apprentice, has told us that, if we once start tampering with natural processes, we unleash even more destructive forces.

As Joni Mitchell once sang: 'Give me spots on apples and give me the birds and the bees. Please.'

20 July 1918
WOMEN FOR FRUIT-PICKING

To the Editor of the *Daily Telegraph*

Sir – Owing to the shortage of seasonal labour in Scotland, it has become necessary to make a special appeal in order to secure at once the services of an additional 2,000 women to assist in fruit picking in the Auchterarder districts for jam for the fighting forces. In view of the shortage of the fruit crop in many parts it is vital that all available fruit should be gathered, in order that the requirements of the Navy and Army be met and as much jam as possible be made available for the civilian population. In securing the necessary labour, however, the Government is naturally most anxious to avoid recruiting workers already engaged to the national advantage. It is believed that there are large numbers of patriotic women who would be willing to devote a fortnight to six weeks to work which is of urgent national importance – Yours, &c.,

Geo. H. Roberts

J. R. Clynes

Full of Eastern Promise

13 August 1995
THE CURRY OF OLD ENGLAND
Amit Roy

Today is an important day for the British curry eater. In Southall, west London, a £7 million high-tech food factory opens to dispatch 50,000 Indian meals a day to the supermarkets of Britain.

From Gulam Kaderbhoy Noon's new factory, packets of pasanda, vindaloo and biryani, of korma, tandoori and balti will flow to Sainsbury's and Waitrose, a tidal wave of curry washing over a nation with an apparently insatiable appetite for the stuff.

Mr Noon, who came to London from Bombay in 1973, has probably done more than anyone to bring Indian food within reach of the supermarket trolley. As a result, the catering industry thinks curry can no longer be treated as an ethnic food. 'It's mainstream,' says Mr Noon.

It is more than that. Although the red meat lobby will protest, perhaps it is time to replace 'as British as roast beef' with 'as British as chicken tikka masala'. The latter appears to have established itself as the favourite food of the British.

Mr Noon started in 1989 with daily sales of 4,000 meals and an annual turnover of £2.7 million. These have risen to 50,000 meals and £15 million. The number of recipes he offers has grown from four to 37.

Chicken alone comes as pasanda, vindaloo, biryani, korma, tandoori, balti, tikka makhani, makhanwala, rogan josh, tikka pasanda and Madras.

'I have yet to meet an Englishman who doesn't like Indian food,' says Mr Noon. Noting the phenomenal growth in the curry culture, the current issue of the trade magazine *The Grocer* asks: 'Where have all the bangers gone?' They are being replaced, it has discovered, by bhajis – a symbol of Indian food.

There was a time when Indian cuisine meant prawn curry and onion bhaji served to the lads in their local Taj Mahal after pub closing to soak up six pints of lager. The restaurants would not have felt right without their flock wallpaper and taped sitar music, plates of poppadoms and stained tablecloths.

It has not all changed – the Taj Mahals still exist – but the world of the British curry has moved on. The Brits, who are becoming discerning about Indian food, now know their vindaloo from their Madras. At the Kurbani in Plymouth, the owner, A. M. Tarafder, recalls a dissatisfied Englishman who sent back his vindaloo. When he was offered a replacement within 10 minutes, the customer gave the waiter a withering look: 'It takes a lot longer to do it properly – three hours of slow cooking to be precise.'

The number of Indian restaurants – the term has come to cover establishments run by Indians, Pakistanis and Bangladeshis, totals 8,000 – the biggest group among the estimated 50,000 restaurants in Britain. Within five years, the number is expected to exceed 10,000.

Foreign travel, the presence of an Asian population of 1.6 million and popular TV programmes such as Madhur Jaffrey's BBC series have all combined to give the British a familiarity with curry. It remains relatively cheap and easily available, often when other eating places rudely turn away late diners.

'Indian cuisine is not a fad,' says Pat Chapman, founder of the Curry Club, an organisation that keeps tabs on everything to do with Indian cuisine. 'Once you become hooked on ginger, garlic, or chilli you are hooked for life.'

He recalls Oz's remark in the popular TV series, *Auf Wiedersehen, Pet*: 'Let's go for a curry. It's a British national dish.' Mr Chapman says: 'Ten years ago the comment might have raised an eyebrow. But not any more. Curry is on the way to becoming the favourite British food.'

Industry surveys show that, each week, 2.5 million people eat at Indian restaurants, spending £2 billion a year. The breakdown by age reveals the relatively short history of curry restaurants in this country: 23 per cent of diners are between 16 and 24, 36 per cent between 25 and 34, 16 per cent between 45 and 64, and only two per cent over 65.

The crucial change has been the willingness of people to eat Indian food at home, and increasingly to cook recipes using authentic spices. 'There has been a huge growth in the ingredient market – Tesco can't keep up,' says Peter Grove, editor of *The Real Curry Restaurant Guide*.

Last year, nearly £100 million was spent on Indian ready-made meals. Another £300 million went on ingredients and sauces – an increase of 90 per cent since 1991.

Mr Grove says: 'During the last few years the market has been changing with the ready availability of herbs and spices in the supermarkets and a far greater knowledge by the public. This has led to the emergence of newer, up-market but still reasonably-priced restaurants offering regional menus.'

To pep up a curry, an increasingly adventurous nation will add a spoonful of pickle. Last year, the Indian pickle market was worth £1.3 million, of which Patak's, the spice firm, had a 71 per cent market share. The favourite is mild lime pickle. According to Debbie Bracegirdle, Patak's brand manager, Britons nibble their way through 10.5 million packs of poppadom at home. 'With 12 to a pack, that's 126 million poppadoms – a hell of a lot of poppadoms,' she enthuses.

The sound of poppadoms being crunched can be heard in even the most English of villages. Outside the heavily ethnic areas, it is not the Indians and the Pakistanis who patronise the Indian restaurants. 'Only two per cent of our customers are Asian,' says a waiter at the Pipasha in the Surrey village of Churt. At the Le Raj, Epsom, the proprietor, Enam Ali, boasts: 'We are in the heart of the stockbroker belt and get people from the Bank of England and a lot of celebrities – Fiona Fullerton loves chicken jhaal which is very hot.'

The British palate will not be the same again. Angela Megson, the director responsible for ready meals at Sainsbury's, says: 'In the prepared meals sector, Indian is the largest. People buy korma and tikka but are prepared to try new flavours and trade up the heat level.'

This is also the view of the manager of Kababish, a balti restaurant in Birmingham, which first found it hard to change a young man with 'very reserved' taste. After three weeks, his attitude was altogether more demanding: 'Would you put in a few more green chillies, please?'

4 February 1931
A LESSON IN FRENCH COOKERY
X. M. Boulestin

We write articles and we write books and we publish recipes which we try to make as attractive and as simple as possible. These dishes, being made in a natural and normal way, with good materials, are nourishing and healthy; they should stimulate our appetite and do no harm to our digestion, the only rule being to avoid things which do not agree with our system.

And now we see, in an almost blinding light, the fundamental difference between the French and the English. For the British Government have announced the appointment of a Committee to advise the public on matters of nutrition; 'The duty of the Committee will be to translate into plain language scientific knowledge of the value of food.' A fact significant in itself.

Just as significant as the American menus, where next to the name of the dish is printed the number of calories the dish contains, this being calculated by a 'food expert' who, of course, never bothers about the culinary quality of the dish.

Some people will say (indeed, have said): 'Ah, but the French are different; they are healthy, have a better digestion, and can manage to eat better food; that is, food richer and more varied, than the English; the Frenchman knows nothing of the anxiety that gnaws at the minds of those whose less nourishing, less balanced diet keeps them always wondering whether they dare risk this dish or that drink' – which may be true.

But the point is that the French have that 'superior digestive power' precisely because of their old-fashioned and natural diet. A little common-sense and pleasant food are all that is required; the health-giving qualities will follow naturally, will be the result of the better food, eaten with more pleasure.

We never hear in France all these sermons on vitamins, calories, and the like, because the French people of all classes eat as a matter of course this or that food which they grow or buy. They do this instinctively, like a cat who, feeling out of sorts, eats a blade of grass in the garden. Teaching dietetic values is a poor inducement to eat, and it is treating a pleasant and normal function as if it were an acquired habit or a disease.

Fonds de Veau

This is an extremely useful reduced stock to be used as a basis for all sorts of sauces when required. Once made it will keep for about ten days to a fortnight, and will help for rather elaborate dishes; it rather belongs to the variety known as chef's cooking, as opposed to the 'cuisine de cuisinière' – in fact, it is to be recommended for a few dishes, but not for everyday use.

Put in a baking-tin two or three pounds of veal bones, with a few onions cut in quarters, and bake this, quite dry in a hot oven for a quarter of an hour or so. By that time the bones have half melted, half browned; put them then in a deep saucepan with carrots, thyme, parsley, bay leaves, garlic, salt and peppercorns.

Fill with cold water, add either a few tomatoes cut in quarters or a glass of purée of tomatoes, bring to the boil and let it simmer for quite six hours. It should be skimmed occasionally and all the fat which comes to the top should also be removed.

When well reduced pass it through a fine colander, colour it either with a little caramel or with burnt onion, and bind it with a little arrowroot diluted in Madeira wine. Cook a quarter of an hour, skim if necessary, see that it is fairly thick, and keep in a cool place till wanted.

This thick veal stock will come in useful to give substance to all sorts of complex sauces, and as it has practically no specific taste it can be used for making a little sauce for either fish or fowl.

Poulet en Croute

1. Prepare a chicken for roasting, well seasoned inside and outside; cook it in the oven, about twenty-five minutes for a spring chicken, a little longer for a larger one. It should be in a fireproof dish, with a good piece of butter, and often basted.

2. Cut in cubes a piece of foie gras and one truffle in smallish pieces, keeping aside the peelings and the trimmings. It is important to use pure foie gras and not pâté de foie gras, as most pâtés contain, as a rule, a certain amount of meat which is not foie gras, and would melt unpleasantly later. When fresh foies are not available the best thing to buy is 'foie entire', that is, a goose liver whole in a tin.

3. When the chicken is done, remove the string and fill the inside with the pieces of foie gras and truffles and keep it hot.

4. Meanwhile you have prepared the batter as follows: make a heap on a board with one pound of flour; in a hole in the middle add, one by one, three whole eggs, a quarter of a pound of butter, a pinch of salt, and half a glass of tepid water, working it the while in the ordinary way. When the batter is smooth and firm flatten it on the board to a layer about half an inch thick, and large enough so that you can wrap the chicken in it. When wrapped paint with yolk of egg, put it in the serving dish and bake ten to twelve minutes in a moderate oven.

5. The chicken should be, of course, shown in its finished state, important looking, and hiding its succulence under its coat of golden crust. With a sharp knife cut the crust all round, so that you can, having removed a kind of lid, take out the chicken and carve it, each person to be given with a piece of chicken a piece of crust, some stuffing, and sauce Périgueux.

Sauce Périgueux

For this sauce you use the trimmings of truffle, which, very finely chopped, you cook in a small saucepan with a glass of Madeira wine. Reduce by half, season well, add twice the quantity of 'fonds de veau', cook slowly for eight to ten minutes, and serve, seeing that it is very hot and highly seasoned.

30 April 1899
COOKS COMPARED:
FRENCH V. ENGLISH
John Strange

In speaking of the French cook, I do not propose to discuss the merits of the heads of the profession, but rather to confine myself to the leading characteristics of the good lady who in France takes the place that the 'good plain cook' takes in England. All English people know to their cost the capacity, or want of capacity, of the good plain cook; they know her stodgy sauces, her greasy gravies, her raw vegetables, her over or under done meat, her sticky puddings, and her impossible eggs. Every married woman whose income allows of her paying from £20 to £30 a year so her cook knows the dreary round of demi-incapacity which usually falls to her portion. She has to rack her brains day by day to give her family some change of menu, and she mostly feels that the house-mistress who does not have to think out her own dinners is a happy and blessed woman indeed. Nor is this her only trouble. There is always a roaring fire going in the great extravagant English range. She is haunted by visions of coal bills, of waste in articles of household consumption; she is pursued by visions of that bogey of all English matrons, the kitchen dinner. She sits down day after day to the same unappetising dishes, with never a relief from the plain roast and boiled which her frugal soul tells her is the least extravagant. There is always a suspicion in her mind, too, that cook is not so particular as she might be about her pans, and if she is at all nervous, she is shy of actually looking at them to make sure that they are as clean as they ought to be. Cook, too, if she is at all out of the common in her art, invariably grumbles if she has not a kitchenmaid, and would think it wholly beneath her to undertake the dining-room or lay a hand on the entrance and front steps.

How different it is in France! To begin with, 50f a week is a good price for a cook everywhere outside of Paris. And what a cook you can get for that sum! She will not only do a bit of the housework, but also will do it cheerfully and as a matter of course. You cannot buy your French cook too many pans, and her soul loves copper in her kitchen. Certainly an English cook would grumble if she was expected to keep a kitchen full of copper pans bright and clean; but a French one has them in a condition akin to burnished gold. Her pride is gratified if her kitchen walls are hung with these ornaments, and even if she does the greater part of her small cooking in little enamelled pans, she will daily rub up the copper ones which hang on the wall.

In a French kitchen there is no waste. It would seem that the French mind does not run to waste or revel in it as the lower-class English mind invariably does. Clémentine uses her crusts for something or other, though it is difficult to say exactly how. Now and again one realises this as one eats scallops (*coquilles de Saint-Jacques*), which have been treated with browned crumbs, herbs, butter, or a little of the white sauce left over from a previous meal or some kindred dish.

Nor is it only in bread that she is careful. Nothing in the shape of untainted food escapes the eagle eye of Clémentine, or is too small for her consideration. The fact that there is not enough of the two fowls cooked for dinner last night, when six persons made the most substantial part of that meal off them, to serve for luncheon, does not daunt her in the least. She sends in the remains of the fowls carefully cut up into viewly pieces, and surrounds the dish with a trimming of cold boiled herbs or slices of sausage bought ready cooked at the *charcutier*'s, and if that seems likely to be short, she has a dozen ideas at her fingers' ends for eking out the meat. She may add an *omelette aux fines herbes*, a dish of stuffed eggs, or of rissoles made of nothing more costly than the remains of yesterday's egg sauce, but browned to perfection and altogether delicious. Or perhaps her addition takes the form of a dish of spinach, with poached eggs, such spinach, too, fit to set before a king.

The large, plain joint, which is the mainstay of ordinary English households, finds no favour in France. Clémentine thinks a six-pound joint ample for a family of ten all told. She will serve it for dinner with new potatoes fried in butter and stewed celery in white sauce. The following day she will serve it up cold – as a favour to her English mistress – with a salad. And then there will be what she calls '*un petit bout*', and that she heats up in some mysterious manner, perhaps two days later, with a rich brown gravy, or rather sauce, in which are gaily jostling each other onions, olives, and mushrooms. It is impossible to tell that this meat is *réchauffée*; indeed I was a long time before I realised that the piece of beef had not been bought fresh for the dish.

Still it is not only in small dishes that Clémentine excels. With a joint she is inimitable. Does she think Madame will enjoy a roast of pork, she will take care to know where the original pig was bred, and then she cooks it slowly till ready. As a matter of fact, she cooks it with the oven door open, wide open, and with no wonderful amount of fire, no more, indeed, than is necessary to keep the various pans going in which the rest of the meal is being prepared. I have known my own cook put a small joint of pork, which would be eaten at half-past twelve, into the oven before nine o'clock in the morning. But mind you, that joint was cooked through and through, neither burnt nor dried, but as tender as a chicken. With it she gave rich brown gravy, apple sauce, spinach and potatoes fried into miniature balloons.

Then Clémentine has a way of cooking veal in a large, deep saucepan, with about an inch of water or stock at the bottom, and an extraordinary variety of herbs and vegetables. For seven o'clock dinner this begins to cook about nine in the morning. She also cooks mutton in much the same fashion. I need hardly say that either of these dishes literally melts in your mouth.

Clémentine gives more, feeds one better, and costs less, both in wages and housekeeping, than her English sister. People who read housekeeping articles often say, 'Yes, it all reads very well on paper, but it is very different when I come to try it.' So I take it there is nothing like actual facts, actual figures when making comparisons, for showing the difference between the cooks of the two countries. My housekeeping and washing for a family of ten is, on the average, £6 a week. Now, every housewife knows that good, that is, careful, housekeeping cannot be done under a certain allowance. The usual rate for a modest establishment is to allow £1 a week each for the master and the mistress, and 10s a week each for all the rest of the family. That makes, for a family of ten, a total of £6. My Clémentine goes but little above that, for we must remember the washing-bill, no small item for ten people. And I must, in justice to her, say that we live more on what we English consider luxuries than we ever did in England, even when we were spending nearly twice as much.

But Clémentine must be taken in her own way. I don't know that Clémentine would be altogether a success in England, even did her mistress speak perfect, or at least colloquially perfect, French. She would not understand our vast kitchen ranges, nor, I fancy be entirely happy in our more restricted life. If one wants to get the best out of Clémentine, one must tell her the work, the hours and style of meals, give her an idea of the money she must spend, and leave everything to her. Clémentine likes to do her work, her cooking, and her shopping, especially her shopping, in her own way and at her own time. If I see her sailing away down the street with a basket as big as herself, no covering on her shining head, unless it be a cap, snowy as chloride of lime can make it, I do not ask where she is going nor how long she intends to be. In fact, I neither know nor care. Clémentine will serve the *déjeuner* and the dinner at the proper time and in perfect condition, her kitchen, pots, and pans will always be clean, she will not worry me about evenings out nor make a fuss if I want to ask a friend to dinner on Sunday; and so I never try to restrict her little gaddings any more than I try to prevent her from turning an honest penny for herself as she makes my bargains, and spares me, a busy author and mother, a thousand petty worries and details in my everyday life.

12 August 1989
HOT STUFF FOR THE ENVOY
Claudia Roden

The new United States Ambassador, Henry Catto, has been hankering for the fiery and exotic flavours of his native Texas, and is now keen to introduce them to London. So he has flown in the best representative of South-Western cuisine to teach the cooks at the official residence in Regent's Park.

Mrs Rosemary Kowalski, who has catered for the Catto family for 20 years, brought with her 16 suitcases full of tortilla mixes, tortilla presses, chilli sauces, assorted dried beans and jars of cumin, as well as multi-coloured paper flowers, streamers, confetti and mesquite chips for burning.

South Texan food is a blend of Spanish with Aztec and other Indian overtones, modified over the years to suit American tastes and to accommodate local ingredients.

It is called Tex-Mex and is quite different from Mexican cooking and different too from other Mexican–American cuisines which have taken root in California, Florida, Arizona, Nevada, New Mexico, Utah and other regions with a Hispanic influence in the kitchen.

Tex-Mex is characterised by a predominance of chilli peppers (at least 200 varieties are grown), tomatoes and beans, and a flavour combination which includes hot chillies, ground cumin, fresh coriander (*cilantro*), oregano and garlic (dark bitter chocolate, cinnamon, cloves, almonds, peanuts, pumpkin seeds and sesame sometimes come into play; meat is mixed with fruit), and everything is served on or with tortillas, the ubiquitous maize or wheat pancakes. Much of the inspiration comes from the new immigrant arrivals from Mexico.

The following dishes make good summer foods. The first two were discovered by my daughter in New York.

I recommend three books: *The Complete Book of Mexican Cooking*, by Elizabeth Lambert Ortiz (Vallantine £3.95), *Authentic Mexican Cooking*, by Rick Bayless with Deann Groen Bayless (Headline £14.95), and *Mexican Cookery*, by Lourdes Nichols (Fontana, £3.95).

Guacamole

Avocado Salad with Fresh Tomato Sauce
(serves 4)
2 medium-sized ripe avocados;
The juice of ¾–1 lime (or to taste);
Salt
For the salsa:
½ a small onion;
1 or more small hot chilli peppers;
3 tasty ripe tomatoes;
A bunch of fresh coriander

Make the salsa first: very finely chop the onion, chilli (stem and seeds removed), tomatoes and coriander – using the food processor if you like. Just before serving chip the avocado and season with lime juice and salt, crushing the avocado a little with a fork (don't turn it to a purée). Serve the guacamole with the salsa for everyone to help themselves and mix the two to taste. Accompanied by tortilla chips.

Queso Fundido con Rajas y Chorizo
Melted Cheese with Roasted Pepper and Chorizos
(Serves 4)

2 peppers – yellow, red or green;
1 small onion, thinly sliced;
2 tbs light vegetable oil;

250g (½lb) chorizo sausage, skins
removed and cut into slices;
Salt;
A pinch of chilli pepper (optional);
375g (¾lb) mozzarella or fontina

Roast the peppers in the hottest oven for about 20–25 minutes until soft and the skin is brown and blistered. Then drop them in a plastic bag, close it, and leave them in for 10 minutes. When they are cool enough to handle, skin, remove the seeds and stem, and cut into ribbons.

Fry the onion in oil till soft and golden, then add the chorizos and fry for a few minutes till soft. Mix with the roasted peppers, season with salt and, if you like, chilli pepper, and spread at the bottom of an oven dish. Cover with cheese and bake for a few minutes until the cheese is bubbling hot. Serve with warmed tortillas or toast.

Rosemary Kowalski's Grilled Lamb Chops with Honey and Mustard Glaze
(Serves 4)
4 chump chops;
3 tbsp olive oil;
100ml (3 fl oz) dry white wine;
A sprig of thyme, crumbled;

A few sprigs of fresh coriander or
mint, chopped;
Pepper or a pinch of chilli pepper;
Salt;
2 tbsp clear Mexican honey;
2 tbsp grain mustard

Marinate the chops in a mixture of oil and wine with the herbs and pepper for 1 hour or longer. Then sprinkle with salt and cook for about 10 minutes over glowing embers, turning over once.

Now brush the top of each chop with a mixture of honey and mustard and turn over, cook for 1–2 minutes. Brush the other side with this glaze and turn the meat over again to finish this side.

Serve accompanied by cabbage slaw made with grated white and red cabbage and carrots mixed with mayonnaise and horseradish sauce.

21 September 1964
THE WORLD COMES TO OUR DINNER TABLES
Claire Butler

There's a new look about the dinner table these days. It's not just the exciting shocking pink or vivid green of dinner mats from Mexico, or that dishes, plates and glasses come from Germany, France, Finland, Portugal and a host of other exciting places but that there is an invasion of foods new to many of us and we are discovering the wines of many more countries.

The recent Food Fair at Olympia helped to open one's eyes to some of the things now around in the shops, such as deep-frozen king crab from America (it lives up to its name, is excellent and not wildly expensive).

I found, too, Spanish olives, deliciously stuffed with almonds or anchovies, sweet red peppers, and sauerkraut in white wine sent over in small cans from West Germany. You can also enhance sweets by using Bulgaria's wonderful strawberry jam or serve the Turkish sweetmeat, helva.

For wines our shops range the globe: inexpensive Turkish white and red are good value, while for a sparkling white wine, try German Sekt. Hungarian and Bulgarian wines are also coming over.

Many housewives have discovered this summer that the slog has been taken out of mayonnaise-making by the sale of *real* mayonnaise, made with the proper ingredients, in small plastic bags. An excellent Danish one, correctly made, using eggs and oil, can be kept in a refrigerator for a few days.

Small plastic packs of mayonnaise are also coming from Germany. These need flavour added, such as a few finely chopped chives but you will find you've made your mayonnaise in the time it takes you to chop them and to cut open the plastic bag.

Britain's restaurants, getting more and more international, are competing with housewives for these foreign foods and so increasingly the demand for them. They are also encouraging our palate for foreign foods.

At the small, intimate and cheery La Vodka restaurant, at 132, Cromwell Road, diners acquire a palate for Russian dishes such as shashlik and blinis – the latter made with a batter and stuffed with sour cream.

The lunch mood may be for a curry, and I can't think of a more pleasant setting for a slight midday meal than the India Tea Centre in Oxford Street, where you can have a simple chicken curry (the dearest) for 5s or a meat curry with dahl (lentils) for 4s.

Speciality shops that sell Indian, Hellenic, Caribbean and other national foods are multiplying all the time and providing a challenge to us to find out how they can be used and to widen our knowledge of the world through our own dinner tables.

28 June 1987
ACQUIRED TASTES
Lizzie Spender

The first memory I have of food dates back to when I was five years old. I was staying with my parents and elder brother in a wonderfully primitive farmhouse belonging to friends off the coast of Wales. The food in question was at this point still very much alive and walking on eight legs, and took the form of local lobsters.

The lobsters lived in a big tin basin filled with sea water on the kitchen floor. However, come children's bath-time, the lobsters were lifted out of the basin and put on to the stone flags, and my brother and I were lifted in. I remember sitting in our tin bath watching with curiosity the several enormous grey armoured creatures as, claws furiously waving, they valiantly attempted to scale the slippery walls of the basin. They must have had a far higher opinion of freezing cold sea-water than my brother and I as we certainly would have climbed *out* if it had not been for the presence of these monsters. Eventually they would retire exhausted in an untidy circle in the middle of the kitchen floor and, from this vantage point, would stare morosely and with bulging eyes at their usurpers, no doubt having decided by now that psychological warfare was more appropriate. Now and then, to make a point, they would attempt to 'swim' backwards. Not being in water but on stone, this would result in a dismal clattering sound, like the alarm of an old-fashioned winding clock as it dies away. Eventually I suppose we must have eaten these poor creatures.

Whether or not lobster was served after children's bedtime, pigeon was certainly served before. The pigeon consisted of less fortunate members of a flock of carrier pigeons which had been blown off-course. The birds, having given up any attempt to resume their journey, had taken up residence on the farmhouse roof, unaware of the steady decline in their numbers.

The next vivid impression of food came three years later. My father was given a job at the University of California, and for one gloriously happy year the whole family decamped to a charming bungalow on the outskirts of Berkeley.

California, to a greedy eight-year-old, was quite simply like arriving in heaven. It was the land of ice-cream – thirty-nine flavours, including lime sherbert and chocolate chip, while still the most that could be hoped for in the England of the early 1960s were slices of spongey yellow vanilla and, on special occasions, raspberry ripple. Joy of joys, the Californian ice-cream lived at home in big tubs in the ice-box, alongside the round metal scoop. In the larder were real sugar cones, a far cry from the two flat pieces of thin cardboard masquerading as wafers in this country. I think it is from these days that I date my passion for the American continent. No Anglo-Saxon austerity for them: they believe in running their country *for* human beings rather than in spite of them.

The next treat was to discover that although I had to attend High School, we did not have to wear uniforms, and school dinners simply did not exist. Slivers of curled-up grey gristle served with soggy over-boiled cabbage are not considered proper food for the future heroes of the USA. We took from home painted tin boxes with handles into which our parents put luscious sandwiches. One thing the Americans have always been able to make, and the English have not, is sandwiches. In an American sandwich, the filling is three times the thickness of the bread. I remember best the tuna fish, mayonnaise and celery, and the bacon, lettuce and tomato.

Unfortunately, my days at high school were numbered. Every break-time I would be chased around the playground by a gang of kids, who would first throw me to the ground, then twist my arm behind my back, demanding that I say the magic word 'Turrll'. Eventually, I interpreted this as a desire to hear the word 'turtle' spoken with a British accent. The effect of the pronouncement of this word was to render them all instantly incapable of further torture as they rolled around convulsed with laughter. After two months, tuna fish sandwiches or no tuna fish sandwiches, my mother decided to continue my education at home.

As a child I had consumed the usual statutory quota of stodgy macaroni cheese and overcooked spaghetti bolognese, but it was only in my late teens, during my first summer in Italy, that I discovered the real thing.

For five weeks I worked at the Spoleto Festival in Umbria, helping to make the costumes for the opera, and for five weeks I ate pasta until it was virtually coming out of my ears: tortelloni stuffed with ricotta and spinach, spaghetti served with fresh tomatoes and basil, with fried aubergines, and with sauces made from every combination of locally available vegetables and meats. Last but not least, at the Gatepone, a charming little restaurant at the top of the town overlooking the Roman Viaduct, a home-made fettuccine, green and white, served with melted fresh mozzarella cheese, mushrooms, and thinly-sliced white truffles.

There was another girl more or less my age working for the festival, and we became friends. Claudia Ruspoli was tall, dark, stunningly beautiful and a Roman princess. She had been everywhere, including up the Amazon, done everything, and very few questioned her natural air of command. Her younger sister, Giarda, had recently married, and so Claudia, missing the presence of someone small, blonde and quiet following a few steps behind, adopted me instead. All summer I trailed at Claudia's heels. We ate pasta in Roman trattorias, on Tuscan hillsides with my brother who by then was living outside Siena, and in grand country villas belonging to Claudia's grandparents – a white gloved footman behind each chair.

The following summer Claudia arranged for us to go to the island of Panarea and run a shop for her aunt, who was called Zia Arabella. Panarea is one of the group of rather strange, ghostly but beautiful Lipari Islands off the coast of Sicily. We were to sell a selection of chic objects of sophisticated modern Milanese design such as Perspex ice-buckets and snazzy chrome photograph frames. It would be hard to imagine anything *less* likely to tempt the city-dwellers who had come all the way to Panarea with the express purpose of getting away from that sort of thing. The smart Milanese set were busy enjoying 'La vita Selvàtica'. They revelled in the absence of basic amenities like electricity and thought it enormous fun when the water on the island ran out as it did every few days and we would have to wait, anxious and salty, for the next boat to arrive.

We rented a little apartment with a balcony overlooking the tiny harbour and almost on the waterfront. (Our shop premises failed to become available, since two waiters were lodging there, illegally, but on account of the heat and the Sicilian attitude to life, no one could summon the energy required to evict them.) We decided to run our shop on our balcony. We put up some signs clearly visible from the port. On one column we painted 'Claudia' and on the other column we painted 'Lizzie', and in between we hung two banners, one saying, '*Bottéga e mostra*' ('Shop and exhibition') and the other '*Salite*' ('Come on up'). The police made us take down '*Bottéga e mostra*' – they claimed we didn't have a licence – so we were left with just the 'Claudia. Lizzie. Come on up.'

We unpacked and then settled down to the job of organising the housekeeping. For Zia Arabella and Claudia this was a real novelty. Before now they had never really had occasion to think much about how food gets from the shop to the table. They wrote a shopping list.

5kg (11 lb) tomatoes;
2kg (4.4 lb) cheese;
5kg (11 lb) spaghetti;
2kg (4.4 lb) olives;
Una scatola *(one box) tinned tuna fish;*
4kg (8.8 lb) coffee

And so on. A small boy was dispatched to the island shop with the order. Claudia and Zia Arabella were mildly surprised when a few hours later a flotilla of small boys returned to the apartment carrying box after box of provisions. Nothing daunted, they decided it was the perfect opportunity to give a party, the only problem being that we had only been on the island twenty-four hours and so did not know anybody. A solution was close at hand. Nothing much ever happened on Panarea, despite the fact that we were within easy sight of a still live volcano – the ominous next-door island of Stromboli with its black sand beaches. The only thing that did happen was that every two days the ferry boat from Naples arrived with a few cargo of holidaymakers, and everybody flooded down to the port to watch. The next day Claudia stood on the balcony and I acted as messenger down below as she pointed out victims: 'That one, no, not heem, the 'andsome boy there…' And so thirty guests were invited, even including a stray movie star, Pierre Clementi, who had played the devastatingly attractive criminal with steel reinforced teeth opposite Catherine Deneuve in *Belle de Jour*. We served '*Spaghetti al pomodoro*' (spaghetti with tomato sauce), and our party with thirty strangers was an enormous success. We had so much spaghetti left over that the following night we gave another party and served '*Frittata di spaghetti*' (spaghetti omelette) to our thirty new-found friends and a few other future friends who had heard in the course of the intervening day that '*Claudia e Lizzie, Salite*' was the only place on the island to be.

The Case of the Pork Pie Widower

31 March 1958
GENUINE PORK PIES
Dorothy Van Rose

While our attention has been on the Cold War, has a sinister underground movement been going on to oust the genuine pork pie from our lives? Mr E. J. Finlay, of Lower Dyserth, sends me a grouse which he says must interest thousands, on a subject which, he says, brings tears to his eyes.

'I have tried pork pies from many shops and in various towns, and have come to the conclusion that the art has been lost – deliberately. Most pies now are dear, doughy, unseasoned and contain a hard core of a minced meaty material which seldom tastes or smells like the pies we used to know, which were made and not manufactured.

'The really good pies were made with cut pork and well seasoned with tasty jelly and crisp pastry.' He concludes pathetically, 'I would like a real pork pie.'

Mrs Flora Webb, of Carshalton Beeches is scathing about the younger generation's attitude to food. 'I am sure you will never get them to bother with good food that takes a little longer to cook and prepare. Life is made so easy for the novice that they seem to have no desire to try experiments with food or to cook a "real meal."'

Empathically I disagree with her. I know scores of young people, of both sexes, who take the keenest interest in food and go to immense trouble in preparing it. What is your experience?

5 December 1958
FOR AND AGAINST WOMEN IN GASTRONOMY
Egon Ronay

'Unless a good plain fillet steak is given eye-appeal, women are likely to underrate it. They will always fall for over-decorated dishes without worrying about what is underneath.'

This is how Col. Leslie A. Dunnage elaborated to me on his criticism made the other night at the annual banquet of the *Réunion des Gastronomes* where, in the conspicuous absence of women, he assured us all that they would *never* follow the example of the House of Lords and admit members of the opposite sex to their banquets.

Said the bold epicure: 'The world of eating and drinking is a man's world. Women can be good cooks but not creative ones, and never gourmets or gastronomes.'

Brian Gardner, director of a firm of City caterers, gave very much more credit to women when I asked him to comment: 'They are much more creative than men once they get the opportunity to experience all the foods and wines we do.

'The luncheon table should be reserved for men because,' he added gallantly, 'women would distract our thoughts from business. The contrary is true of the dinner table.'

Though having enjoyed the banquet, I am afraid I, too, disagree with my host's views. The world of food and wine is artificially limited to men through the prevailing habit of 'all male' functions.

The British system of public schools has fostered this habit. For too many years boys look upon women only as mothers, matrons and nurses.

I am with the Continental and American male who does not really enjoy a good dinner unless he can, at the same time, enjoy feminine company.

19 March 1959
22 WOMEN WHO LOVE COOKING HOLD INTERNATIONAL DINNERS
Claire Butler

Could Eastern and Roman banquets have been any better than this, I wondered as I sat and feasted in an attractive Westminster flat recently?

The night was young. There were over 20 of us – all women except for our hostess's husband – and the dishes were to be sampled slowly and enjoyed. 'Take only a little. There's plenty to come,' warned my neighbour as we had a delicious soup made by a woman on the staff of the French Embassy.

Then a Chinese guest provided delicate meat balls special to her country's cookery.

The International Kitchen Club, where this fabulous evening continued with about 12 dishes of various countries, must be one of the most exclusive in the world. Membership is limited to 22, all women. Each is talented in the cookery of her own country.

This was a Spanish evening, with Mrs Tom Burns, who is Spanish, as hostess. Thanks to a member's efforts, you can now find true paella dishes hanging from the ceiling of a Soho shop and costing from 8s to 35s.

I was the first journalist to be invited to this dining club. It started, Dame Vera Laughton Mathews, the president, told me, when talented women cooks of many countries met at the International Cookery Exhibition run by the Gas Council in 1952.

'We got to know each other then,' said Dame Vera, 'and some time after we met in my flat. Everyone said, "This can't be the finish." So the club was born and we now meet monthly.'

They meet to cultivate the friendships born of a common interest in cookery and to get to know the exciting dishes of one another's countries.

8 July 1899
STARTING HOUSEKEEPING
A Matron

Cooks nowadays are, comparatively speaking, but few, whilst the numbers of mistresses requiring them are ever on the increase. As to the why and wherefore of these two facts, I do not now propose to inquire, though I shall hope to deal with the subject later on. For the time-being let the bare fact suffice, since it has to be faced. It is twice as difficult to obtain even a moderately good cook today as it was even a year ago, whilst the wages demanded by that estimable person when found are, in my humble estimation, quite out of all proportion to her merits. Now, this fact in itself constitutes one of the greatest stumbling-blocks in the path of the young and inexperienced housewife, who, as a rule, cannot afford to pay very heavy wages, and is yet wishful to have a dainty, well-kept table. The remedy, though, to a certain extent, lies in her own hands. Train your cook for yourself, and, if you are careful when selecting your 'raw material', only unqualified success should, in the long run, be yours.

To begin at the beginning, however. Let me advise you to, if possible, choose a country girl, and for this reason: Most of them, even the very ignorant, have some slight idea of cooking to start with. There are no fried fish or ready-cooked ham and beef shops in small villages, and, as a general rule, Hodge likes his Sunday joint properly cooked and is particular to a degree over the potatoes served with his daily bacon, and the practice in all these things, simple as they are, gives a girl some insight into the first principles of cookery. 'Yes, but where am I to obtain a country girl?' says the puzzled young housewife. Well, your best and safest plan is to advertise in one or more of the country papers. For instance, Suffolk, Norfolk, Yorkshire, Gloucestershire; most of the girls from these counties make admirable cooks. State your requirements as briefly as possible, and I daresay you will not have to complain of any lack of answers.

And now the question arises, How much, or how little, should the cook to be trained actually know when she enters your service? First and foremost, she must be able to roast and boil thoroughly well and to cook vegetables properly, as also to produce such simple dishes as beefsteak and kidney pudding, Irish stew, shepherd's pie, hot-pot, &c., whilst if she can, in addition, make and bake bread, so much the better for you. She should also know how to produce mutton broth and beef tea. That her pastry is likely to be as heavy as lead, and of the consistence of a bullet, need not trouble you in the least, since if you follow my advice and the recipes I hope later on to give, both these defects may be easily remedied. It will be, I fear, too much to expect her to be able to cook fish, with any degree of properness that is, since fish, as a general rule, is very dear in country and non-seacoast towns. In fact, her ideas of frying are likely to be fundamentally wrong altogether, but as this, too, is a defect which can be easily cured, it need not worry you any more than the preceding ones. I do not suppose she will be able to produce stock either, since this is a branch of the culinary education of the English lower-class girl which is invariably neglected; but if she can, as I have said, roast well and cook vegetables properly, your path as instructress will be comparatively an easy one.

One golden rule, however, you must observe: Do not overload her with instructions. Try to put yourself in her place for a moment, and remember how strange and confusing everything must appear to her untutored eyes. Why, the very kitchen range itself, with its up-to-date improvements and appliances, must be almost a terrifying object to a raw girl fresh from the most primitive of cottage ovens or one of the old-fashioned open grates. Having then shown her how to manipulate and overcome the mysteries of the kitchen stove, your very first lesson should be devoted to stock-making. I have so often given the recipe for the preparation of simple stock that it is unnecessary to repeat it here; but you should impress upon her that after being brought gently to the boil it must be drawn to the side of the fire and only allowed to simmer; and, if you make her clearly understand that upon this simple precaution the whole success of her soup depends, you should have no cause for complaint.

And now as to frying. As I have already said, what she knows of this art is likely to be worse than useless. Potatoes are as good as anything else to fry, so let them serve for our object lesson. First, then, having duly peeled, washed, and sliced them as thinly as half the thickness of a shilling, wash these slices again, and dry them on a clean vegetable cloth till perfectly free from even a suspicion of moisture. Select a deep stewpan and place in it sufficient lard to, when melted, half fill it. Then bring this to the boil, explaining that it must not only be hot, but actually boiling, and that, moreover, fat does not boil so long as it bubbles; that, indeed, the potatoes must not be added until it is perfectly still, with a faint blue smoke arising from it. The instant this appears, add a few of the potatoes and fry till of a bright gold colour, shaking the stewpan occasionally; then taken out quickly, drain upon clean kitchen paper, and transfer to a hot dish; sprinkle with salt, and reserve until the rest are cooked, when serve at once. Explain also that if too many potatoes are put into the fat at once the latter will be 'chilled' and successful frying becomes an impossibility. Having disposed of all the potatoes, you may, with advantage, strain the fat through a clean gravy strainer into another saucepan. Make her bring it to the boil again, and, having meantime initiated her into the mystery of egging and bread-crumbing a sole in approved fashion, let her plunge that into the bath of boiling fat, and fry on until it also is of a bright yellow gold colour, shaking the pan occasionally as before directed; then take out, drain on clean kitchen paper, and serve with a beetroot salad, Italian fashion, which is made by slicing the beetroot thinly, and then dusting it with pepper, and pouring over it some sweet mint sauce.

A fried entrée of meat should never, if possible, be selected to follow a plate of fried fish. Nevertheless, if you wish to serve a dish of cutlets, you may, perhaps, surprise your new cook, and, at the same time, teach her a valuable lesson, by making her carefully strain the fat in which the fish was cooked through a fine gravy strainer into a clean saucepan; bring it to the boil again, and, having egged and breadcrumbed the cutlets in question, fry them in the same fat, which, if carefully strained, will not betray even in the faintest degree the fact that it has just previously cooked fish. But note first that the straining must be properly done; second, that a clean saucepan should be used, and, third, that the fat must again actually reach the 'blue smoke', i.e., boiling point. While upon the subject, too, let me call your attention to the fact that, unless you have a very large quantity of fish and cutlets to fry, a single beaten egg should suffice for the egging process, if it is divided, and an egg-brush used instead of the old wasteful fashion of dipping the article to be fried bodily into the egg. This, by the way, is the reason of the bare patches sometimes seen on fried fish, since naturally, if imperfectly coated with the egg, the bread-crumbs will not adhere properly.

Having got so far with your raw chef, you should, bearing in mind what I said as to the necessity of not overloading her awakening culinary intelligence with too many instructions at one time, leave her to cook, dish-up, and serve the remainder of the dinner in her own fashion, having beforehand taken the precaution of only selecting such dishes as you are sure she can achieve with distinction 'off her own bat', so to speak. For instance, a roast fowl might follow that fried sole, accompanied by bread sauce and the chipped potatoes aforesaid; or a roast forequarter of lamb, with potatoes and green peas, by way of second vegetable. And if sweets are not as yet her strong point, a junket accompanied by stewed apricots – the bottled ones are excellent for this purpose – might serve as entremet. You will note, perhaps with surprise, that I am only naming the very simplest dishes. My reason for doing so is, I hope, obvious; since it is only by pursuing this course, and letting her, as it were, 'feel her feet gradually', that you can hope to train your cook successfully. Too elaborate directions and recipes must be avoided at first, otherwise she will never attain anything like all-round excellence in her art.

10 August 1905

THRIFTLESS WIVES

To the Editor of the *Daily Telegraph*

Sir – I have already told you that I am by marriage Anglicised, if that is the correct word. In my previous letter I dealt with, among other things, the shunning of the kitchen in England by the mistress and the family. A little sympathy would help so much between maid and mistress. If the domestic misconstrues a visit, or an intended kindness from her mistress, it must be that there is a want of trust previously created, some 'abime' between the two.

How is a naturally dainty woman, and nearly all women are so, to get any heart to do cooking, to work among pots and pans? It is essential that the kitchen should be bright and clean. An airy, cheerful room, with smokeless fires, no unnecessary corners nor pipes all over the walls, nor fixed cupboards to harbour dirt and hidden things. Away also with the ugly iron saucepans, and replace them with the light and prettily coloured enamel ones. The floor should be tiled, and the walls as well, if possible, so that plenty of water can be used every day to keep the place sweet. I believe in cupboards that can be moved about, one for crockery and glass, the other for food, with a snowy white table. Given these conditions, what is to prevent the courageous Englishwoman donning an apron and rolling up her sleeves. Then, whilst the girl is doing the rough work, paring potatoes, &c., the mistress can attend to cooking dainty, simple dishes for her husband. The Englishwoman does not find much help outside her home. If she goes to the butcher all he can supply is a chop, or roast of beef or mutton, or a veal cutlet. Should she wish a certain kind of cut, the butcher is willing enough, but his imagination conceives naught beyond solid joints and fat chops, for even to him a cutlet is a chop.

Abroad, if you go to the butcher, he will contrive for you a couple of dozen of different dishes. It all comes out of beef, mutton, veal, or pork, but you get a variant from the eternal, costly joint. He will supply you with such and such tit-bits, or bones, to make delicious soups. And your Continental greengrocer has always an endless variety of vegetables. What, then, is an Englishwomen to do thus handicapped? She cannot be always making soup out of cabbage supplemented with turnips, carrots, or potatoes; she may eke these out with dried 'legumes', but they do not make palatable soup. In England the wife has only about half-a-dozen varieties of vegetables to select from; so-called 'spring greens', mostly fit for the stable, for there is so much waste. But your Englishwomen are great on puddings; with these she can hold her own against the world which includes every foreigner. I have always enjoyed the nice home-made English puddings.

Here are a few ways I have for improving tasteless greens:

For cabbage: Wash well and boil quickly till tender, add enough salt when ready, strain thoroughly, almost dry. Then chop very fine, put in a small saucepan, add one spoonful of dripping or butter, plenty of pepper, a little sprinkling of nutmeg, and salt if still needed; put on lid of saucepan and stand on side of stove; let steam until time to dish up. Try this – it is only cabbage, but delicious.

For carrots: Scrape a bunch, or as many as are required; cut into very small pieces; do same to four large onions; add one good lump of butter, season with pepper and salt, put in three lumps of sugar, just cover all with water (no more), boil quickly, then put aside and let stew gently for one hour and a half, stirring now and then. Water should be almost steamed away. With an entrecote or sausage it is a feast.

For endives: Wash them well and cut into small pieces, put into a saucepan with a cup of boiling water, pepper and salt. Steam thoroughly, adding a lump of butter when ready. Serve hot.

For red cabbage: Cut up very finely, add sweet apples and large onion, also finely-cut; season with vinegar, oil, pepper, and salt. Makes a good salad. Also cut very fine a red cabbage with one pound of sweet apples, two chopped onions, add sauce-spoon of dripping, pepper, salt, put all together in saucepan; put on lid and let cook in its own steam. Serve with *côte de boeuf* or veal or pork – yes, or mutton.

There are many wholesome and cheap dishes which give very little trouble to make. To learn young the secrets and mysteries of 'cuisine', is the best way. Let not Englishmen grumble over much if their wives cook badly, but think how they have been spared the risk of overeating and red noses.

Yours truly,
Mrs Bertha B.
London, S.W.

COOKING STRICTLY FOR STAND-INS
Jean Robertson

It was just 10 minutes before breakfast when the disc slipped. The kettle was on, but the coffee was not ground or the toast made. That was three weeks ago and ever since, my husband has had sole charge of the kitchen.

It's the sort of minor catastrophe that could hit any household any time – one friend of mine has just brought his wife home from the ski slopes on a stretcher, another is coping with the children while his wife has bronchitis, a third is the anchor man in a home confinement. All of them have suddenly been brought face to face with the culinary facts of life.

Excluding the professionals, male cooks generally come in three guises – occasional competent, occasional flamboyant, and occasional reluctant.

Luckily for us my husband comes into the occasional competent category which means that, while he may not relish regular cooking, he does not regard it as degrading to apply the full force of his intelligence to the trivia of domestic economy.

The kitchen has not been blue with smoke and obscenities or work-top high in dirty dishes, but if it had been, the first rule of survival in such circumstances is not to let the chaos disturb you – or at least not to let *him* see that it disturbs you.

Try to choose dishes for which precise cooking instructions can be shouted from the bedroom (like cutlets) rather than those requiring judgment (such as steak), and favour packets and cans carrying unequivocal cooking instructions.

Abandon conventional two-course two-veg meals, which make too much washing-up and involve bringing three or four things, all with different cooking times, to the dishing-up stage simultaneously – the Waterloo of most novices.

If fish appears at all at such times, it should be either hot-smoked (which needs no cooking) or out of the freezer. Smoked trout (4s 6d each) and Arbroath smokies have both given us good meals, so have Findus fillets of plaice.

Pork chops cooked in foil have been a success on two accounts. They tasted good and there were no pans to wash. Paint the seasoned chops with olive oil, season and lay them in the centre of a large double sheet of foil. Add a few chopped mushrooms, a little parsley if you have it, and a touch of garlic if you like it. Seal the packet tightly so that no juices can escape and bake for 30 minutes at Regulo six (400°F) and 30 minutes at Regulo four (350°F).

There are some packeted foods which may not appeal as a meal in themselves but which provide an encouraging ground-work on which the enterprising male can improvise. Prawns, green peppers, celery, tomato, any or all of these could be added to a quick, dry, packaged *paella*. A jar of Cirio tomato sauce could be used as it stands, or it could be improved with chopped chicken, olives, frozen shrimps, cooked mushrooms – what you will. Or it could be added to a fry-up of onions and minced beef to improvise a bolognese sauce.

 143

During this emergency we have inflated the sales figures for 'granary' bread (bought sliced to save crumbs in the kitchen), which has replaced potatoes; fruit and yoghourt, which has replaced pudding; Bennett's 'home-made' mayonnaise from the U.S., Baxters soups and Green Giant Mexicorn.

We had some lucky breaks, of course – like the private meals-on-wheels organised by a benevolent sister-in-law who brought round casseroles, which only needed heating up, and the good friend who treated us to a dinner laid on by the Home Meals Delivery Service.

These people deliver a complete meal or just a main course to your door at the time you want it. It is ready to eat and its containers are thrown away afterwards (minimum order 27s. 6d. for the total bill, not each dinner; minimum notice one hour). To get them dial C-H-I-C-K-E-N.

Since that first meal we have 'dined out' at home once a week. After all, every cook deserves a day off, even the stand-in.

9 February 1969
AN END TO THE LONESOME PORK PIE TRAIL
Jill Tweedie

Bend your mind to the Case of the Pork Pie Widower, recently recorded in a medical journal. This poor gentleman subsisted entirely upon pork pies, beer, unsweetened coffee and a once-weekly portion of fish and chips, which meant (apart from frightful indigestion) that he had no vitamin C or A, hardly any iron and less than half the protein an adult needs.

This unthinkable menu underlines what doctors already know; today's most vulnerable group nutritionally are old men who live alone. And who is largely to blame for their sad state? Old women, that's who.

For generations, no female art has been more jealously guarded than that of cookery. Mothers, wives and sweethearts down the years have spent their lives insinuating that the four walls of a kitchen witnessed culinary rites of such intricate skill that no mere man could hope to emulate.

Among the monotonous repetitive chores of a housewife's day, cooking stands out in solitary splendour – creative, emotionally satisfying and deeply appreciated by anyone within sniffing distance. No wonder we clasp its mysteries to our bosoms. It would be hard to milk the full drama out of cooking a meal if you knew your daughters, sons and husband could cook it equally well with only half the fuss.

'John?' say middle-aged wives, gazing fondly upon their husbands' bald pates, 'why, he couldn't cope at all. I honestly believe he'd die of starvation if I were away for a week.' And their faces glow with honest pride at the thought of John's incompetence and their own indispensability.

An immediate answer to the problem is happily being provided by the enterprising Electrical Association for Women, with their annual series of three hour-long cooking lessons conducted under the motherly eye of Mrs Pickford.

'Of course, many night schools give cookery classes but, you see, men won't go to them because most of the pupils are women. We run strictly men-only classes and we try to pick dishes that are nutritional (though we don't tell them that) and simple to make without being dull.'

But the younger generation of men is a different story. Nowadays they can whip themselves up at least as good an Irish stew as most young women and few bachelors today would touch the diet of old socks their fathers' generation found quite tolerable. And, with more and more women spending at least part of their time working outside the home as well, the aura of exclusivity is fast giving way to a passion of gratitude towards any male who'll boil an egg at the end of a long day.

Not that there aren't some disadvantages to possessing a cooking husband. You are taking the risk of unleashing a fastidious, temperamental chef and then all hell can break loose.

Women cut their coats according to their cloths in cooking: if the budget's tight they'll braise gristle. But men always insist on the best of everything – double cream where milk would do, T-bone steaks where stewing meat is perfectly suitable. And, carried away by their own creativity, men invariably use a 10-gallon bowl to whisk one egg and use every single dish, cup, saucer, saucepan and piece of cutlery in the entire house to make one omelette. At the end of a session with the liquidiser the kitchen looks like a gastronomic hurricane.

Nor do men rest on their laurels. My husband started out modestly enough, content to toss an onion into some mincemeat, boil pasta, call the whole spaghetti bolognese and throw in a glass of wine. Now, the sauce requires a cornucopia of rare spices, he knits the spaghetti himself and every available cupboard is packed with fermenting grape juice because he makes his own wine.

But we should be glad. If we leave our husbands wifeless, they may live in utter squalor but malnutrition will be unheard of.

Dawn of Couscous Parties

6 November 1966
PIES FOR PARTIES
Jean Robertson

Putting a pastry crust round a dish of meat, fish, eggs or fruit is like putting make-up on a girl or a frame round a picture. It cannot make a masterpiece out of a mess, but it does make the most of a modest talent. And even a real gem is all the better for a pretty setting.

This halo effect of pastry is something worth exploiting, especially when one of the most panic-free formulas for feeding a small crowd is to produce three or four massive pies, or a trayful of savoury tarts, hot from the oven.

The pies can be made the day before and reheated on the night, while the tarts can be prepared early in the day, laid out on a baking sheet, shrouded with a damp cloth, and shoved into the oven as the first guest arrives on the doorstep.

The pastry must be good of course, but that is no problem these days when the heavy-handed or pre-occupied among us can find good paste in the deep freeze cabinet of every corner grocer.

I am not going to waste space here giving yet another recipe for steak and kidney pie. However, very few manuals tell you how to reheat it:

Lightly crush a couple of sheets of greaseproof paper, make them damp and then fit them over the pastry. Put pie into a preheated oven (Regulo 5 or 380°F) for 30 to 40 minutes according to size.

Almost any large meat pie can be reheated in this way, including the chicken pie recipe given below. However, as the raw pastry goes over a filling that is already cooked, it is no problem to bake the pie on the evening of the party.

Chicken Pie
Ingredients for two large pies:

1 large or two small boiling chickens;
2 onions, 2 carrots, 1 stick celery,
½ turnip, 2 leeks, bouquet garni,
salt, peppercorns and blade mace
(if you have it) – all for boiling
with the bird;
¾lb boiled ham in the chunk;
3 canned pimientos;
¼lb button mushrooms (the canned
ones will do);
2oz butter for colouring the chicken

For the sauce:
3oz flour (scant);
3oz butter (generous);
2½ pints of the liquor in which the
chicken was cooked;
1 gill cream;
salt, freshly ground black pepper
and powdered mace;
2 large packets of frozen puff pastry
(Jus-Rol for choice)

Using a really large saucepan capable of holding the bird and all the vegetables, melt the butter and let the chicken colour all over. This will take at least 25 minutes. Then surround the bird with vegetables and *bouquet garni* and pour over enough boiling water to cover. Add the seasonings, cover and leave to simmer for 2½ to 3½ hours, according to the age and size of the fowl.

When it is cooked pour off about three pints of the cooking liquor and leave the chicken to cool in the rest of the liquid.

To make the sauce: Using a fairly large, heavy pan, melt the butter. Remove from heat and stir in sieved flour. Return to heat and cook for a minute or two without stirring *too* vigorously. Stir in one-third of the stock (hot but not boiling) and, when that has been absorbed and the mixture is smooth, add the rest in two equal instalments.

Leave this to cook very gently on an asbestos mat for ten minutes, or a little more if it seems too thin, then stand it in, or over, boiling water for 30 to 40 minutes. Season generously with salt, freshly ground black pepper and mace, and add the cream.

While the sauce is maturing over hot water, strip the flesh off the chicken bones and dice it into stamp-size pieces. Cut the ham into large matchsticks and the pimientos into slivers, and, if you favour fresh mushrooms rather than tinned, toss them in a little butter. Pile these ingredients into two large pie dishes.

Roll the pastry (which needs at least an hour at room temperature to thaw out) to the thickness of a half-crown. Cut off a couple of strips at the edge to lay on the dampened rim of the pie dish, paint the strip with water and then cover the pie with the pastry.

Make a hole in the centre for the steam to escape, decorate and paint with an egg yolk beaten up with a little salt. Bake for 35 to 40 minutes in a hot oven (Regulo 7 or 425°F).

Flamiche or Leek Flan

Mention the word 'savoury flan' and the first thing everyone thinks of is *Quiche Lorraine*. Good as this is there are other equally good fillings such as cheese, mushrooms, seafood, smoked salmon with cream and eggs, onions or leeks.

The pastry in the recipe that follows is a basic quiche paste and can be used for any savoury tart. It is virtually fool-proof and takes only three or four minutes to mix.

Contrary to the rather harsh comments in *Larousse Gastronomique* our quiche from Picardy, where the roses come from, is a remarkably delicate dish. Although I am suggesting it as a party recipe the ingredients listed below are for a four-person flan only, as you are more likely to have small flan rings than large ones.

However, the arithmetic of these ingredients is so simple that it is easy to increase the quantities by 50 or 100 per cent should you have a flan ring big enough. If you double the quantities, allow an extra five minutes' cooking time.

The pastry:

8oz plain flour;	*½ gill cold water;*
4oz butter;	*salt*

Make the pastry by tipping softened butter, water and salt into a well made in the centre of the sieved flour, and quickly and lightly drawing the flour into the liquid mixture until all the ingredients are smoothly combined. Leave the pastry to rest in a cool place for at least one hour.

The filling:

12 very thin leeks (or 6 fat ones);
2 rashers bacon;
½ pint milk (seasoned with slice of onion, peppercorns, parsley stalks, bay leaf and mace);

1 heaped tablespoon butter;
1 level tablespoon flour;
½ gill double cream;
butter for sautéing the leeks

Set the thinly sliced leeks, using white and very pale green parts only, to sauté in butter. They should soften but not colour. Meanwhile, make a white sauce by stirring the tablespoon of flour into the melted tablespoon of butter (off the heat), and then stirring in the milk, one third at a time (on the heat).

Let the sauce cook for a few minutes, and then stand it in or over a pan of boiling water for up to 40 minutes. Then add cream, leeks seasoned with salt and pepper, and the bacon (cut into matchsticks and tossed in the same butter as the leeks).

Roll out pastry, line a seven- to eight-inch flan ring, pour in filling and cook in the centre of a preheated oven for 20 minutes at Regulo 7 (425°F). Cool slightly before serving.

14 November 1969
CANAPÉS COME BACK
Robert Carrier

Canapés are back. First popular in the twenties as a sop for the important quantities of dry martinis consumed at private parties, the canapé makes its reappearance today as a streamlined pre-dinner party snack designed to rouse the taste buds and give your guests a sense of confidence in what is to follow.

Whether you are serving vintage dry martinis, dry sherry, champagne, bull shots, or just plain vodka on the rocks – you'll find your first arrivals will appreciate a tiny pre-dinner snack while waiting for the other guests to arrive. And if you are throwing a super shindig with drinks for millions – then the canapé is a necessity not a luxury.

In the list of canapé recipes that follows you'll find a few trifles which will take you only about ten minutes to assemble. For more ambitious cooks, there is a group of *bonnes bouches* which will prove a little more time consuming. None, however, is complicated to the point of absurdity. Each is individually delicious. So, take your pick.

Salame cornucopia – thin slice of salame set in a tin ham cornet; filled with cream cheese flavoured with lemon juice and finely chopped parsley and chives. Note: salame cornucopia is removed from tin cornet before serving.

Wedge of fresh pear – dipped in lemon juice to preserve colour; dusted with freshly ground coriander or black pepper; wrapped in a strip of *prosciutto* (Parma ham) and fastened with a cocktail stick.

White mushroom cap – dipped in lemon juice to preserve colour; dusted with freshly ground coriander or black pepper; piped with a mixture of equal parts blue cheese and cream cheese flavoured with salt and freshly ground black pepper. Topped with a shiny black olive.

Indonesian beef *saté* – cubes of beef skewered on a wet cocktail stick (to prevent burning); brushed with soy sauce and honey; rolled in chopped nuts and sautéed in butter or oil (or grilled) until tender.

Radish canapé – pimento cream cheese mixture piped around radish and rolled in finely chopped parsley.

Steak tartare canapé – put 1 lb sirloin steak twice through the finest blade of your mincer. Add the yolk of one egg, season and taste.

Grilled Cheddar Canapés

2 level tablespoons butter;
1 level tablespoon flour;
6 tablespoons milk;
6oz freshly grated Cheddar cheese;

1 egg, separated;
White bread, sliced and cut into 2in
rounds; paprika

Melt butter in the top of a double saucepan; add flour and cook over water. Stir continuously until blended. Add milk and grated cheese and stir until the sauce is smooth and thick. Remove from heat and allow to cool.

Beat egg yolk until lemon coloured; add to sauce. Beat egg white until stiff; fold into sauce.

Toast rounds of bread lightly on both sides. Spread rounds with cheese mixture. Spread canapés on a well-buttered baking sheet. Dust canapés lightly with paprika; place under a heated grill and cook until cheese is puffed and golden brown. Serve immediately.

1 July 1905
BRIDES' CAKES

June is the month of weddings as of roses, and this year there has been a phenomenal harvest. It has given a substantial impetus to trade, particularly to the confectionary trade, which naturally includes the caterer. Few brides have to order so colossal a cake as that designed for Princess Margaret, but it is ordained that a bride's cake must grace every wedding feast, however humble; though some would have us believe brides' cakes have ceased to be 'fashionable'. The confectioners refute this theory by their experience, particularly during the present season. They maintain that fashion has interfered with this, one of the oldest marriage customs, only to the extent of requiring greater elaboration and finer workmanship in the preparation of the bride's cake. Brides' cakes of today represent only the best of the confectioner's art. The cook may master the intricacies of the actual cake-making, but the master hand gives it character in the piping. It is sad almost to think of the painstaking work that is spoiled by the ruthless knife in cutting the cake, but, after all, the sugar coating is only a cover meant to be broken. Fashion has certainly exerted an influence on the exterior character of the sugar casement, demanding, as the first essential, delicacy of treatment. Excessively heavy ornamentation was the fault of a few years back, and the three-tier cakes of even the best makers showed no attempt at artistic effect.

Then the architectural phase came into force. Grecian columns and severe Grecian patterns, more delicate tracery in definite design and heraldic embellishments, were the main factors that governed the ornamentation and gave splendid opportunity for free and bold treatment. Gradually the atrocities in artificial flowers that were supposed to ornament the top were discarded in favour of daintier specimens and real flowers, with long strands of delicate ferns, quite the happiest factor conducing to the beauty of the modern wedding-cake. Colour has never been tolerated on brides' cakes, at least in the scheme of the sugar piping. There is a wealth of opportunity for the colour-artist in the icing of tea cakes, birthday or christening cakes, but the bridal cake must needs be white.

There is no doubt that the recent competitions instituted among the professors of the culinary art and sugar artists by the promoters of the Food and Cookery Exhibition have done a great deal to popularise this branch of confectionary, and to conduce to the higher standard of excellence to which it has attained. The results this year, in all classes, were distinctly good, sugar architecture being most splendidly represented. It is in these exhibits that novelties are introduced, but this year the exhibitors seemed shy of new departures, the exhibition being distinguished more for the delicate interlacing and lattice work.

19 June 1935
'CHAMPAGNE' THE COTTAGE: TESTED RECIPES FOR HOME CELLARS
A Country Housewife

The outstanding ingredient in the making of 'champagne' of the countryside is cheapness – 4 lb white sugar costs 9d, a pint of clean wheat about 1½d. The products from the gardens are made up for less than 1s per gallon, and the winemaking needs only the simplest management in the vessels available within the home.

The three essential points are:

1. Mash or brew to gather flavour or substance from flowers and fruit.
2. A period of fermentation.
3. Time to mature and break up the crude brackish liquid into a mellow wine holding all the fragrance of the mash.

Green Gooseberry Champagne

Pull the gooseberries when they are large and juicy – but remember they must be bone-dry.

Allow 1 gallon of gooseberries, 12 grape-leaves, 1 gallon cold water, 4 lb white sugar.

Put the gooseberries into a bowl with the vine-leaves down amongst them. Cover with water.

Mash the fruit and stir occasionally; leave 21 days, and then squeeze every drop of moisture from the gooseberries and leaves before throwing them away. Strain the liquid and add the sugar. Stir until it is dissolved and put in a warm room to ferment. Leave eight days; then skim and bottle.

Raisin Champagne

2 lb large raisins, 4 lb sugar, 1 lb wheat, 2 large old potatoes, 1 gallon hot water, and 1oz yeast.

Clean but do not peel the potatoes, grate them up and put in a bowl with the raisins, sugar and wheat. Cover with the hot water and leave until it is lukewarm. Crumble up the yeast and sprinkle it on top. Allow this to ferment for three weeks, but occasionally stir it with the hand, breaking up the raisins.

Strain twice through a jelly-bag, bottle and keep four months.

Grape Champagne

I made this from grapes produced in a cold greenhouse which were not nice enough to market. Ordinary green grapes will do, but make the wine when grapes are fairly sour – at the beginning of the season, or when they are cheap. Quantities: 6 lb grapes, 1 gallon cold water, and 4 lb sugar.

Put the grapes and water into a bowl. Squeeze and mash every three days for three weeks. Then strain, squeezing every drop of moisture from the grapes before throwing them away. Add the sugar to the liquid and stir until it is dissolved. Then allow to ferment 14 days. Strain and bottle.

Marigold Champagne

3 quarts marigold flowers (the whole heads), 1 gallon water, 4 lb sugar, 1 lb wheat, 2 lemons, 1oz yeast. Pour the water over marigolds – gather them on a dry day. Let them stand seven days, pushing them down in the water until they get sodden. Strain and squeeze all the moisture from the flowers before throwing them away. Add wheat and sugar to the liquid. Squeeze the lemons, cut up the rinds, and put in the bowl. Lastly, sprinkle over the yeast and leave to ferment ten days. Strain and bottle and keep six months.

4 November 1960
GUESTS COOK THE DINNER – AND BREAK THE ICE
Beryl Hartland

Favourite party dish of Mrs Annette Lasley, an American hostess living in Knightsbridge, is a Fondue Bourguignonne (served with red Italian wine). 'It's a wonderful ice-breaker,' she says, and sooner or later the guests exclaim, 'Isn't this fun.'

Guests cook their own food (small cubes of rump steak) in a butter oil mixture sizzling in copper pans on top of small burners in the centre of the table.

Each guest has a special long fork and a plate of the raw cube steak surrounded by all sorts of delicious condiments and sauces into which they dip the meat when cooked.

Fondue Bourguignonne sets (forks, burners and rounded copper pans) can be bought in Knightsbridge and Greek Street, Soho, but they are fairly expensive. If, of course, you already possess a small heavy copper saucepan, you are half-way there.

12 February 1971
APHRODITE IN THE KITCHEN
Clement Freud

I do not suppose they did it on purpose, but I feel badly about going metric immediately after Valentine's Day. Taking your love for a four-guinea dinner only to find that, as the clock strikes midnight, they slap a bill for £4.20 into your lap, is a very, very unromantic happening.

However, leaving decimalisation to others, I shall write about wooing food.

A Valentine's Day dinner must not be simple. I know you can get fantastic results by administering an overdose of shepherd's pie to the right person, but such people would behave in precisely the same way if they got lentil soup, fish fingers or a luncheon voucher. Remember, I am writing about wooing, not seduction.

The unsimple Valentine dinner must be capable of being prepared well in advance so that the perpetrator of the feast can spend the maximum amount of time on personal appearance, without taking the risk of spoiling the evening by reeking of leeks, or whatever. Let there be a candle on the table, and a fingerbowl: a minimum of cutlery and a large glass because, if you are going to be fussy about the food, you must keep the wine simple. Champagne is a pleasant drink, or a cool white Beaujolais if you are less than rich.

Prepare prunes, soaked for two or three hours and then wrapped in rindless streaky bacon, speared with a toothpick. This is called a devil on horseback and can be cooked in the top of a hot oven for ten minutes.

Make a dip by peeling an aubergine, simmering the slices in butter, liquidising them when tender, and adding to the sieved aubergine some finely chopped garlic boiled for a few seconds in milk – which takes away the pungency and retains the perfume.

Serve toast Melba with the dip. You make this by toasting a thin slice of bread, cutting off the crusts, slipping a knife between the toasted out-sides and then putting the two slices, raw side up, under a medium grill. In case your loved one does not care for the aubergine dip, make flavoured butter. To make 3oz of anchovy butter, add two fillets of anchovy minced or rubbed through a sieve and blended with a fork.

To make egg butter, add one sieved hard-boiled egg and a good pinch of salt to 3oz butter.

Herb butter is best made with a teaspoon each of chopped parsley and chopped chives or spring onion tops, again per 3oz.

All will keep.

Jellied soup is woosome fare. Turtle soup put in the refrigerator comes out jellied – but even good tinned tomato soup, lengthened with cream and set with gelatine, wobbles eagerly in a cup and gives the right sort of impression.

Then fish. Make heartshaped pancakes by cutting a V out of a round pancake, and between two of these place slices of Mediterranean prawns simmered in brandy bound in tomato purée. Roll the pancake in buttered paper of foil – keep it in a cool oven, or wrap it in two lots of foil if the oven is hotter: to serve, take off foil, unwrap pancake and anoint it with a spoonful of brandy heated over the candle and then ignited by it.

Buy the finest sausages – price is a very good guide when it comes to excellence in the sausage field – and cook these slowly in a pan. Serve them with a salad incorporated in the dressing at the last moment. Tomatoes are quite suggestive, perhaps with thin slices of raw onions.

I am not at all sure that you will need a pudding. If you do, I have failed, so you might as well send the guest out to a decimal takeaway shop. There cannot then be any doubt about your original intentions.

But, if all goes well, Grape-Nuts and cream, toast and ginger marmalade, and some good hot strong coffee should be the next kitchen chore for you.

12 March 1972
WHEN IT PAYS TO BE A DAY IN FRONT
Winefride Jackson

Recently on this newspaper we were quite overawed when one of the young married secretaries produced a cold buffet lunch for her office farewell party.

She had cooked it the previous evening – turkey, ham, pâté, quiche, a variety of salads, treacle tart, mince pies, trifle . . . oh, yes, and cheesecake. Her husband packed it all into the Mini the next morning and there we were with a superb luncheon.

This story works up to the most important point in today's cookery books (apart from decent recipes), the need for directions in planning and cooking meals. The latest under this banner is *Cooking Today – Eating Tomorrow*, by Jan Hopcraft, to be published 23 March (£1.95 by Methuen). The recipes are arranged as complete menus for the family and for parties.

There is nothing to stop you changing the menu items, and each recipe carries a note of just how much can be prepared or cooked the preceding day. Here are two examples:

Lamb Chops en Croûte
The sauce can be made and the chops prepared a day ahead.
Action time: 45 minutes. Cooking time: 25 minutes.

*6 boned loin of lamb chops
(keep bones for sauce);
1 pint brown sauce;
14oz puff pastry (frozen puff pastry
can be used);
6oz mushrooms, thinly sliced;
1 small onion, finely chopped;*

*1oz butter;
1 lightly beaten egg – for brushing
pastry;
A pinch of rosemary and thyme;
Salt and freshly ground pepper;
Parsley, finely chopped*

Method: Grill the boned chops for three minutes on each side to brown them. Remove them from the heat and set on one side to cool. Meanwhile melt the butter in a pan and gently fry the onion for five minutes. Add the mushrooms, two tablespoons of water, the parsley, rosemary, thyme, freshly ground pepper and a little salt and cook until the water has been partially absorbed by the mushrooms. Take the pan off the stove and let the mushroom mixture cool. Roll out the pastry until it is thin and cut it into six strips about 8in long. Place the chops on the pastry strips and spoon a share of the mushroom mixture on to each. Moisten one edge of the pastry with a little water and fold it over the chop, pressing it down firmly on the other side: then close in the sides.

At this stage the chops can be kept in a cool place until the next day. Just before cooking, brush lightly with egg, place on a buttered baking tray and cook in a 'hot' oven (425°F, Mark 7) for 25 minutes. Serve with brown sauce, new potatoes and red cabbage.

Brown Sauce

Can be made a day ahead.
Action time: 15 minutes. Cooking time: 20 minutes.

1 carrot, grated;
1 small onion, finely chopped;
1oz butter;
¾ pint beef stock or cube;
2 tablespoons sherry (optional);
2 teaspoons flour;

¼ teaspoon French mustard;
⅛ teaspoon salt;
Freshly ground pepper;
1 bay leaf;
1 tablespoon sugar for caramel or few drops of gravy browning

Method: Melt the butter in a saucepan and gently fry the onion and carrot for five minutes. Add the flour and continue cooking for a further two minutes before placing the stock, bay leaf, mustard, salt and pepper in the saucepan. Meanwhile, in another saucepan put one tablespoon of water with the sugar and, stirring, boil until the syrup turns dark brown (alternatively use gravy browning though you will lose the bitter taste the caramel provides); add to the stock in the pan. Simmer for 20 minutes, stirring occasionally. Remove from the heat, put half the vegetables through a sieve and discard remainder. Return the liquid and the sieved vegetables to the pan and add the sherry. Keep in a cool place. When required, reheat and serve with chops.

Yachting, Motoring and Picnics

1 July 1971
EATING *AL FRESCO*
Mary Brogan

One thing which has been made plain by the sudden spell of good weather is that, if the British want to take to the great outdoors to eat, it is now a great deal easier for them to do so than ever before. It would be an exaggeration to say that every street is bursting with gay, Continental-style cafés, but it is true that every kind of eating place, from pubs and pizzerias to top-grade restaurants are busy bringing out the tables and umbrellas, if they have a spot of ground to call their own.

There, of course, lies the snag. The ground really does have to be their own: none of the messy Parisian cluttering up of the public footpaths for us. As Westminster Council put it: 'You *could* apply to use the pavement and the application would be considered, but it's highly unlikely to be granted. And even with your own forecourt you could still run the risk of obstruction.'

With this distinct lack of encouragement from the authorities, it is surprising that so many restaurateurs make the effort. However, if they can manage it, it is well worth their while. Stella Brett, who owns L'Artiste Assoifé in Westbourne Grove, decided two years ago to make use of her garden and deck it out with tables, umbrellas and lanterns.

'It's been a great success,' she says. 'People love the idea of eating in a garden in spring and summer and we're taking orders up to 12 o'clock.'

Mr John Pitcairn, of the Mardi Gras in Harrington Road, S.W.7, has had the same experience. He used just to have coffee tables on his terrace, but now it is a full-scale dining area and on warm nights he's turning customers away.

Obviously, given the chance, we are as fond of *al fresco* eating as any other nation, so wouldn't it be possible to make it just a bit easier for restaurants to give us what we want?

'Of course it would,' says food guide writer Egon Ronay. 'All this talk about obstruction is nonsense. Obviously, you wouldn't take up half the pavement in Oxford Street, but there's no reason why it couldn't be done in side streets. We should have the Continental system, whereby cafés rent pavement space from the local authority.'

It might be thought that, with our climate, anyone taking on the extra trouble and expense of outside tables was risking a poor return for the money, but not so, apparently. Come the first blink of sun or the first day which isn't positively freezing and we're out having lunchtime pints in pub gardens and even *diners à deux* on the terrace.

One explanation for this growing enthusiasm is that all over the country restaurants are being opened by French and Italians who take outdoor eating for granted. As well as this, the long-standing complaints by tourists on the subject are now having an effect. Our visitors have done us a good turn.

26 May 1906
EFFERVESCING DRINKS

Millions of dozens of aerated waters are now made annually, involving the employment of probably at least 50,000 persons in this country alone. This fact, coupled with the numerous devices which enable the consumer to prepare his own soda-water at home, seems to indicate, says the *Lancet*, that the introduction of aerated waters fill a place in the requirements of modern life, and the question arises as to whether the frequent drinking of waters strongly impregnated with carbonic acid gas has any prejudicial effect upon the health of the economy. It is an interesting feature of the case that total abstainers formed at one time the chief patrons of aerated beverages. But undoubtedly the present popularity of whisky is very closely connected with the demand for an aerated beverage. Soda-water has increased the sale of whisky enormously. The man who drinks whisky for the sake of its flavour rarely mixes it with aerated water. A bubbling liquid, endowed, moreover, with stimulating properties, proves to be a singularly attractive beverage and harder to resist than the non-sparkling fluid.

What is the charm of effervescence? Champagne would be miserable stuff without it, and beer that is not brisk is not only unattractive but unwholesome. Probably there are two reasons for it; first of all, carbonic acid gas gives piquancy to a beverage, a briskness to it, and an acid taste; moreover, effervescence implies freshness, and the eye is pleased with the continuous succession of tiny bubbles upwards through the liquid. Secondly, there are reasons for believing that the effervescent properties of a liquid promote digestion in two ways – first, by the carbonic acid acting as a stimulant to the movements of the stomach, and, secondly, by assisting in the disintegration of the contents of the stomach. Certainly, the alcohol in an effervescing liquid is more rapidly diffusible than in a still liquid. Champagne exhilarates more quickly than is the case with still wine. On the other hand, the introduction into the stomach of so much gas may lead to the embarrassment of the heart's action. It has also been stated that carbonic acid gas is rapidly absorbed from the stomach and that it may thus induce a condition of cyanosis, in which an excess of this gas is invariably found in the blood. In certain cases, therefore, the use of aerated water should be avoided. On the whole, however, it is possible that the moderate indulgence in pure aerated water is not only without prejudice to health, but serves as an aid to digestion when such help is needed. The frequent consumption of immoderate quantities of aerated water may be safely condemned, as such a practice undoubtedly has possibilities for evil.

25 June 1935

THE CHEF AND THE SALAD BOWL

The chefs of the West End restaurants revolutionised their menus yesterday. After an Ascot Week in which hot soups and savouries were welcome at the end of each day's downpour, the sudden heat wave created a demand for cooling salads and iced dishes.

This year's fashions in salads are interesting, owing to the extent to which new blends of flavour are being tried out in the salad bowl.

Hot Londoners were enjoying yesterday unusual mixtures of fruits and vegetables and the mingling of herbs in endless variations of the modern salad. Here are some of the most popular midsummer salads, according to a leading West End chef, M. Lebegue, of Grosvenor House.

Arrange the heart of a lettuce in basket form, filled with thin slices of apples, quarters of oranges and grapefruit, beetroot and *fenouil*, a species of celery which has an aniseed flavour.

Another fashionable salad of the day consists of lettuce, cold globe artichokes, sliced cold potato, and slices of pimento, tomato and chives.

Here is a third suggestion, the proportions given being for one person: Blend together half an alligator pear, half a cos lettuce, half a dozen grapefruit quarters, slices of pickled walnut, strips of pimento, slices of tomato and cucumber.

Alternative ideas for salad creams to accompany the tasty salad of today are as follows:

Take one teacupful whipped cream, juice of a lemon, one tablespoonful ground horseradish, one tablespoonful tomato ketchup, salt and pepper to flavour. Mix well together.

The other recipe has as its ingredients one tablespoon pulped Roquefort cheese, two tablespoonfuls salad oil, one tablespoonful vinegar, one teaspoonful chopped chives or very young spring onions and salt and pepper to flavour.

Salads of all kinds are likely to be found on both luncheon and dinner menus in Mayfair during the rest of the season. The Duchess of Kent has revealed to her friends that her ideal lunch is a mixed salad with cream, cheese and tomatoes.

Her guests at 3, Belgrave-square for luncheon have made the acquaintance of many new varieties of salad, in which sweet corn, avocado pears and cold asparagus make their appearance.

Tastes in salads are so individual that many hostesses may like to follow the example of Lady Portarlington, who had a table set aside with all possible salad ingredients at a buffet luncheon the other day in her Chesham-place home. She invited each guest to mix his or her own salad.

12 May 1943
AL FRESCO MEALS

To the Editor of the *Daily Telegraph*

Sir – Since we are urged to have stay-at-home holidays this year, cannot the Ministry of Food and local authorities encourage more facilities for taking meals in the open air?

British Restaurants might be persuaded to place a number of tables outside when space and weather permit, while riverside towns, such as Richmond and Kew, could cater much more effectively for war-time holiday-makers if more open-air cafés were provided.

Yours sincerely,

Maurice Caerburn, Putney, S.W.

23 April 1977
KEEPING COOL, WITH THESE INDIAN THIRST QUENCHERS FOR THE LONG, HOT SUMMER
Bon Viveur

India produces her own wines from grapes grown in the north and then sent to the Goan Peninsula for pressing and bottling. Drinking them was not, to us, one of the highlights of our trip.

Everything is against them: the climate is lethal to the very finest of the world's wines, reducing the better Indian ones to the level of the poorest Provençal reds or those produced around Collioure.

Conversely, the Indians produce highly palatable lager-type beers which are both light and refreshing. They are also eminently suited to Indian fare.

Even so, the drinks we liked best were the many non-alcoholic beverages which range from the simplest of all, fresh lime juice and Indian soda over crushed ice, to survivals of the old days of the British Raj.

We have authentic recipes for these, but we have notable omissions due to the fact that the average British housewife is unable, in most cases, to get hold of mangoes, asafoetida, guavas, kumquats and sweet limes.

The ones left to us are rich in vitamins and minerals and do much to stimulate appetites jaded by the intense heat – which, if we are to have a summer which in any way resembles last year's, becomes extremely relevant to this island.

One day last summer it was hotter in London than in Calcutta. This is when a jugful of well-chilled Assam Pineapple Quencher or Assam Orange Squash becomes a boon; or, as a prelude to European or Indian luncheon on terrace or patio, a Tomato Orange Refresher as served throughout all India is useful.

In both the north and the south, the Indians are definitely buttermilk addicts who serve either the Sweet or Savoury Buttermilk mixtures which we often encounter at vegetarian buffets.

From the Punjab comes the famous Khurmani Sherbet made with tinned or fresh apricot purée. North India also gives us a Gajar Kanji which is based on carrots. For this we may need to substitute pink ones for the fresh purple variety found in Indian markets. Here are some of the recipes:

Assam Pineapple Quencher

Use 1 lb of tinned pineapple or 1 medium fresh one; the strained juice of 2 oranges; 4 fl oz milk; sugar to taste (scarcely any with tinned pineapple); 12 fl oz cold water (only 3 with tinned pineapple); 1 tumbler crushed ice.

Put the peeled fresh, or rough-cut tinned, pineapple into a liquidiser with water, or water and tinned fluid, add sugar to taste and orange juice and reduce to a total purée. Add the milk, pour over crushed ice, swizzle and serve.

Assam Orange Squash

This can either be made in small quantities for immediate use or, as in India, be made in bulk, funnelled into sterilised wine bottles, corked and the corks sealed with hot paraffin wax. To do this, drive corks home firmly, then invert bottles and dunk each cork in the hot liquid wax.

Use 1¾ pints of strained orange juice; 2 lb 12oz granulated or soft brown sugar; 27 fl oz water; 1¼oz citric acid (from the chemist); the thinly peeled rind of 4 limes or lemons and a mean 2 grammes potassium meta-bisulphite (also from the chemist).

Place sugar in roomy pan with water and lemon peel. Stir over low heat until every grain of sugar has dissolved, then bring to boil. Cool, strain, stir in citric acid and orange juice, holding back 3 fl oz in which to stir potassium. Add, pour through funnel into bottles, and seal as explained.

Tomato Orange Refresher

Use the strained juice of 2 thin-skinned oranges; 9oz ripe tomatoes; 1 flat teaspoon sugar; a mean, flat teaspoon of cooking salt; ¼ flat teaspoon of freshly milled black peppercorns; strained juice of 1 large or 2 small lemons; 1 generous teaspoon Worcestershire Sauce; 1 flat teaspoon chilli powder (can be omitted); 1 rounded teaspoon of milled, fresh parsley heads or chopped, fresh mint leaves; 6 fl oz water; ½ pint crushed ice.

Simmer rough-cut tomatoes in water for 5 minutes. Press through a sieve to expel all juices. Stir in sugar, salt and fruit juices; then

Worcestershire Sauce, pepper and chilli powder. Finally add parsley. Refrigerate.

For service, one-third fill small glasses with crushed ice, fill up with Tomato Orange Refresher.

North India's Flavoured Buttermilk

Take 4–6 tablespoons yoghurt; 1 pint water; salt; black pepper; 1 rounded teaspoon toasted cumin seeds.

Mix all ingredients thoroughly and refrigerate. At moment of service, stir well again.

South India Buttermilk

Make a paste in a coffee-grinder, or mortar with pestle, of 6 tablespoons yoghurt; 1 green chilli; 1 thin slice of green ginger; 1 flat teaspoon coriander leaves; 1 peeled garlic clove, and have ready one pint of cold water.

When all ingredients except water form a perfectly smooth paste work in water gradually. Refrigerate until moment of service.

Khurmani Sherbet

Use 8 tablespoons fresh or tinned apricot purée (we tested with a baby food); 6 flat teaspoons sugar; the strained juice of 1 orange and 1 lemon or lime; 10 fl oz water; 4 fl oz cold milk.

Hold back milk and put all remaining ingredients into liquidiser. Switch on full for about 1 minute. Then add milk, stir, pour straight into fridge-frosted tumblers, and add at least two ice cubes to each serving. In India, a sherbet is a drink and not a water ice.

Gajar Kanji

Take 18oz fresh pink or purple carrots; 4 flat tablespoons salt; 1½ flat tablespoons red chilli powder (could be modified); 2 tablespoons mustard seeds crushed to powder; 6 pints or 3½ litres cold water.

Wash and scrape carrots. Slice thickly, place in pan with about 2 teacups water and cook for 10 minutes. Add all remaining ingredients. Stir well, turn into large stone or glass jar and place either in hot sun for three or four days, or in hot room. If using pink carrots, add a small cooked peeled beetroot, sliced to same thickness as carrot. Serve each small glassful with two ice cubes and two slices of carrot.

8 July 1973
SETTLE FOR A SORBET
Marika Hanbury-Tenison

Water ices or sorbets were originally served between courses to sharpen the appetite and settle the gastric juices and this is still a practice at some grand banquets today. Whenever they are served, a light, well-flavoured water ice makes a delicious contrast to the ingredients of any main course; they are easy to make and far less rich than a true cream ice.

The finished ice can be served in well-chilled champagne or wine goblets, in small glass dishes or in a fruit shell such as an orange skin, hollowed out melon or partially scooped out half pineapple. They look cool and attractive and can be made in a vast kaleidoscope of colours and flavours. Like cream ices, the sorbet can be stored for some length of time in a deep freezer providing it is well packed into a polythene container and tightly sealed. If the ice is made with wine or a liqueur flavouring, it should be left for at least 24 hours before being served to allow the flavourings to ripen and mature.

To give water ices more body and a lighter, smoother texture, whipped egg whites can be added to the recipe.

Gooseberry and Blackcurrant Leaf Sorbet
In this recipe an infusion of blackcurrant leaves give the gooseberries an unusual musky flavouring.

2 lb gooseberries, topped and tailed;   *Juice of 1 lemon;*
1½ lb sugar;   *2 handfuls blackcurrant leaves;*
½pt water;   *1 egg white*

Combine the sugar and water, bring slowly to the boil and boil as fast as possible for five minutes. Add the gooseberries and simmer for five minutes if the berries are soft and ripe, or for 10 minutes if they are hard and green. Add blackcurrant leaves and leave to infuse in the hot fruit for 20 minutes. Remove leaves and strain the juice through a fine nylon sieve. Press fruit gently to extract all the flavour. Add the lemon juice, pour syrup into a shallow tray and freeze at the lowest possible temperature.

When the mixture has frozen to a depth of ½in around the sides of the tray, give it a good stir to break up the ice crystals. Continue to stir every now and then until the ice is almost solid.

Whip egg white until stiff. Turn ice into a bowl and beat until it is mushy. Fold in the egg white, mix well and return to a freezing tray. Freeze until solid.

Strawberry or Raspberry Water Ice

1 lb strawberries or raspberries;
¾lb granulated sugar;
¾pt water;
Juice 1 lemon;
Juice 1 orange;
2 egg whites;
2 tablespoons brandy (optional)

Combine the sugar and water, bring slowly to the boil and boil as quickly as possible for five minutes. Mash fruit with a fork. (The fruit can be puréed but I find mashing gives an additional fruity texture to the ice.) Add fruit juice and brandy. Freeze and add egg whites as in the preceding recipe.

Liqueur Water Ice

These are frankly prohibitively expensive but next time you really want to splash out, make an impression and not have to break your back doing so, here is a sweet which is made in minutes and is blatantly luxurious. Use crème de menthe, crème de cassis or an orange-flavoured liqueur such as Grand Marnier. Serve the ice in fine glass goblets, topped with a little sweetened whipped cream. Pour over a little more liqueur just before serving and hand round a plate of almond biscuits to go with it.

12oz sugar;
1pt and ½ gill water;
Juice of 1 lemon;
¼pt liqueur

Combine the water and sugar, bring slowly to the boil and then boil as fast as possible for five minutes. Leave to cool and mix in the lemon juice. Pour into a freezing tray and freeze, stirring every now and then as the sides become solidified. When the mixture is all granulated, mix in the liqueur and continue to freeze until almost solid.

AUTUMN

Inspecting the Marmalade

20 June 1914
HOME-MADE JAM

Less than a decade ago the British housewife took a pride in her home-made jam. Nowadays it is different. The woman who makes a point of preserving at least a few pounds of every kind of fruit is looked upon by her friends as having wasted valuable time which might be devoted to bridge. If age and activity permit, it may be the tennis court that claims the *mère de ménage*, whilst golf is looked upon as indispensable to the well-being of all women who can afford to indulge in the pastime.

Explanations and contrasts are of little avail. The fact is that two good old-fashioned institutions are rapidly disappearing. They are home-made jam and Christmas pudding. Not that either has declined one whit in point of popularity, for both are consumed in large quantities than ever. Almost past is the day when the husband argues enthusiastically that his wife's jams and puddings are by far the best he ever tasted. Men are content today to praise the domestic attainments of their mothers, especially in regard to the cuisine.

Enterprising firms have stepped in and relieved Materfamilias families of much of her work. 'Who will be bothered to make jam when it can be bought so good and so cheaply?' is the unanswerable question of the moment. Before the public are aware, for example, that strawberries are plentiful they are offered 'new season's jam' by the alert grocer or the manager of a department in the 'stores'. It is all done so quickly that people do not realise what is taking place. There is no denying the fact that leading British firms do the work remarkably well. A visit to a well-conducted jam factory is sufficient to convince the most exacting of folk that 'bought' preserves are as good as, and perhaps better than, those made at home. The statement may be iconoclastic, but it is none the less true. Jam makers know their business.

Jam-making as a topic might well be introduced by a series of 'don'ts'. It is not so much a question of what to do as what should be avoided. First of all the idea that fruit which is not good enough for dessert is just the thing for jam is utterly and hopelessly wrong. Unripe or overripe strawberries are equally objectionable, preserved or raw. The addition of sugar and the application of heat do not change the quality of the fruit. In factories noted for good jam the work of selecting the fruit is done with the greatest possible care and precision, inferior samples being rejected without hesitation. To make palatable preserves the fruit must be of good quality and in thoroughly sound condition.

To have jam in perfection the fruit should be gathered in dry weather early in the day with the morning sun shining on it. The British climate makes adherence to those conditions difficult at times, and it is not much use telling Londoners and suburban dwellers to rise early in the morning and pick the fruit they do not grow. They can, however, get good fruit if they will take the trouble to look for it. Modern life with its rush and pace has its advantages as well as its disadvantages. One of the former is the wonderful supply of fruit which is brought to the door within a few hours of being gathered. To all intents and purposes the fruit offered nowadays might have been gathered under the ideal conditions suggested. Fast trains and motor services have revolutionised the fruit supply.

Assuming then that a proportion of home-made jam is still appreciated it must be borne in mind that the very best fruit, and the best only, will give good results. This does not necessarily mean large, handsome specimens – especially in the case of strawberries. The best variety of strawberry for preserving is the Sir Joseph Paxton, commonly called the Paxton. Unfortunately, as pointed out yesterday in an article dealing with strawberries, it is not always possible to get Paxtons, at any rate without a little trouble; but it is well worth an effort to secure that excellent variety.

A few pounds of jam made of Paxton strawberries will delight all who have a discriminating palate.

Care is required in regard to the use of sugar. Coarse kinds quickly destroy the delicate sub-acid flavour of any kind of fruit. One is almost timorous of suggesting the use of pure cane-sugar, because the public seldom stop to think whence the sweetening substance is derived. In these times, when rival chemists can prove almost anything to the lay mind, it is indeed difficult to convince anyone that cane sugar is the best the world produces. Let those versed in analyses and synthetic preparations quarrel as they will, it was old-fashioned Nature that provided the sugar-cane, and after all she is the greatest of all chemists. It is delightful to return to a few ancient ideas, amongst which good fruit and can-sugar for jam must be included.

There are fruits other than strawberries to which the housewife might with advantage turn her attention. Black currants are always useful in the preserved state, and it so happens that France will this season provide an ample supply. Then the richly-flavoured raspberry, and many kinds of plums, including the damson, should not be neglected. In all cases the rule about quality and condition holds good.

Large factors frequently affix a notice on the jars to the effect that a little fruit acid has been added to the original ingredients of fruit and sugar. This practice has arisen from observation, it having been found that the addition improves the confection and does away with some of the excessive sweetness of fruit and sugar only. The use of acids except in the hands of experts is not to be recommended.

Many urge the superiority of home-made jam because 'they know what it is made of'. In all probability that is precisely what they do not know. Few of the public are acquainted with the different varieties of fruit. How many consumers can discriminate between a Paxton, Sovereign, or Stirling Castle strawberry? It were well not to venture a guess. The making of jam is a business which requires as much understanding and experience as numerous other culinary preparations which the uninitiated do not attempt. The avoidance of mould is in itself a lesson that needs much learning; so perhaps the women of today are wise in their generation when they buy preserves prepared by experts of repute.

18 September 1926
BLACKBERRYING

During the pleasant season on which we are entering, when the stimulating air and autumn tints of the countryside attract so many ramblers from town, many industrious people will be gathering blackberries, the chief harvest of the English hedges. Numerous roads which now form part of suburban London once offered a feast to the youngster at this time of year – a fact that is within the memory of many Londoners. Even today the bramble flourishes between Hampstead and Golders-green. The only widespread English fruit that is free to all, it ripens at a time when there is little fruit in the garden. Yet the first that most Londoners know of the blackberry season is when the berries are brought to town and sold in the shops. Indeed, it is strange how many splendid blackberrying centres in Kent and Surrey, within twelve or fifteen miles of Charing-cross, are missed by City workers in their week-end exodus. The great London traffic undertakings are organising publicity on this matter with a view to popularising the idea of the 'blackberry excursion'.

The harvest is exceedingly fine this year, the fruit being large, firm, and plentiful. The long hours of sunshine just as the berries were darkening have helped to bring them to perfection. So often, if the summer is late, they grow hard under the sun's rays, and seem to be nothing but pips, while if they ripen in bad weather they taste watery and acid. But this year they give promise of attaining to the full the delicate flavour which is so prized in bramble jelly and in the home-made wine. During the next week or so every day will add to the number which hang black and ready for the excursionist's crook on the upper branches. In most places the lower branches cannot hide their prizes for long from the fingers of schoolchildren. The long arm usually wins in the inevitable race to see whose basket fills quickest, but there is another factor besides height. It is knowing the ways of this most variable of British fruits, of which, according to botanists, there are about twenty-one sub-species. Somehow or other some of the finest berries ripen behind leaves. The picker who wants to explore for hidden fruit, however, should provide herself with a really stout pair of old leather gloves if she wants to save her hands from unsightly scratches.

12 March 1940
INSPECTING THE MARMALADE
Daily Telegraph Woman Reporter

Housewives who have made marmalade for which they received special grants of sugar are now expecting a visit from a member of the local Food Controller's staff.

Inspection of the store cupboard is beginning now that the time for obtaining the sugar allowance is over. This period ended on Saturday, and officials want to be sure that the sugar has really been used to make marmalade.

The chairman of the Chesham Food Control Committee, Mr Swann, was out on the marmalade round early yesterday morning. He planned his tour to include every type of home.

Housewives had no idea at whose homes he would call. But he had a welcome everywhere and was taken into kitchens to see neat rows of glass jars labelled 'Marmalade, 1940', containing the newly made preserve.

London Food Control officers differed in their attitude to the question of inspecting the marmalade pots.

'We have other things to inspect and there will be no time for looking at marmalade,' said one official. 'But we have not entirely trusted the housewife. We carried out the Ministry of Food's instruction to take the bill for Seville oranges and see the ration books.'

Another London official pointed out that women in his district had to give a written undertaking that they would use the sugar to make marmalade. 'We have relied mainly on this, but although we have no cut-and-dried plan for inspecting marmalade, we may decide to select a few cases and put them to the test. We have the power to call on anybody to whom we issued a permit for sugar.'

19 November 1958

JAM-MAKING IS MISS CARTER'S HOME INDUSTRY
Claire Butler

This is the season when some of the choicest, but half-forgotten, old-world preserves can be brought back to English tables.

You seldom see quince jam or jelly nowadays. But I have been talking to Miss Dorothy Carter who, from making marmalade and jam from good family recipes for herself and her friends 30 years ago, has built up a thriving home industry.

She is not only making the two quince preserves, but other specialities, including crab apple jelly and apple jelly flavoured with geranium or elderflower. Soon she will be making medlar jelly.

After Christmas comes marmalade-time. This Miss Carter makes entirely from Seville or other bitter oranges – no sweet ones are used, nor does she use lemon as do so many home-makers. Long boiling is the secret for dark colour and flavour.

It was during the war that Miss Carter first looked for a market for her home-made preserves and today she supplies shops from her own home in Iden, Sussex. Until this year she made them in two old-fashioned coppers. She now has installed three Calor gas burners in the kitchen workshop beside her house.

Into these fruit jams, made as you would make yours in your own kitchen, go local-grown fruit and sugar, with no colouring or other additions. Strawberry jam, made from punnets of strawberries, is another of her specials.

The 16,000 to 18,000 lb she makes a year are done with the aid of one assistant all the time and two in the busy season. Demand increases, but this country- and home-loving woman has no intention of enlarging her premises. She prefers to keep up the home-made quality and personal touch of her products, rather than to develop it into a small factory.

Two other people who share Miss Carter's attitude towards the factory approach are Mr and Mrs E. M. Davie, who have a pottery studio in Rye. Our sense of design was lost, they think, during the industrial revolution. Before then designs were passed on from father to son.

In Sweden it was never lost, and today there is a great revival in designs of all kinds, stimulated by design centres in the various towns.

Mr Davie uses a kick wheel for his pottery. He prefers this to an electric one which, he says, does not give the co-ordination of brain, hand and food. Some of his designs are in an enchanting deep, soft glaze, which can only be achieved by using a lead glaze.

Another new glaze he is using is celadon Korean. It is a soft grey-green, a wonderful colour for flowers of any colour. It is undecorated on the basis that a good pot can stand on its own merits. There are beer mugs, flower bowls and vases, too.

The Davies share a shop in the Mint, Rye. They came there eight years ago, taking over two derelict cottages, which they have now turned into a shop and a pottery. Mr Davie was trained as a painter, and teaches art in Rye. Mrs Davie does weaving. Farmers bring in their own fleece which are spun, then woven, into suits or costumes.

They are often woven in their natural colours of black and white, and are not dyed at all. Her tweeds are very popular with Americans, too, and she can never make enough tweed. Hand-made woven and linen ties for 12s 6d are also favourites. She makes evening stoles in any colour you like, with French silver thread.

Another man who believes in doing things himself is Mr Roberts, the biggest apple-grower in the Rye district. Not only has he built his own cold store, but he has also designed and made a grader and a sprayer that does the work of two men and is much cleaner to handle.

There is a touch of the family business here, too, for his eldest daughter helps with the fruit packing. Apples, of course, figure often on the menu. Mr Roberts' favourite sweet is Apple Amber, and his wife makes it like this:

Line a flan tin with short pastry. Peel, core and slice about 1½ lb apples. Cook with a little butter and only just enough water to prevent burning, until soft.

Beat to a pulp, add 2 egg yolks and beat well again. Pour into the flan case and bake in a moderate oven for about 30 minutes, until set.

Whisk 2 egg whites until stiff, fold in about 3oz caster sugar. Pile on top of the apples and return to a cool oven to set.

Another great favourite is fried rings of Cox's Orange Pippin with bacon.

13 October 1952
MAKING JAPONICA JELLY

The old japonica or Japanese quince which bears flowers like red apple blossom in early spring, is a favourite shrub in country and suburban gardens where it is generally trained on the house wall, though it flourishes also as a bush in the open garden.

It often bears a crop of large, apple-like fruits. Are these edible, and if so, what can be done with them?

The answer is that they are useless unless cooked, but make an excellent jelly of reddish amber shade with a slightly tart flavour suitable with rabbit, game or mutton. The fruits are extremely hard and never seem to ripen, but they are ready for gathering in October–November.

After wiping the fruits, cut them into pieces but do not peel or core. Place in a saucepan, cover with water, bring to the boil and cook until soft. Strain all night through a jelly bag and, for every pint of juice, allow 1 lb of sugar.

Bring juice to the boil before adding sugar, which should be previously warmed. Stir until the sugar is dissolved. Boil for 10 to 15 minutes, testing in the usual way, pour into small jars and tie down.

5 May 1984
MARMALADE IN VARIETY, BUT REMEMBER THE VITAL TIPS

Bon Viveur

We have been researching and testing throughout last year, cooking and compiling recipes for storage and preserving. We stopped counting after we had collected 5,000 marmalade recipes.

These include tangerine, ortanique, ugli fruit, grapefruit, sweet orange, bitter Seville orange, lemon and lime marmalades but not one included the salient points to remember.

All must now be made with well-scrubbed fruits in order to dispose of the preservatives with which they are painted for export. All must be made with pure cane sugar (unless we settle for rapid crystallisation by suing beet sugar).

Fortunately we had a little pure cane sugar, so we made a test batch. The jams and marmalades lasted two to three years in perfect condition whilst, after three months, entire jarfuls made with beet sugar were filled with crystallised grits.

Hating to throw away food, we emptied the contents of a few jars into a wide, shallow pan, set them over a mere thread of heat and re-potted after all crystallisation had melted away. Alas it returned shortly afterwards.

Remember, too, that it is never necessary to use bottled pectin for any marmalade, provided the pips are bagged up in muslin, steeped in cold water to cover and this bulk of jelly/fluid counted in with the given water quantity.

Warm all jars before filling them and never tie down until contents are cold and set.

For our prime selection then, four of us, all serious cooks of long standing, chose an Orange and Ginger Marmalade; an old French Recipe still used all over France; a Lemon; a Grapefruit and a Dundee Marmalade given to us by a famous Scottish cookery writer.

The Recipes

Dundee Marmalade
Ingredients:
4 Seville oranges;
1 quart of water to every weighed 1 lb of prepared fruit;
Pure cane preserving sugar

Method: Place oranges in a preserving pan of very lightly salted water. Boil steadily until a skewer pierces skins easily. Plunge into cold water. Retain water in which they were boiled. Quarter the oranges, scoop off all soft pith from the peels and cut these into 1in x ¼in pieces. Rub pulped interiors through a coarse sieve. Weigh the pulp. Return the pan with an equal quantity of sugar and add 1 breakfast cup of the reserved water for every pound of mixture. Put preserving pan over a moderate heat. Raise contents to a slow rolling boil and maintain until mixture 'jells'.

French *Confiture d'Oranges*
Ingredients:
10 sweet, thin-skinned oranges;
Pure cane sugar;
Unsweetened shop-bought apple juice;
Ice cubes;
Boiling water

Method: Pierce the well-scrubbed oranges, using a wooden skewer to make 6 holes in each. Place in a roomy pan and just cover with boiling water. Leave for 30 minutes. Lift all fruit into a dry pan. Empty 2 trays of ice cubes in with them and top up to cover with cold water. Rest a further 30 minutes then drain, wipe and quarter them, removing all pips and discarding central cores. Either mince the remainder or put through a food processor and switch on for a burst of 5 to 10 seconds to reduce to pulp, but not purée. Weigh this pulp. Put all into a jam kettle or preserving pan, raise to boiling, steady off at a simmer until a drop on refrigerated plate sets without spreading.

Pale Lemon Marmalade
Ingredients:
3 lb of very fresh, well-washed lemons;
1pt cold water and 2½pt ditto;
pure cane preserving sugar

Method: Peel lemons extremely thinly. Shred peel very finely with a small, sharp knife. Place all shreds into a small pan. Cover with the 1pt water. Raise to boiling and simmer for 40 minutes. Meanwhile pare white pith off lemons and remover inner white cores. Cut up remaining flesh fairly small, place in a preserving pan, add the 2½pt water and simmer for 1 hour 15 minutes. Strain through a jelly bag without exerting any pressure, add the fine lemon peel shreds with their remaining liquor. Measure the combined quantity. Add exactly double the amount of warmed, pure cane preserving sugar. Raise to boiling, maintain for about 30 minutes. Test on a refrigerated plate before potting.

Grapefruit Marmalade
Ingredients:

4 grapefruits;

Water;

6 small, thin-skinned oranges;

Pure cane preserving sugar;

6 medium lemons

Method: Wash fruit carefully, wipe and simmer the grapefruit in well-covering water until tender. In a separate, smaller pan, simmer the oranges until tender. Turn both lots into roomy bowls and rest overnight. Half the grapefruit (across the centre). Scoop out pulp into a coarse sieve thus retaining all pips and coarse pith to discard. Cut remaining rinds into the finest possible hair-like shreds. Slice whole oranges into very fine threads. Add to shreds of grapefruit. Add 2 quarts (4pts or 80 fl oz) cold boiled water. Heat through in a preserving pan fairly slowly to allow heat to penetrate. Meanwhile heat 1½ lb pure cane preserving sugar to each measured pt of mixed fruit and fluid. Turn on to well-heated fruit with the strained juice of the lemons. Simmer to a good 'jell'.

Orange and Ginger Marmalade
Ingredients:

1½ lb thin-skinned oranges;

3pts cold water;

4oz preserved ginger chopped fairly finely;

Strained juice of 1 lemon;

1oz bruised root ginger;

½oz unsalted butter;

Cane sugar

Method: Tie ginger in muslin. Put in preserving pan with whole oranges and water. Cover and simmer until skins are quite soft when pierced with a wooden skewer. Halve fruit across centres. Ease out pips and remove all pith including centre cores. Open up ginger bag and add pith and pips. Re-tie and return to pan. Chop orange peel and add with strained lemon juice. Cook for 15 minutes. Squeeze out muslin bag. Weigh the mixture and add equal weight of preserving sugar. Stir in until clear and only then raise to a good rolling boil. Add butter and boil to setting point for about 20 minutes adding chopped ginger only for last 5 to 8 minutes.

28 February 1931
FROM AN OLD MANOR HOUSE:
ORANGE MARMALADE 1825
M. E. S.

Of recipes for marmalade there are no end, but the following, from a M. S. of 1825, differs from those of present-day use. Very good is this old marmalade, and worth trying.

Take any quantity of good Seville oranges and their weight in loaf sugar. Cut the oranges in halves and press out the juice well. Boil the sugar and juice together till it will slightly jelly. Meanwhile, boil the rinds in water till perfectly tender. Then cut them into long, narrow strips, and add to the syrup and sugar about five minutes before it (the syrup) has finished boiling. Put in jars and cover as usual.

6 July 1986
THOUGHT FOR FOOD:
STRAWBERRY CONSERVE
Denis Curtis

The scene was a discreet hotel in the South of France, more like the home of a rich friend than a commercial enterprise. I sat by the pool for *petit déjeuner* and dug a spoon into a dark red jelly in a white porcelain dish, pulling out a beautiful whole strawberry. I dribbled it all on to a chunk of hot croissant. There was fresh fruit and black coffee and more strawberry conserve. Beside this concoction all the strawberry jams I had tasted fade into insignificance. All winter long I experimented with expensive imported fruit and now I have achieved near perfection – though without the pool and the sun it still does not taste *quite* the same.

Rub the base of a preserving pan generously with glycerine and in its place 1 lb strawberries and 1 lb redcurrants. Cover with 2 lb preserving sugar and stir all together. Place in the refrigerator overnight. Next day add 2 pints of water and place over a high heat. Bring to the boil, stirring. Boil for 10 minutes and drip through a jelly bag. Place the liquid (about 1 litre) in a cleaned and re-glycerined preserving pan. Add the juice of 3 lemons and their pips tied in a piece of muslin. Bring to the boil, and fast boil until a set is just achieved. Reduce the heat and add 3 lb of slightly under-ripe, medium-sized, hulled strawberries and simmer until the set is achieved again. (Do not overboil, because the strawberries need to remain whole and the jelly must not set rigidly, but dribble when spooned. Should the berries show signs of disintegrating remove them to the pots and boil up the liquid on its own). Let stand for 20 minutes. Spoon the whole fruit into sterilised jars to within ½in. of the top. Pour in the liquid. Cover with greaseproof discs, seal, label, and store in a cool dark place. Excess liquid should be poured into sterilised jars and used as jelly.

Let Light into the Larder

BOTTLE THOSE WINDFALLS – USE THEM FOR A WINTER TREAT
Bon Viveur

The last storms played havoc with our apple trees with the result that we have been forced to salvage windfalls a great deal sooner than usual. One of our great winter standbys is apple *purée* from these windfalls – bottled in jars or frozen in waxed cartons – always without any sugar so as not to throw the balance of flavour in whatever we may choose to make with it.

The range of uses begins with Apple Sauce, and because our stocks are made in bulk now it is a good deal quicker to do since the *purée* demands only a brief dressing up.

Then, adding sugar to taste, we use it for Layered Apple Cake. The layers are pancakes, each thickly spread with apple *purée*, these are then piled one above the other and the same *purée* is spread thickly around the sides and over the top with a generous sprinkling of fairly coarsely chopped walnuts overall.

Baking is done under a loose tent of kitchen foil at 350ºF (gas mark 4), one shelf above centre, for 15 minutes. Served with cream – about which we shall have something to say in a moment – it is by no means undistinguished!

The simplest way of all with this *purée* is one of the most popular. You empty a large jar or cartonful into a casserole and, after weighing, add 2½oz of really moist sultanas to every pound. Stir them in with a couple of very thin lemon peel leaves and sugar to taste, and heat through on middle shelf of oven, at 325°F (gas mark 3), for 20 minutes – this allows the sultanas to swell up nicely. Chill and again serve with cream.

We had a little cream-making machine many years ago in which we used to make a very acceptable thick 'cream' from 4oz unsalted butter and ¼ pint (5 fl oz) gold label milk. So we were delighted to find an improved, modern version which enables us to be positively Norman in our lavish use of 'cream', available in return for a brand of trading stamps. Now, 7 or 8 fl oz cost us about 3d for the milk and 1s 3d for the butter – a total of 1s 6d; if it had been ordinary dairy cream it would cost us nearly 4s.

The Recipe

Blackberry/Elderberry Syrup

Cover the picked, stem-free, chosen raw fruit with cold water. Bring to the boil and simmer until purged exactly as for any fruit jelly. Strain overnight through a jelly bag. Measure the fluid and allow 4½oz of pre-serving sugar to every pint. Heat liquid to boiling point, stir in the sugar until completely dissolved, raise to a slow roiling boil and maintain for 20 minutes. Bottle and store.

At the moment we are harvesting cultivated blackberries from the kitchen garden. So, for teaming with both apples and pears, notably the hard ones (driven too soon from our young trees by the same howling gales), we make and bottle a goodly supply of Elderberry or Wild Blackberry Syrups. The method, given above, is constant for both fruits.

Then, when we come to use our bottled or frozen, peeled, sliced apples or winter-available cooking apples, we slice them, put them into a casserole, give them generous libations of either of these two syrups and cook them slowly at 300°F (gas mark 2) low down in the oven. They are quite delicious.

Hard pears are not only windfall ones. In our last garden we had a gigantic tree which defied all attempts to make the pears edible even when carefully cooked. Then, as a last attempt, we peeled some of them whole, left the stalks on, packed them into stone jars, covered them with blackberry (or elderberry) syrup, then gave them foil lids and put them on the floor of the oven (lower racks removed) at 250°F (gas mark ½) overnight.

Next day we fished them out bright pink and completely transformed into something really fit to eat. You can serve them with the revived 'cream'; you can give them a dollop of ice-cream, or you can simply reduce the cooking liquor by simmering until it achieves a coating sauce consistency. Then arrange the pears in a circle on a serving dish, and pour the sauce overall.

We find that our own Apple Ginger makes an acceptable addition to our preserve shelves.

You will need 4 lb cooking apples; 4 lb preserving sugar; 2 pints water, 1oz bruised root ginger in a muslin bag. You begin by peeling the apples and then, thoroughly wastefully, you cut out preserved ginger shapes in the flesh (without any core). Then weigh the shapes and remember to use up the residue for more apple *purée*.

Put sugar, water and ginger bag together in a roomy pan, bring the mixture to boiling point very slowly so that the sugar has time to dissolve first, and simmer steadily for 25 minutes until it is of a good syrupy consistency. Then with the syrup still simmering steadily, drop in the prepared fruit shapes and reduce the heat until the simmering is very gentle indeed as otherwise, when the apples start softening, the force of fierce bubbling will make them collapse.

Prod the pieces down if they tend to rise above the syrup – do this gently, too – and avoid stirring as much as possible. It will take anything from three-quarters of an hour to one hour for the apple pieces to become transparently clear and yellow. Then just skim any foam off the top surface and pour into (ideally) rubber-ringed, clip-topped French bottling jars (these are becoming more and more easily obtainable).

When quince time comes along, make a Quince and Apple Jelly. Use these fruits in the proportions of 2 lb cooking apples to 1 lb quinces. Cut all up roughly, place in a pan, cover with cold water, bring to the boil and simmer steadily until the fruits collapse. Strain through a jelly bag overnight. Weigh, and allow 1 lb sugar to every pint of the final strained liquid, exactly as for any other jelly; but do remember to heat your strained syrup with added sugar, and stir over a low heat until all is dissolved and bring to a slow rolling boil. Maintain until a little sets on a saucer. Then skim, put in pots, but do not cover until absolutely cold.

You might also like to try your hand with Elderberry Jam – just remember that berries must be pitch-black, and be prepared to pick them free of every scrap of stalk.

Allow 1 lb of sugar to every pound of berries, plus the strained juice of 1 large or 2 small lemons, and the grated rind of 1 lemon.

Begin by putting the berries in the pan and bruising them with a wooden spoon. Then draw them over a low heat until the juice runs freely; add one-third of the measured sugar and simmer up to boiling point very slowly. Then rub all through a sieve, return pulp to pan, add all remaining ingredients, and continue to cook; pot and tie down.

19 December 1925
'MARMITE': ITS GENERAL UTILITY

There are on the market a number of special food products that, although offering an individual quality, are strictly limited in utility when combined with other food. Marmite, the vegetable extract richest in vitamin B, can be employed in so many ways and for so many different purposes that there appears to be no end to the use to which it can be put. For instance, apart from its quality as an individual vegetable extract, from which can be prepared a number of most delectable dishes, it can be combined with other foods in order to impart to them the necessary standard in vitamin B value.

Moreover, Marmite is probably the greatest preventive of certain food deficiency diseases, as was amply proved during the course of the war. It was discovered that owing to the lack of the anti beri-beri, or vitamin B, factor in the rations served out to the troops on the Eastern fronts during the war various deficiency diseases resulted which rapidly disappeared when a small quantity of Marmite was added to the diet of bully beef, bread and biscuits.

While Marmite has a positive nutritive value in itself, its principal function is performed in the marvellous effect it has on other food in the course of the digestive processes, releasing, as it were, their stored-up energy, so that all their value is delivered to the body. Much of the food eaten, especially meat and fish, requires the presence of certain substances of vegetable origin in order to ensure perfect assimilation and digestion, and it is in these qualities that Marmite proves its utility in a most agreeable way. The stimulating properties of Marmite, which are so necessary in cases of illness, have proved of much use to invalids. It is during convalescence that such form of food, pleasant to take and easy to assimilate, is sought for by those in charge of the sick. In this connection it should be remembered that Marmite is specially useful in cases of influenza and severe chill, and is most beneficial to those who are troubled with sleeplessness if taken immediately before retiring. Full information may be obtained from the Marmite Food Extract Co. Ltd.

12 February 1991
DON'T PANIC: IT'S ONLY CONTINGENCY PURCHASING
Oliver Pritchett

It has been difficult lately just to go into a shop and buy a large loaf. You dread being mistaken for a panic buyer. So you set your jaw, gaze serenely into the eyes of the shop assistant, and put on the special calm voice of the captain of a British Airways jumbo jet preparing passengers for a spot of turbulence.

After all the frantic shopping that was reported to have taken place at the beginning of this spell of unusual weather (note the measured tone of the prose) I have become inhibited about going to a shop and asking for two of anything. People might accuse me of hysterical over-reaction and of excessive stocking-up.

'Just having a few people over for a custard-tasting evening,' I remarked casually to explain why I have asked for an extra pint of milk. 'Yes, they're driving over in a very relaxed way from Dorking, actually. I gather that the petrol was bought quite a while ago.'

Not everybody has the same attitude to panic buying. I happened to meet a man in the supermarket the other day who had interesting views on the subject. We were having a dignified, imperturbable tug-of-war with the last bunch of celery in the store.

'What do you think of panic buying?' he asked, jabbing me in the ribs with his elbow.

'It is something I would never indulge in,' I replied, stamping on his foot with equanimity.

'It can be a worthwhile activity,' he argued, sweeping an armful of pomegranates into his shopping basket.

It turned out that his name was Dr Justin Case. He was a member of the economics faculty at the University of Bexleyheath and he ran a course in panic buying – although it was officially called Contingency Purchasing.

As we made our way round the supermarket, Dr Case pointed out that after this cold weather was over the next big panic buying event would be Easter, when the shops were closed on Good Friday and Easter Monday and the nation's shoppers had to take desperate measures to ward off privation. 'People need to be properly trained to panic,' he observed.

'You can't teach people the art of panic buying,' I protested. 'It wouldn't be proper panic buying if you did.'

Before he answered, Dr Case persuaded me to buy five extra tins of pineapple chunks, as a little bird had told him that a State of Pineapple Chunks Emergency was to be declared on Thursday.

'There is a difference,' he went on, 'between running wild-eyed up and down the frozen veg shelf and genuine creative panic buying.'

Having advised me to stock up with 30 tins of brown shoe polish as it was shortly to be made illegal, Dr Case explained his dream of creating a whole Panic Economy.

'The idea is to get the rumour and alarm that are rife in the Stock Exchange and spread them round the wider economic system,' he said. 'One Budget day, I believe, the Chancellor of the Exchequer will come out of No 11 Downing Street, but he will not hold up his Budget box for the photographers. He will be holding two plastic carrier bags and will make a mad dash to the nearest off-licence.'

In this new Panic Economy, advertising will no longer be necessary. It should be possible to quadruple the sales of, say, fish fingers merely by hiring some person to drop the right overheard hint in an Andover bar.

'You really ought to take the course in Contingency Purchasing,' Dr Case told me. 'If you do, you had better enrol quickly,' he added, his voice rising an octave. 'It is a very popular course and it is certain to be over-subscribed,' he screeched.

29 January 1962
MEALS FROM SHREDS AND TATTERS
Elizabeth David

I am still thinking about the point of chief interest at this year's Hotel and Catering Exhibition (at Olympia until Thursday) – the food processed by the system known as Accelerated Freeze Drying, or A.F.D.*

Half the food firms represented at the show seem to be displaying trays and bowls of these brittle, brightly coloured little shreds and tatters.

They require no more than a few seconds' dip in cold water to reconstitute themselves into carrots and onion slices, green peas and prawns. Like Japanese flowers in a glass of water, they swell and expand as you watch.

I tasted two soups (from two different firms), one mixed vegetable, one chicken and leek, both made from A.F.D. ingredients. Both appeared to me the same – no better, no worse – as most commercial soups.

Green peas (soaked but raw) tasted much the same as ordinary fresh frozen peas. Prawns (soaked *and* cooked) had much the same flavour – no more, no less – and the same characteristically chewy quality which one associates with routine deep-frozen prawns.

A.F.D. chops and steaks, in their fossilised state, looked like relics dug up from a Pharaoh's tomb. Not that this would have dampened my curiosity, for it seems to me that it is the meat which will be the great test of this process – but the meat was not for tasting.

None of these products is yet on sale to the general public. It will certainly not be long before they are, but until we have had a chance to test them out in our own kitchens it is impossible to form any balanced judgment.

It would hardly, for instance, be fair to base an opinion upon a soup made by a firm which boasts that its products cost the caterer from 0.887 of 1d to 2½d a helping.

One thing is certain, though. As far as conservation, storage and distribution of foodstuffs for the hungry countries, for the famine-stricken, for emergencies (and of course for space flights) is concerned, this new development makes infinite sense.

Just one ugly question remains. In the case of that direst emergency at the back of our minds, would there be the water to rehydrate our food?

According to the brochure of one firm using these products, the basic process of Accelerated Freeze Drying is the removal of the water content from food by sublimation, i.e., direct conversion of the water content from ice to vapour without passing through the liquid stage.

When food is frozen no liquid phase is present, so that when the ice is sublimated from this solid frozen food, the structure and spatial distribution of salts and other components in the then dried food is the same as in the original frozen food.

4 November 1984
NUTS WITH EVERYTHING
Josceline Dimbleby

'Dear God, we thank you for our British friends and for the interest in peanuts which has brought them here.'

This unusual grace, spoken in an old colonial house in Tifton, Georgia, was only one of the many which preceded the meals of a group of us who went on a peanut harvest tour through the southern states of America last month. For a week we saw peanuts at every stage; from vast fields of low, leafy plants with knobbly roots to the factory where gallons of peanut butter dripped into jars.

Then we tried peanuts cooked in different dishes at every meal. These included peanut muffins, which we felt would have been better without the peanuts, peanut ice-cream, which we all hated, and peanut soup, which we were all certain we would hate. But this proved an excellent surprise, both in taste and texture.

The experience confirmed my feeling that, in cooking peanuts should only be used for savoury dishes.

Williamsburg Peanut Soup (serves 4–5)

1oz butter;
1 medium onion, chopped;
2 stalks celery, chopped;
1½ level tbs plain flour;
3 rounded tbs smooth peanut butter;

¼ pint single cream;
Salt;
2–3 pinches cayenne pepper;
Garnish of chopped celery leaves
and/or chopped peanuts

Melt the butter in a largish saucepan. Stir in the chopped onion and celery and cook gently, stirring occasionally, until soft. Remove from the heat and stir in the flour. Put back on the heat and bring to the boil, stirring. Bubble for 2–3 minutes.

Remove again from the heat and whizz in a food processor until smooth. Add the peanut butter and whizz in, followed by the cream. Season to taste with a little salt and the cayenne pepper. Reheat in the saucepan but do not boil. Serve with the garnish.

Cod with Peanut, Ginger and Avocado Sauce (serves 4–5)

3 tbsp groundnut oil;
1 rounded tsp ground coriander;
2in piece fresh ginger and 3 cloves
*   garlic, peeled and chopped finely;*
1 medium red pepper, deseeded and
*   chopped finely;*
½ level tsp cayenne pepper;

Juice of 1 lemon and 1 orange;
3 tbps water;
2 rounded tbsp crunchy peanut
*   butter;*
1½ lb cod fillets, skinned;
1 medium avocado;
Salt

Make the sauce first. Heat the oil gently in a medium-sized saucepan. Stir in the coriander followed by the chopped ginger, garlic and red pepper.

Put the lid on the saucepan and cook over a very low heat for 15–20 minutes.

Remove from the heat and add the lemon and orange juice and the water. Then stir in the peanut butter, add salt and cayenne and put on one side.

Steam the fish for 15–20 minutes according to thickness. Then halve and stone the avocado, peel off the skin and slice across thinly. Reheat the peanut sauce gently, stir in the avocado and keep over the heat for a minute or so, just to heat the avocado.

Drain the steamed fish on absorbent paper before transferring to a shallow serving dish. Spoon the sauce over the top but try to leave plenty of pure white fish showing. Serve at once.

23 January 1939
FOOD STORAGE

To the Editor of the *Daily Telegraph*

Sir – As one of the only two women inspectors at the Ministry of Food during the war, I am particularly interested in Sir Auckland Geddes's advice to housewives.

One of your correspondents puts the onus of food storage on the Government. But, in reality, could not housewives provide the nucleus of a far more widespread provision for emergency than ever could be accomplished by a Government, however active?

What is more, there need not be any delay or additional expense. Most modern houses are well equipped for safe storage of foodstuffs in excess of the ordinary requirements. Most good housewives, not dwelling on the possibility of war, have learnt by experience the wisdom of being prepared for any emergency which might interfere with the normal delivery of foodstuffs, and so will be more than willing, if their purse allows, to facilitate the working of a scheme for the good of the whole community.

Yours very truly,
(Miss) Violet P. Scriven,
Saltdean, Brighton

Lumpy Custard

2 August 2013
GOOD-MOOD FOOD
Bee Wilson

Asked on what occasions she drank champagne, Lily Bollinger used to say that she drank it when she was happy and when she was sad; in company and alone. 'Otherwise I never touch it – unless I'm thirsty.'

Most of us have a similar attitude to food, I suspect. We eat when we're happy, and sad. Solitude and company are both occasions for food. Otherwise, we never touch the stuff – except when we are hungry.

The role of our moods in shaping eating patterns has long been studied by psychologists. But until very recently almost all research focused on bad moods. The term 'emotional eating' referred to the way that negative feelings could trigger a binge. Experiments have shown that, if you induce anxiety by giving people an impossible puzzle to solve or forcing them to watch *The Shining*, they eat more afterwards.

There are two theories about why a bad mood has this effect. The first is that many of us – particularly the overweight – cannot distinguish hunger from unpleasant emotions. The second is that we use food – especially sugar – as a drug to calm ourselves down.

It's only recently that psychology has recognised that happy moods can make us eat more too. A study was published earlier this year by

Catharine Evers and colleagues from Utrecht University in the Netherlands on 'good-mood food'. It showed that a group of 70 students consumed significantly more snack foods (M&Ms, peanuts, wine gums) after being put in a good mood by watching a heartwarming film about a baby panda sneezing. After the film – which lasted just two and a half minutes – the students consumed 100 more calories than a control group who'd been shown a boring film about birds in the desert.

The thing I find most surprising is that the baby panda film was so universally loved. Was no one immune to its cuteness? As for the radical discovery that an enjoyable film encourages snacking, this is less astonishing. The whole economy of cinema snacks is founded on the premise that emotions on the screen can manipulate us to eat popcorn by the bucket.

It stands to reason that we eat more when we are happy. We are conditioned from childhood to use excess calories to celebrate, whether it's birthday cake or the orgy of Easter chocolate. Besides, food tastes better when you are feeling chipper. The psychologist Michael Macht has done several experiments showing that chocolate tastes more delicious and 'stimulating' in a state of joy than in a state of sadness.

So we eat more when we are happy as well as when we're sad. Except for those whose appetites are dampened by strong emotion (which sounds enviable, but comes with its own problems). So what to do? We could avoid having fattening foods in the house, except when our mood is entirely neutral. Which is probably never. Or maybe we could condition ourselves to turn to better treats at times of heightened emotion. Instead of meeting joy with confectionery, buy yourself a punnet of juicy plums, a loaf of rye bread or some very good prosciutto. Then go and watch a film about baby pandas.

28 August 1983
A BANK HOLIDAY COOKERY COMPETITION
Josceline Dimbleby

This Bank Holiday competition, put together as it has been in the middle of the crowded hurly-burly of the family's summer holidays, could not fail to be a joint effort. Every member of the family has contributed, including my youngest daughter, who suggested the question on cranberry sauce. An uncle decided to do a section on Biblical food, and has, as you see, come up with some fascinating questions. For me, it has brought back all sorts of interesting memories of different kinds of food I have eaten on my travels throughout the years.

The Questions*

1. (a) What is the main ingredient of sauce soubise? (b) From whom does it get its name?
2. Who invented cranberry sauce?
3. What do sarni and colibki have in common?
4. Each of the following people might be offended if you offered them one of these dishes. Match the person with the dish.
    1. A Muslim
    2. A Jew
    3. A Hindu
    4. A Sikh
    5. A Parsee
    6. A Jain
        a) Smoked salmon
        b) Caviar on a silver dish
        c) Oysters
        d) Garlic bread
        e) Fillet Steak
        f) Halal meat
5. Which fruit is the odd one out? Guava, Mangosteen, Custard Apple, Medlar, Rambutan.
6. Who said: 'The destiny of nations depends on how they eat'?
7. What distinguishes a roux from all other methods of thickening a sauce?
8. Is lamb *vert-pré*: (a) Under one year old? (b) Grilled with butter and parsley? (c) Raised on grass by the sea?
9. *Who* thought that *what* should be 'well sliced and dressed with vinegar and then thrown out as good for nothing?'
10. (a) Which tropical fruit is not allowed to be taken into hotel bedrooms or on to aeroplanes? (b) Why not?

11. What is: (a) A Roulette? (b) A Diable? (c) A Paella?

12. A cook has a knife, a bowl of iced water and some radishes. What is she about to make?

13. Which is the odd one out? Shirred, jellied, coddled, clarified.

14. If you sat down to eat turkey cooked with chocolate: (a) What country might you be in? (b) What would be the name of the dish? (c) In what other countries is chocolate used in a savoury dish?

15. How many varieties of British apple are known today? 10, 100, 1,000, 3,000, 6,000 or 10,000?

16. Answer the following on eggs: (a) How many people will an ostrich egg feed: 3–4, 10–12, or 16–18? (b) Approximately how old are the Chinese 'thousand-year eggs'? (c) What are the most expensive eggs in the world?

17. Now for three questions which will test your knowledge of the Bible: (a) On what occasion and to whom was broiled fish and honeycomb served? (b) Who refused to eat the sacrificial goat? (c) What did the besieged mother of Samaria boil and eat in desperation?

18. Give another name for: (a) Eggplant; (b) Jamaica pepper; (c) Physalis fruit; (d) Zucchini; (e) Plantain; (f) Groundnut oil; (g) Papaya.

19. Which of the following are considered to be aphrodisiacs? Celery, Beetroot, Marmite, Oysters, Hardboiled eggs, Asparagus.

20. What is the origin of the word Pizza?

21. What fruit is richest of all in protein and vitamins and can be served either savoury or sweet, cold or hot?

22. Answer the following fish questions: (a) How do you 'cook' fish without heating it? (b) What is the name of the dish which epitomises this? (c) Where does it come from?

23. How do you: (a) Stop cabbage going blue when cooked? (b) Stop avocado pear discolouring? (c) Stop eggs bursting while being boiled? (d) Stop cabbage smelling when cooking? (e) Stop pasta and rice from sticking?

24. Who do the following foods bring to mind? (a) Madeleines; (b) An omelette made with smoked haddock; (c) Lampreys; (d) An upside-down apple tart; (e) Peaches with raspberries; (f) Cannelloni stuffed with beef and pâté; (g) Marinated herring with sour cream.

25. Where would you have for breakfast: (a) Goose fat with onion and maple? (b) Idli? (c) Ensaimada? (d) Papaya with fresh limes? (e) Churros? (f) Sardines?

*Answers can be found on pages 319–320.

16 May 1976
JELLY MAGIC
Marika Hanbury-Tenison

I suppose we all have our childhood hangups. Mine is jelly. Jelly in any form, from a chilled jelly consommé to a psychedelic, wobbling, pyramid of brightly coloured layers, slumping slightly in its dish.

Today's mould is only a mere shadow of the jelly magic that used to be performed in the Victorian days.

Puddings from those Victorian days play a role in an attractive little book, with a practical cover that can be wiped clean, called *Perfect Puddings*, by Christine Collins.*

Red Wine Jelly (Serves 4–6)
½ bottle red wine;   *¼ pint hot water;*
6oz redcurrant jelly;   *½oz powdered gelatine*
6oz caster sugar;

Melt gelatine in hot water and stir until completely dissolved.

Mix sugar and redcurrant jelly thoroughly together in a saucepan and dissolve gently over a low heat. When melted add gelatine and stir well. Lastly add wine and remove from the heat, pour into individual glasses and allow to set.

These jellies are best eaten just as they are without further adornment in order to savour to the full their delightful flavour, although a little light whipped cream may be used to decorate.

Devonshire Flavour, compiled by Elizabeth Lothian, published recently, also has some good pudding recipes amongst its collection of recipes gathered from those living in the country and interspersed by attractive little vignettes of country life.

Honey Jelly (from *Devonshire Flavour***). Serves 4
½oz gelatine;   *6oz clover honey or 4oz clover honey*
½ pint hot water;   *and 2oz heather honey;*
Juice of 1 lemon;   *1 gill cold water*
Chopped apple or orange segments;

Dissolve gelatine in hot water, add lemon juice and honey and stir till dissolved. Add cold water and fruit and pour into a mould.

* *Perfect Puddings*, by Christine Collins – price £2.25, published by Faber and Faber.
** *Devonshire Flavour*, compiled by Elizabeth Lothian – price £1.95, published by David & Charles, Newton Abbot.

6 January 1961
NEW DISHES IN OLD GUISES
Daily Telegraph Reporter

Prof. Vernon Mottram, the dietician who, at 78, does most of his household's cooking, offered some down to earth advice yesterday on how to persuade children to eat food they do not like. He advocated the use of a little 'hypocrisy' rather than any sort of force.

'I don't believe in force at all,' he said. 'In my own home youngsters were introduced to a new food by stealth, flavouring it with the old food they were used to.'

Prof. Mottram, formerly of Queen Elizabeth College, Kensington, was giving the opening lecture at a two-day catering course arranged by the Incorporated Association of Preparatory Schools, at University College, London.

He quoted as an extreme example the mother who put cod liver oil emulsion on bread and butter pudding because her child had been accustomed to cod liver oil from babyhood. 'It would have made me sick, but the child loved it. No child likes new food. All children are frightfully conservative.'

He suggested that another worthwhile method was to treat the eating of new food as a kind of adventure 'like climbing Everest'. The sprightly, white-haired professor had a variety of other ideas for making valuable, but sometimes unpopular foods, more appealing.

Boys' Problems
These included:

Milk: 'Some boys think it is a "sissy" drink and prefer tea as more grown up. Try giving it to them with a dash of coffee.'

Herrings: 'Young boys often can't fillet them properly and there is a dreadful lot of waste. Why not get the filleted kind, put them through the mincer and serve them with toast as "sardines?"'

Liver: 'Some say it is "insides" and won't eat it. Make it into paste.'

Raw cabbage: 'They may not take this unless it is cut up and thoroughly camouflaged with a few lettuce leaves or something.'

Prof. Mottram told his audience of housekeepers and others responsible for school catering that he was in favour of snacks at 11 a.m. and mid-afternoon as a means of keeping up the level of sugar in the blood. 'But these snacks should be protective foods rather than biscuits and doughnuts usually found in the school tuckshop.'

All Pie-Eyed

12 February 1931
FAVOURITE PUDDINGS FROM ENGLISH HOMES

What a wonderful variety of puddings and sweets there is in daily use in our English homes, dishes that have come to be known in the family as 'Our Favourite Pudding', and how extraordinarily interesting many of these home recipes are!

The entries for 'Our Favourite Pudding' Recipe Competition have been very numerous, and in many cases novel, for it is in this bunch of cookery that home cooks seem most inclined to introduce those variations and new ideas that are, as it were, the spice of daily fare.

Simple and old-time nursery puddings, for instance, have been given a modern touch. The growing use of canned fruits has prompted women to devise new ways of serving these popular delicacies. Another important point is the attention paid to appearance. Puddings to please must look nice, as well as taste good.

The award of one guinea has been made to MRS C. D. OLDHAM, BELLAMOUR LODGE, RUGELEY, STAFFS, whose recipe for Bellamour Charlotte is printed on this page. All the ingredients for this prize pudding would be found in the ordinary larder.

Each of the following selected recipes, for which consolation prizes of 5s are being given, has some special point of interest:

January Pudding

This pudding owes its name to the fact that the first month of the year finds remains of Christmas mincemeat in the store, waiting to be used up. 'It is delicious and very quickly made,' is the comment of the competitor.

Take a 1 lb jar of mincemeat, mix it with 1 lb of flour and an egg. Turn into a buttered basin, cover, and steam for two hours.

The fruit, suet, and so on, being already in the mincemeat, it is exactly the pudding to make on a busy morning, and it is at the same time nourishing and delicious. – Tested by Mrs M. A. King, Lansdowne, Hadley Wood, Middlesex.

Semolina Souffle

The familiar semolina pudding is given a new lease of life when treated in the following way:

Into a saucepan put two tablespoonful of fine semolina and one tablespoonful of sugar. Gradually add one pint of milk, stirring well. Flavour with coffee, chocolate, vanilla, &c., or not, as desired. Stir over the fire until the mixture boils. Remove pan from fire and stir in beaten yolk of one egg. Then fold in the stiffly-beaten white of one egg. Put mixture into dish or individual dishes, and put into oven of 300°F for ten to fifteen minutes. – Tested by Mrs Alex. Powell, Foo An, S. Hayling Island, Hants.

Dorsetshire Apple Cake

Here is a farmhouse sweet to rejoice the hearts of the children in this cold weather. They can eat it for dinner or nursery tea:

Take a cupful of self-raising flour and rub into it half a cupful of butter. Add a cupful of apple chopped so finely that each piece is the size of a currant. Next stir in half a cupful of castor sugar and half a cupful of cleaned currants.

Mix to a soft dough with two well-beaten eggs, and turn quickly into a shallow, buttered baking-tin. Bake it for about three-quarters of an hour in a fairly hot oven, until it is puffed up and a golden-brown colour.

Thrust a skewer into its midst, and when it comes out clean it is done. Slip on to a hot dish and split open horizontally. Spread the bottom layer generously with fresh butter, sprinkle thickly with brown sugar, and replace the top. Now dust it with castor sugar and eat it at once. – Tested by Mrs Frances Cox, Sharnbrook Park-avenue, Watford.

Kentish Well Pudding

A recipe for that old favourite, Kentish well pudding, comes with the intimation that it has become a new favourite in New Zealand, where the competitor's two sons are learning dairy farming. 'Their employer's wife finds it very satisfying to hungry lads after a morning's strenuous work on the farm!'

Equal quantities of suet, fine breadcrumbs and flour. Mix to a slack dough. Grease a pudding basin and place some currants, a little sugar and a knob of butter at the bottom of basin. Fill up with crust and fruit alternately, finishing with crust, cover with grease-proof paper and steam 2½–2 hours. – Tested by Mrs H. M. Reed, High-street, West Malling, Maidstone, Kent.

Chocolate Mousse

A more ambitious sweet is the famous Mousse au Chocolat of the Paris restaurants and a favourite dish in the household of the sender.

For six people: Take ½ lb best eating chocolate, six fresh eggs. Melt the chocolate in a pan in a slow oven until it is soft, but not liquid, and do not add any water to it. Separate the whites of eggs from the yolks, and whisk the whites to a stiff froth. When the slab of chocolate is melted and still hot, mix it slowly into the yolks of eggs and beat the mixture well with a wooden spoon. When well beaten, add the whites and mix well for some minutes. No other cooking is necessary.

Pour the mixture into a glass dish or small dishes, one for each person, and allow several hours for it to set. It can then be decorated with whipped cream or burnt almonds. – Tested by Mrs P. R. Antrobus, 64, Prince of Wales's-mansions, Battersea Park, S.W. 11.

The Prize Recipe
Bellamour Charlotte

Spread the inside of a cake-tin with butter, or margarine, seeing that the whole surface is thickly covered. Line with neat fingers of stale bread (from a tin loaf) which have been generously spread on both sides with golden syrup. Fill with the following mixture, and bake in a brisk oven for forty minutes.

THE FILLING – Cream two ounces of butter, add 1½ ounces of flour, one egg, half a teacupful of milk, a heaped table-spoonful of golden syrup and four and a half stale penny sponge-cakes well crumbled. Flavour with a little ground ginger, and lastly, when all is well mixed, add a pinch of baking powder.

This is sufficient for four persons. Serve with cream or custard, handed separately, not poured over the sweet.

12 November 1961
BANGERS AND MASH
J. R.

'I must admit,' Mr Amory once confided to the Commons, 'that I find the sausage to be a much more complicated entity than I ever imagined.'

And after reading some of the parliamentary discussions about the contents of the so-called 'honest British banger' I cannot help sympathising with the failure of his imagination – though not with his failure to do something about the sausage.

Ever since 1956, when the Food Standards Committee recommended that meat content of the sausage should be regulated by law, Members on both sides of the House have been badgering the Minister of Agriculture to protect the sausage-eating public from those manufacturers who still look upon the sausage as a profitable dustbin.

Last week the subject came up again with a slightly original twist. The Member for Stoke-on-Trent asked whether, in view of the 'high consumption of sausages in this House,' the Minister did not feel he should regulate their meat content. There was no originality in the Minister's response.

Sausages can be made of 100 per cent pure pork, but they very seldom are. The average British banger contains at least 45 per cent starchy filler, which makes even good sausages a pretty expensive way of eating meat. But when this proportion goes up to 60 or 70 per cent (and is made to taste meaty with synthetic meat flavourings) the house-wife has been tricked into paying a lamb chop price for a largely vegetarian product.

5 January 1962

BRAISED OXTAIL

C. B.

With this cold spell our thoughts turn to all kinds of warming foods, especially if they are easy to cook. Here is an old favourite which is better prepared the day before wanted. Before re-heating, remove the fat which has risen to the top.

1 oxtail (2½ lb-3 lb);
2 onions coarsely chopped;
2 carrots cut in thick slices;
A stick of celery;
Bouquet garni (bay leaf, sprig of thyme, a few parsley stalks);
8 peppercorns, crushed;

3 cloves;
Salt;
1½ pints water;
Stock or a beef bouillon cube dissolved in hot water;
1 glass cheap red wine;
1 dessertspoon flour

Have the oxtail cut into joints by the butcher. Wash and dry it, remove surplus fat. Melt fat in pan, fry oxtail until lightly browned, then put into a casserole or saucepan.

In the same fat fry the onions golden brown and add to oxtail. Sprinkle flour into fat, cook until nicely browned. Add stock or water by degrees, and pour over the oxtail. Add salt to taste, and remaining ingredients.

Bring to boil, cover with greaseproof paper and lid. Lower heat and simmer gently for 3–4 hours. The meat should be very tender when cooked.

22 August 1993

DUNK FOOD THAT TAKES THE BISCUIT
Hugh Fearnley-Whittingstall

Hail dunkers, a new biscuit on the supermarket shelves, specially made for those who like to dip something crisp and dry into something hot and wet, and suck on the resulting gunge.

If that sounds crude, then I make no apology. Dunking is crude. At least it *is* regarded as crude by a hefty minority of the population. According to a Mori poll taken earlier this year, 52 per cent of us think that it's 'all right to dunk', while 38 per cent regard the habit as 'socially unacceptable'.

The young (15 to 35 year olds), it transpires, are more inclined to dunk than the old, with the over-55s branded 'least likely to dunk'. This comes as no great surprise, when you consider the prevalence of dentures among the upper age bracket. Dunking is not denture-friendly.

The geographical epidemiology of dunking was also considered. The survey revealed that the concentration of people who will not stoop to dunk is particularly high (54 per cent) among the genteel Scots (who are also inclined to hold their saucer in one hand, their cup in the other, and cock their little finger when they sip their tea – a body language which leaves no hands or digits free for dunking).

Like so many polls, this one sadly leaves the really interesting questions unanswered. For a start, the survey is only concerned with whether or not people dunk.

This assumes that all dunkers are the same – which is, of course, nonsense. For a start, dunkers must choose their biscuits. There are those who dunk only one sort, and those who are promiscuous. Other variables include time, depth and frequency of immersion.

Number-crunchers like me want some harder facts about the wet biscuit-munchers. This is my suggested list of questions for the next major poll on Britain's dunking habits:

1. What biscuits do you regularly dunk?
2. What biscuits would you never dunk?
3. How much of the biscuit is dipped in the drink?
4. How long do you leave it there?
5. Do you dunk before every bite, or do you intersperse drinking with dry biting?
6. Do you eat the soggy crumbs left at the bottom of your cup?
7. If the soggy end falls off, do you scoop it out with a teaspoon and eat it straightaway?

Such imponderables aside, we must consider the future of the new-comer to the biscuit shelf, Prewett Food's designer Dunker. With so many exponents of this activity at large in the UK, a biscuit specifically designed (oval, no less) for dunking, sounds, on the face of it, like a cunning marketing wheeze. I have my doubts.

My own theory – which I have no intention of asking Mori to investigate by poll – is that regular dunkers (I don't mean the new biscuit, I mean those who dunk) are by nature very conservative people. The act of dunking – rendering sloppy and amorphous, and eventually disintegrating, a biscuit that was, only moments before, crisp, pristine and complete, is about the most rebellious thing that most of them ever do. To dunk, for them, is to commit an act of anarchy.

Such defiant gestures are not undertaken lightly; in particular, they are not undertaken with unfamiliar biscuits. Dunkers have their favourite biscuits, and they are not likely to switch overnight to some new-fangled, Johnny-come-lately brand.

The only way in which Dunkers (and now I *am* talking about the biscuit) can succeed is if they prove to be so far superior, when hot, wet and soggy, to other biscuits, that a single trial will convert even the most die-hard dunker of digestives, or the most avid ginger-nut nutter.

With this faint possibility in mind, I have conducted a comparative dunking of the new pretender with nine brands known to be among the nation's favourites.

The points of comparison are those I consider to be most salient to dunkers everywhere (even if they've never actually thought about it). They are: the speed with which the liquid is absorbed (some knowledge of this is essential for good timing of your dunk); the pleasantness (or otherwise) of the consistency of the totally saturated biscuit; and the advisability of dunking the biscuit in coffee as an occasional alternative to tea (which is, of course, the primary dunking beverage).

To dip or not to dip? And for how long?
The good dunker's guide to the perfect coffee break
SOA = Speed of Absorption
CWS = Consistency When Soggy
CWC = Compatibility With Coffee

Dunkers (Prewett's)

SOA: Fast.

CWS: Retains some crunch, which is sugary rather than biscuit. Never goes completely soggy, even after three minutes' immersion.

CWC: Good. Unsweetened coffee helps to counteract the biscuit's excessive sweetness.

Verdict: Good for a couple of dunks, but ultimately too sweet. Dunkers who like their biscuits to become completely soggy are likely to be disappointed. 6/10

Rich Tea (McVitie's)

SOA: Medium slow.

CWS: Totally soggy – smooth and creamy, melts in the mouth.

CWC: Takes on plenty of coffee flavour, as its own taste is mild and bland.

Verdict: A fine dunker. With good timing (about five seconds immersion), it can be eaten when slippery and wet on the outside and still crunchy in the middle. 7/10

Digestive (McVitie's)

SOA: Medium fast.

CWS: Soggy, but retains some granular texture (the nutty bran from the wholemeal flour can still be caught between the teeth).

CWC: Good, if you don't mind the saltiness (see below).

Verdict: A classic for dunking which is above criticism. The Digestive is saltier than most other sweet biscuits, which I have a problem with. Millions don't. 8/10

Garibaldi (Crawford's)

SOA: Fast.

CWS: Totally soggy and wet, but for the middle layer of jammy, water-resistant currants.

CWC: Currants and coffee are not a great combo – best stick with tea.

Verdict: An acquired taste – for speciality dunkers only. 4/10

Nice (Peak Frean)

SOA: Medium.

CWS: Retains a pleasant, finely grainy texture even when soggy.

CWC: The hint of coconut in a Nice goes rather well with a strong cup of coffee.

Verdict: Better dunked than undunked, when I find them rather uninteresting.

5/10

Ginger Nuts (McVitie's)

SOA: Medium slow.

CWS: A pleasant granular texture even when completely soggy.

CWC: Excellent, and the basis, in fact, of a rather fine pudding: ginger biscuits soaked in strong coffee and sandwiched together with whipped cream.

Verdict: A truly great biscuit, whether dunked or not. Particularly good after a very short (three-second) dunk, when they are wet but still crunchy.

9/10

Bourbon Creams (Crawford's)

SOA: Fast.

CWS: Dunk an inch for more than 10 seconds and it is guaranteed to fall off when you bring it back to the horizontal.

CWC: The chocolate combines with coffee for a delightful mocha effect.

Verdict: The creamy bit in the middle adds a whole new dimension; it melts, thereby allowing a deeply satisfying technique of combined dunking and licking.

7/10

Malted Milk (Elkes)

SOA: Medium.

CWS: Very soft, but not slimy; good, even when cold.

CWC: Coffee destroys the subtle maltiness of this rather sophisticated biscuit; far better with tea.

Verdict: A remarkably good dunk. I will be returning to this one.

9/10

Maryland Cookies (Lyons)

SOA: Very fast.

CWS: The biscuit part becomes slightly slimy, and a high fat and sugar content mean the dunked biscuit is rather sickly. The melty bits of chocolate are some compensation.

CWC: As with the bourbon creams, the mocha effect is interesting.

Verdict: A good cookie, and generous with the chocolate, but on balance, best undunked.

4/10

Abbey Crunch (McVitie's)

SOA: Medium fast.

CWS: Pleasantly soggy, with residual graininess – the oat flakes give a nice nuttiness.

CWC: Good. Suck the coffee from the biscuit after a short (two-second) dunking. Very satisfying.

Verdict: These light, very crispy biscuits have plenty of airspaces, and hold plenty of tea/coffee. By repeated, rapid, dipping and sucking you can drink almost an entire cup without raising it to your lips.

7/10

20 January 1980
ALL PIE-EYED
Marika Hanbury-Tenison

My husband Robin, who is not known for his culinary sensitivity, recently rang me from America to tell me of the fantastic winter pies he was enjoying there.

'Darling,' he said, 'they really do know how to please a man over here. You have just *got* to learn how to make a Pecan Pie and Deep Southern Apple Pie with plenty of butter and spices in it.'

What Robin had not noticed was that for the past couple of years I had served a Pecan Pie for lunch at our yearly rough shoot over the moors in Cornwall, and that his American Apple Pie is merely a variation on the traditional Apple Pie of Olde England.

Well, I suppose all that jet lag does dull the brain – so here for him and for anyone else who enjoys warming and hearty winter puddings are recipes for those two American winter favourites.

Pie Pastry

A rich shortcrust pastry that is ideal for sweet pies. Any left over can be wrapped in a polythene bag and refrigerated or frozen for later use. The amount you use for each pie will depend on how thin or thick you like your pastry. This amount should be enough for two pies.

12oz plain flour;
6oz butter;
1 medium egg;
1 tablespoon caster sugar;
1 tablespoon dry sherry

Cut chilled butter into small shavings and rub it into the flour with your fingertips until the mixture resembles fine breadcrumbs. Add the sugar and egg and work with the hands until the mixture is lumpy but beginning to stick together. Add the sherry and continue to work with the hands until the mixture forms a smooth dough – if necessary add a little cold water at this stage if the dough does not stick together. Do not work the pastry more than is necessary to get it smooth.

Turn the dough onto a floured board and roll it out once; if the butter was ice-cold it should not be necessary to chill the pastry before using it but it is worth chilling the pastry case or filled case in the refrigerator before baking.

American Apple Pie

Pastry as above;
2 lb cooking apples;
4oz dark brown sugar;
½ teaspoon cinnamon;
½ teaspoon ground nutmeg;
1½ tablespoons cornflour;

1 teaspoon plain flour;
1½oz butter;
½ teaspoon vanilla essence;
1 tablespoon lemon juice

Line a 9-inch flan case with thinly rolled out pastry. Peel, core and thickly slice the apples. Sieve the cornflour and add it to the apples with the brown sugar, cinnamon, nutmeg and lemon juice, tossing the ingredients to mix. Melt the butter and add the vanilla. Add the butter-vanilla mixture to the apple mixture and mix well. Pile the ingredients into the flan case. Roll out some more pastry to cover the pie, dampen the edges and press them firmly together. Prick in two or three places with a fork and bake in a hot oven (400°F, Reg 6) for about 40 minutes until the crust is golden brown and the apples soft (test by sliding a sharp, small pointed knife through the crust). The pie can be served hot or cold and is traditionally accompanied with a sharp tasting Cheddar cheese on the side – lashings of cream is also provided for those without a waistline problem, Robin told me with glee since he is one of them.

Pecan Pie (Serves 6)

Pastry as above;
6oz shelled pecan nuts;
3 eggs, beaten;
3½oz soft brown sugar;
5oz golden syrup;
6oz maple syrup (or use all golden
syrup or half golden and half
molasses);
½ teaspoon vanilla essence;
2oz melted butter

Line a 9-inch flan case with pastry. Roughly chop 4oz of the nuts and spread them over the bottom of the case. Combine the sugar and syrups in a saucepan and heat over a low flame, stirring until the sugar has melted. Leave to cool and then combine with the beaten eggs, vanilla essence and melted butter and mix well. Pour the mixture over the nuts in the case and top with the remaining halved pecan nuts arranged in a pattern over the top. Bake in a moderately hot oven (375°F, Reg 5) for about 40 minutes until the filling is set. Serve warm or cold with plenty of cream.

22 November 1974
THOUGHT FOR FOOD:
STEAMED SPONGE PUDDING
Denis Curtis

What I missed most when I came to London was my grandmama's steamed sponge pudding. Those served in the college canteens tasted like baked loofahs (they had been overcooked with too little fat content in the mixture – the more fat that is added the more difficult it is to get the pudding light). Half-fill a large saucepan with water and bring to the boil. Well butter a 1½ pint basin and deposit in it 3 level tablespoons of jam or syrup. (Have ready your greaseproof, string and cloth: everything should be prepared in advance for once you've added the flour all the air you've beaten in will rush out as rapidly as from a pricked balloon.) Cream together 4oz butter and 4oz vanilla impregnated sugar until *really* light and fluffy. Beat in a little at a time two well beaten eggs. Fold in 6oz SR flour with a metal spoon. Swiftly add a little milk to give a soft dropping consistency. Spoon mixture over the jam. Cover with greaseproof. Tie on the cloth and steam for 1½ hours (top up with boiling water after 1 hour).

Variations: Add 3oz mixed fruit or cut-up glacé cherries before folding in the flour. Instead of jam as a topping use 2oz currants, 2 level tablespoons syrup and a lemon's juice. Or slice two apples thickly (slice thinly and they'll be tough) and sprinkle with 2oz sugar. Put 3oz soaked dried apricots, 3oz sugar and a lemon's juice in the basin. For chocolate pudding blend 1oz cocoa powder to a cream with tablespoon hot water – add to the creamed butter and sugar.

5 September 1968
BLACKBERRY PUDDING SEASON
Marika Hanbury-Tenison

Blackberries always seem to have a shorter season than any other fruit but from now until the end of the month they are in their prime and it is worth making the most of them. Daily the fruit is ripening on tangled brambles in every hedgerow and anyone who has the time can wander down almost any country lane and pick blackberries by the bucketful, choosing the largest, blackest berries.

As an alternative to pricked fingers and purple stained nails the fruit can be bought in boxes from most greengrocers for around 1s 3d for half a pound.

In the West Country there is a saying that the Devil spits on all blackberries on the first of October. How this saying came about I have never been able to discover and I have always imagined that the Devil must be too busy with other things to go round spitting on every bramble bush in the country.

Perhaps it is the cooler, wetter weather coming at the end of September which causes the fruit to become soggy and tasteless by the beginning of October; whatever the reason, at the moment they are at their best and now is the time to enjoy them.

I love the taste of traditional blackberry pies and tarts but I seem to have a continual battle with all those pips and on the whole I prefer to sieve the fruit before using it. The following recipes both use *purée* and are great favourites in our family.

The first, Blackberry Fluff, comes originally from New Zealand and is a light, deliciously coloured pudding ideal for serving at the end of a dinner party or after a heavy main course.

Blackberry Fluff
1 lb blackberries;
4oz sugar;
Juice of half a lemon;
½oz gelatine;
3 egg whites

Simmer the blackberries with the sugar and a tablespoon of water for ten minutes. Press the fruit through a fine sieve. Dissolve the gelatine in the lemon juice and add it to the *purée*. Leave the *purée* in a cool place until it thickens and begins to set and then fold in the stiffly beaten whites of eggs. Pile into a glass dish and chill well before serving. Enough for four.

Blackberry and Apple Summer Pudding

1 lb blackberries;
1 lb cooking apples;
6oz sugar;
1 small loaf sliced white bread

Peel, core and roughly chop the apples. Simmer the blackberries, apples and the sugar for about 15 minutes, until the fruit is soft. Strain off the juice and rub the fruit through a fine sieve. Cut off the crusts from the slices of bread and soak each slice in the fruit juice. Line a basin with some of the slices of bread and fill the centre with half of the fruit *purée*, cover with a layer of bread and the remainder of the *purée*, and finish with a final layer of bread.

Place a small plate over the top of the pudding and press it down with a weight. Leave to set in a cold place for at least six hours before turning it out. The pudding should be well chilled before serving and is particularly good if it is covered all over with a layer of sweetened whipped cream.

Enough for four large or six medium servings.

The *Frite* of Your Life

CHIP SHOPS TAKE DOOM WITH A PINCH OF SALT
Ann Morrow

That British institution, the fish and chip shop, is likely to lose customers to take-away shops selling 'fast food' like hamburgers in the next decade, according to a City investment expert.

But the owner of one of London's best known fish and chip shops laughed at this gloomy prediction yesterday.

As cod and chips and halibut and chips were handed to office workers who had stood outside his 'Sea Shell' fish and chip shop in Lisson Grove, Marylebone, 42-year-old Mr John Faulkner said: 'I have been in the trade for 30 years. I can't see this ever happening. We have Rolls-Royces turning up here and customers like Ian Mikardo and Twiggy.'

The first fish and chip shop is said to have opened in the East End of London between 1860 and 1865 by a Mr Malin.

But northerners say John Lees started a shop in 1863 at Mossley, Lancs, and the north has the biggest fish and chip shop in the world at Guiseley, West Yorkshire.

Mr Faulkner gets up at about 3.30 a.m. to go to Billingsgate to buy fresh fish. Frozen fish is never sold in his restaurant.

His shop was the first of its kind to be listed in the *Good Food Guide*.

Mr John Hulbert, a taxi driver and a keen fish and chips eater, often takes American tourists to the 'Sea Shell' or to a shop in Theobolds Road.

He said: 'Every Thursday night I spend three to four pounds on fish and chips for the wife and children.'

He remembered the days when fish and chip shops sold delicacies like 'skate eyeballs' and packets of 'crackling'.

'And you don't hear about bloaters anymore,' he said.

The man who predicted that fish and chips would lose out to more modern ready-cooked food was Mr James Bax, 25, who works for the stockbrokers Hoare Govett in London.

'Actually I was talking about the trend in take-away foods,' he said last night.

'I said that over the next decade fast foods like hamburgers might be more successful than the more traditional fish and chips.

'Actually I am very fond of fish and chips and have been to the Sea Shell.'

8 November 1968
GIVE A HOT DOG A GOOD NAME…
Clement Freud

I was not among the crowd who welcomed home the Beatles at London Airport, nor did I stand outside the Comedy Theatre on Thursday evening to catch a glimpse of Prince Philip. I shall not attend the Lord Mayor's Show either, for attendance at popular functions is something I ceased to enjoy at the age of 12.

In March, 1937, my mother, for some still unaccountable reason, had gone into the local Co-operative store, asked for 2 lb of butter, 6oz of short back bacon and five tickets for the Coronation… and got them. As this was before the age of togetherness, the tickets were dotted about one stand and after breakfast on that distant May morning, we were each given a ticket, a packet of sandwiches and some money in case we got lost on the way home. At St James's Park Station my mother counted us, our luncheons and our tickets. My ticket was missing.

I was an orderly child and remembered propping it against the tooth-mug when I had been sent back to wash my hands directly prior to our departure, so I changed platforms, went home, got my ticket, came back and on returning to the Coronation route I realised that I had left behind my lunch.

I forget who said that starvation is the last resort of the patriot; but I didn't go back and was fortunate to have quite near me in the Co-op stand in The Mall, a white-coated man who spent the long eventful day calling out the memorable words: 'Lookee lookee, real Viennese Frankfurters!'

I patronised him on a number of occasions.

This month of November, you may well have thought, was quite simply the month before this December, a time for bonfires in the garden, the very end of the season of mists and mellow fruitfulness. If you were desperate to find further identification, you might have recalled that the 5th, 11th and 28th were days put by for the utilisation of Catherine wheels, poppies and pumpkin pie respectively. If that is what was in your mind, you would doubtless have been as surprised as I, when a public relations firm's handout reached me last week stating categorically that November was National Hot Dog Month. 'Hot Dogs of the World Unite' it only just didn't proclaim, and among the wealth of pennants and stickers that landed on my front door mat was a picture of a chuck-wagon . . . which turned out to be a sort of Wild Western tea-trolley.

Did you know that the number of hot dogs eaten in one year, laid end to end, would span the world?

Be perfectly honest: did you?

Or that, if they were piled in a heap, they would occupy the same volume as the *Queen Mary*?

A wagonburger is like a cheeseburger . . . only you use sliced frankfurt-ers and baked beans – I bet you didn't know that. And a hot roll was originally a cowboy's bedding.

There was such a wealth of unexpected information given by the firm of consultants that I galloped over to South Kensington, loped through the rush-hour traffic of Pelham Street and eventually knocked on the door of the first-floor flat that serves as their office.

Why is November Hot Dog Month? I asked an American lady, who told me that the scheme was her brainchild. Why not? she said, smiling pleasantly, while a picture of a sausage hiding in a soft roll and bearing the legend, Yippee, crouched just above her on the wall. She offered me a sherry.

The promotion of Hot Dog Month is being achieved without regard to race, colour or creed – or, as she put it, sausages could be pink or brown, contain more beef or less pork, and be smothered in a variety of relishes ranging from mustard yellow to pickled walnut black – as long as they were eaten. The aim was to get the younger generation 'tuned in' to hot dogs, in particular the skinless dog, the sausage with the synthetic casing. The younger generation were the target, teenagers had the money; she was certain of that.

I told her that I was uncharmed by the name 'hot dog', felt embarrassed when I asked for one and tended either to say, rather quietly, 'I'll have one of those,' or to buy a packet of crisps instead. I suggested that the increased sale of this confection, by any other name, might serve her purpose as well.

She said absolutely not. She was projecting a brand image. Anyway, resentment of the name didn't come from the young (who had the money); the young were tuned in. We inspected a picture of a hot dog. Hot dogs were an American way of life; a ball game without a hot dog was unthinkable; if all the hot dogs were laid end to end . . . we worked it out; it is 25,000 miles around the world and a hot dog is four inches long.

I asked whether the hot dog had any social barriers. It certainly had not. The Roosevelts had offered hot dogs to King George VI and his Queen. They hadn't known what they were, but they had enjoyed them.

Now I knew that she had gone too far, because they had known perfectly well what they were. I remember that when the coach came past during the Coronation I was just eating my fourth hot dog. They must have seen me, because they waved.

29 April 1979
LUNCH BOXES FROM THE MOON
Godfrey Anderson

Box lunches, once developed for moon-bound astronauts, are beginning to provide nutritious meals for some housebound American pensioners. There are between 20 and 30 million Americans age 60 or older; an estimated five million of them live alone. Some are invalids. Congress has been concerned that some of them do not eat adequately because they cannot afford to do so, lack skills to prepare nourishing and well-balanced meals in single servings, or have feelings of rejection and loneliness which stop them from preparing or eating a meal alone.

Although there is a national nutrition programme for older Americans, which provides hot meals at community centres, schools and churches – and Meals on Wheels even delivers at home – these projects are limited to the larger cities. Now those unable to take part in these programmes because of their personal handicaps or rural isolation are also being fed through research carried out at the Lyndon B. Johnson space centre in Houston, Texas.

About 30 per cent of the food being supplied to the old folk is identical to that eaten on the 1974 Skylab mission. Inside each box are shiny packages of freeze-dried foods which require only the addition of hot or cold water. Other foods are in single-serving tins that just need heating and others are contained in so-called retort pouches of aluminium foil with an inner plastic lining. These containers, only recently approved by the Federal Drug Administration, are believed to preserve the taste of foods better than the freeze-dried method.

The astronaut meals were developed originally over a long period of study and experiment since the fifties – a process still going on at the Space Centre.

Meals on the early Mercury flights were squeezed out of plastic tubes but by the later Apollo missions, the astronauts had discovered that food did not fly around the cabin in the weightless atmosphere of space as had been expected, so Nasa went over to what it calls its spoon-bowl programme.

It was found, for example, that the juice in a bowl of diced peaches would keep the segments anchored and, although some conscious effort was needed to raise the spoon quickly and smoothly to the mouth, there was no great problem about eating in the normal earthbound way.

As to what astronauts thought of the fare provided for them, Rita Rapt, a physiologist working on the flight food programme for Nasa, said: 'Men in space are very like men in the street when it comes to their preferences. They select what they want and we arrange it in menus.

'On the early Apollo flights, the food could not be heated and there was a universal dislike of the cold potatoes, but by Apollo 8 we had progressed to thermo-stabilised heat-processed Christmas dinners.

While virtually anything can be served from *Boeuf Stroganoff* to tuna à la *Neptune* – and special menus are prepared for invalid or ethnic tastes – a few problems remain. Ron Ritz, who has also worked on the programme, says that no way has been found to provide astronauts with a salad; you cannot freeze-dry fresh lettuce. A radiation process for preserving bread is not ready to be put into general use.

What do America's senior citizens think of eating astronaut food? Dr Jurgen Schmandt, of the Lyndon B. Johnson's School of Public Affairs at the University of Texas in Austin, has made a nine-month study, during which 168 elderly Texans tested 21 packaged meals on a daily or weekend basis.

The survey showed 77 per cent of those involved said they liked the meals 'very much', while 90 per cent praised their convenience.

They did not become bored with boxed meals, though not all of them ate everything at one sitting. Some saved portions for later snacking while others opened several boxes at once and mixed the contents to create their own menus.

A few complained of too many starchy foods and stews. There were objections that green beans were repeated three times in a 21-day cycle, while mixed vegetables and corn were repeated four times and macaroni with cheese twice. Peanuts and almonds proved difficult for those with dental problems, though some said they could eat the nuts after pounding them.

Generally, tinned foods were more popular than the freeze-dried variety, which some said had a 'crunchy' taste they did not care for. Some thought the rice tasted 'gritty'. Most unpopular item? So-called 'English peas'. Dr Schmandt thought the peas were possibly not prepared properly according to the instructions provided with each menu.

So far the government has shown little interest in pushing for nationwide adoption of the project. A proposed amendment to the Meals on Wheels Act of 1977, which would have provided for wider use of the astronaut meals, came to nothing.

But about 200,000 meals are being provided for social service agencies and individual senior citizens who order them from Skylab Foods, a non-profit company at Elmsford, New York. Each box contains a well-balanced meal consisting of an entrée, two side dishes (usually vegetables), dessert and beverage. A typical meal might consist of Vienna sausage, macaroni with cheese, green beans, a peanut butter bar and hot cocoa.

The boxes can be delivered with the help of volunteer workers or directly by air freight or parcel post. They may be stored without refrigeration until needed. Only a saucepan is required to convert their contents into a hot meal in ten minutes.

Skylab meals cost 75p for lunch and 95p for dinner. Cases containing six lunches cost about £4.50 while six dinners cost about £5.70. A shipping charge of about 75p is added to each case.

These Nasa-pioneered ideas are among those which have been considered at the University of Leeds for possible introduction in Britain. As George Glew, Director of the university's Catering Research Unit, has said, 'Some elderly people need more help than others to feed themselves properly.' His team had been studying the best ways to provide help for each person – perhaps meals heated by a portable microwave oven in a van and delivered ready to eat, or else prepared by a responsible neighbour; pre-prepared food (needing a refrigerator for storing) to make a complete dish such as a beef casserole; or, as in the American project, meals treated and packed to last a long time without special storage.

5 February 1992
OODLES OF GOOD NOODLES
John Whitley

The noodle bar is the latest addition to the fast-food culture that now dominates our high streets. Like the burger baronies, it's an import, but this time from the East – and it supplies an infinitely more nutritious and interesting meal.

The bars are closer to the traditional British fish and chip shop, in fact, and they favour the same policy of simple, fresh ingredients and low prices – something particularly welcome for recession-hit consumers.

Out East, the noodle is laden with religious significance; deciding what sort to have demands deeper consideration than the fish and chip shop.

Happily, this does not apply to the basic noodle bars. They are devised essentially for worker bees off to catch the bullet train home from their Tokyo offices: it's pit-stop catering. No one's proposing a three-course menu and a snifter from the drinks trolley here; the deal is a single bowl of strong soup, filled with noodles, and a choice of toppings.

Because it's cooking to a traditional pattern, rather than to a fixed formula like the fast food we've become used to, there is room for a bit of flair in the kitchen – though the noodles themselves are factory-made. Turnover is the only way to keep to these rock-bottom prices, so the most prized factor is consistency – not easy when the manager is hoping to push 500 people through on a busy Friday.

This means there is no encouragement to linger: the drinks list and front-of-house trimmings are minimal.

The need for a big customer base has concentrated the worthwhile bars in London. Probably the most authentic is Hamine; it's certainly the least comfortable. It is a snack-bar corridor which balloons out at the far end, and you either queue to get a table there or eat at counters. Most of the Japanese customers – which means pretty well everyone – belt through their bowls in 20-minute sprints while goggling at the Nippon news videos on the overhead television screens.

The menu is brief and to the point: two dozen noodle and rice specials, Coke, beers and Chinese tea; orders and pre-payment are taken, politely but rather disconcertingly, at the door. Plastic and cheques are not welcome – this is the land of the folded fiver.

The dressings are mainly pork, plus a good range of crispy veg. Gomoku-Larmen (£6.50) is the top of the range, with extra dollops of everything; these are piled up in a rather ungainly fashion and the slices of meat may seem excessively greasy to a Western palate. Wang Tang Men is 50p cheaper and better balanced: mushrooms, mangetouts, prawns and slices of scallop alongside the pork, all in a meaty, soya-based soup.

The bowls all seem rather too small for their loads so it's a bit of a struggle to get to the noodle mountain stage. Laid-back waiters explain the menu, which is more elaborate than Hamine's and calls noodles 'ramen'.

The house special, Ramen Wagamama (£4.50), is heaped with a fascinating mixture of flavours: prawns, delicately scented and smoked slices of meat, tofu and exotic cabbage leaves.

Kai Sen Men (£4.50) is a successful variant: fried noodles served in a light fish sauce on a flat plate, which makes them easier to handle, covered with a refreshing combination of squid, prawns, red peppers, mangetouts and wafers of Oriental fishcake. Each helping is really enough for two.

WINTER

Squirrel Pie for Lunch

24 November 1974

JUGGING A HARE
Marika Hanbury-Tenison

I often seem to be asked somewhat ticklish questions about the origins of various dishes or recipes. Recently my father, after one of those delicious gourmet meals still enjoyed by members of City livery companies, telephoned one evening to inquire why jugged hare was so called and why hare, or for that matter venison, came to be cooked in this rather peculiar manner.

The manner of cooking game in a jug, it seems, is an ancient one designed to stew the ingredients gently so that they emerge 'delicately tender, without being over-done, and the whole of the nourishment and gravy preserved'. To do this the ingredients of the dish were packed in an earthenware, cylindrical vessel called a 'jugging pot'.

The top of the jugging pot was tightly sealed with a bladder and then the container was placed in a large pan of gently simmering water that came to within about four inches of the top of the jug, the same principle as the *bain marie* method of cooking.

One 18th-century recipe I found requests that a layer of hay is put at the bottom of the pan of water and this, I suppose, was in order to protect the bottom of the jug from excessive heat. (Do not put earthenware pots on direct gas flame or electric hot plate.)

To cook hare or venison by this method today one needs to use one of those country-style, earthenware jugs that can be found in most pottery shops. I find the best way of sealing the top is to cover it with a double thickness of tin-foil and bind to the jug with that heavy duty Sellotape used for sealing packages for the deep freeze.

The word 'game' seems to smack, to many people, of food in the luxury class. This isn't necessarily so. Last week I bought a couple of casseroling grouse for a dinner party at a very reasonable price and produced a really delicious meal.

Jugged Hare (Serves 6)

1 hare jointed (ask the butcher to reserve the blood);
1½ tablespoons dripping or bacon fat;
Flour;
2 onions;
2 large carrots;
2 sticks celery;
A bouquet garni;
1½ pints good strong stock;
2 tablespoons redcurrant jelly;
1 glass port;
Thinly pared peel of ½ lemon;
Salt;
Freshly ground black pepper and cayenne

Peel and thinly slice the onions; peel and dice the carrots; thinly slice the celery. Dredge the hare joints in flour and fry them until golden brown on all sides in the hot dripping. Place the joints in a thick earthenware jug with the vegetables, bouquet garni and lemon peel. Season with salt, freshly ground black pepper and cayenne and pour over the stock. Seal the jug tightly with tin-foil and place it in a large saucepan. Add enough water to come to within four inches of the top of the jug, bring to the boil and then simmer gently for about 2½ to 4 hours until the hare is tender. Using slotted spoon, remove hare and vegetables from jug to heated serving dish. Remove the bouquet garni and lemon peel and our juices from the jug into saucepan. Add the hare's blood, the redcurrant jelly and the port and heat through, stirring continually until jelly has melted. Check the seasoning and strain sauce over the fare and vegetables. Serve with extra red currant jelly on the side and small balls of sausage meat fried until crisp golden brown.

17 April 1948
PIGS OR SHEEP?

To the Editor of the *Daily Telegraph*

Sir – I see that Mr W. R. Scoble, in his presidential address to the National Federation of Meat Traders' Associations, says that we should concentrate on one animal – the pig. I do not agree with him.

A great many acres in this country are suffering from over-cropping with corn and potatoes; there is no better alternative than to lay that land down to clover and grass.

There is one animal that will turn that clover and grass into meat without being continually fed with coarse concentrates, of which we are so short and at the same time will produce material for our textile industry and, lastly, but most important, will restore fertility to our land. I refer to the sheep.

Here on the Cotswolds and in many other parts of England sheep were for centuries the keystone of prosperity. To-day it is the exception rather than the rule to find a sheep on a farm.

I submit that if any one animal needs encouragement more than another it is the sheep.

Yours &c.,

Horton.

Mark Harford

3 February 1951
REINDEER FOR DINNER?

Reindeer is here! Yesterday cookery expert Claire Butler cooked a joint – half a shoulder of reindeer. First she cut off two slices to grill, then roasted the rest, using both recipes below, given to her by a Swedish housewife.

Her comments were, 'Delicious! The joint browned beautifully, was tender to cut and tasted like beef. Soon after I put it in the oven there was an appetising smell, rather like pheasant roasting.'

The Smithfield firm importing the reindeer says that loin, shoulder and leg are among the best cuts. If frozen, meat must be thawed out before cooking. It is dry meat for roasting; fat and liquid must be added before cooking, basting is important. Butchers expect to have reindeer on sale in their shops within 10 days at a price of about 3s a lb.

To roast:

2–3 lb joint of reindeer;

2½oz fat bacon or lard;

1 onion;

1½–2 tablespoons butter or margarine;

1½ teaspoons salt;

¼ teaspoon pepper;

1 cup meat extract or top of milk (instead of cream)

For the gravy:

2 tablespoons fat from stock;

2½ tablespoons flour;

2–2½ cups meat extract;

Some redcurrant jelly;

1 teaspoon butter

Prepare joint by cutting off all skin. Lard it. Rub half the salt and pepper into meat, heat up butter in a baking tin and place meat in it. Put in oven at 525°F, gas No. 11, to brown; baste some of the melted butter over it. After 10 minutes, reduce over to 450°F, gas No. 8, and pour ½ cup meat extract into the pan (not over the meat), add onion whole. Keep basting, and add if necessary remainder of extract. Cook for 1½ hours.

Prepare gravy in usual way making a roux, seasoning to taste and flavouring with redcurrant jelly.

Serve with roast potatoes, sprouts, fried mushrooms or onions. Red or blackcurrant jelly should accompany the meat. If you have a bottle of claret – this Swedish cook recommends St Julien – your guest will appreciate you as a perfect hostess.

13 May 1971

SQUIRREL PIE FOR LUNCH
Kenneth Clarke

Squirrel pie was accorded the cautious verdict 'quite nice' when it was tried out on pupils and staff at a Devon school in an experiment by the biology master.

Mr Cyril Morgan, who teaches biology at Torrington secondary school, regards the grey squirrel as a menace.

He decided one way to reduce them would be to shoot them for the table. The experiment was to test reaction.

Miss Janet Secker, the cookery mistress, made savoury squirrel pie, squirrel casserole and even 'squirrel burgers'.

'The children enjoyed it,' said Mr Morgan.

Mr Morgan is concerned at the damage grey squirrels do to trees and their effect on the native red squirrels. Farmers and amateur sportsmen ought to regard them as a cheap delicacy, he said. Americans have been eating squirrels for years.

Mr Robert Carrier, the cookery expert, said the taste was 'a cross between chicken, frogs' legs and rabbit, with a slightly gamey flavour'.

At the Savoy, a spokesman said: 'If anyone wanted squirrel, we would do it.' Officially, however, a squirrel remains a rodent – pot roasted or in a pie.

16 January 1945

STILL BETTER SAUSAGES

'The British people can now look a sausage in the face,' said Col. Llewellin, Minister of Food, at the annual conference of the National Federation of Meat Traders' Association, in London yesterday.

'By increasing the pork content from 37½ per cent, to 50 per cent, the sausage can now look us in the face. As soon as we can improve the sausage still more and get back to the pre-war standard I hope to do it.'

He said that it was five years to the day since the meat and livestock control started. He thanked the federation for making the scheme one of the most successful in the food control system.

'I want to provide the shopper with the fuller choice of meat which she loves,' he went on, 'This year is going to be very difficult.'

'We are not out of the wood yet. The strain on manpower is going to be the greatest ever.

'We have never in the history of this country put forth such mighty military strength. All these men have to be well fed, and we as civilians are determined to deny them nothing.

'As soon as we can do it I want to see the meat ration increased. I am not holding out any immediate hope. We shall bring in all the meat that we can get, but it is going to be in short supply for some time.

'Increased quantity and better quality will not come overnight when Germany is defeated. It has not been possible to keep up large herds of cattle and to get fertilisers or machinery, and the world population of cattle has decreased.

'Owing to transport difficulties we have had to restrict some classes of meat to certain areas. I hope that immediately after Germany is defeated we shall be able to have a more equitable distribution.

'As soon as possible I hope to be able to put you in the position of being able to serve your customers in the way that it is your ambition to do.'

24 March 1937
MUTTON PIES: A RECIPE FROM THE KITCHEN OF GEORGE IV
Florence White

Little mutton pies, not raised pies, but those baked in patty pans lined with English puff pastry like Christmas mince pies, if properly made are incomparable as delicious and easily carried refreshments.

The following recipe has been adapted from one that was used in the kitchens of George IV. The secret of their superiority consists in blending the mutton with the Italian sauce as directed.

Cut part of the fillet from a loin or neck of mutton in dice, put 1–2oz of butter in a stewpan with chopped eschalot, parsley, half a dozen chopped mushrooms, salt and pepper; let these simmer over the fire a few minutes; mix the mutton with this, and set the whole to cool.

Then mix with some of the following Italian sauce. Line a dozen or more tartlet moulds with the trimmings of puff paste; fill them with the meat mixture when cold, cut out the cover, from the centre of which cut a piece the size of a wafer; egg the patties and bake them.

When done take them from the patty pans and dish on a napkin or dishpaper and serve.

For the brown Italian sauce, chop an eschalot, pass it in a stewpan with a spoonful of oil or a little butter, a clove, a blade of mace, a few peppercorns, a little ham, and a small piece of bay leaf. When fried a little add two tablespoonfuls of Spanish sauce and one of brown stock. Stir the whole over a fire till it boils; draw it to the corner and let it simmer 15 to 20 minutes; skim it and strain through a cullender.

1 July 1954
TAKING THE MYSTERY OUT OF MEAT
Winifred Carr

It can take a lifetime to become an authority on meat for names of cuts vary according to different districts and even experts differ about the way these cuts should be butchered and cooked.

To-day's article will help to explain some of the long-lost meat terms and will tell you how to grill.

Back on the menu next week, after the end of meat rationing, will be that fine old English dish with the intriguing name – the carpet bag steak.

If you have never heard of it before and you are under 35 you are excused. For it needs an outsize – by rationing standards – cut of sirloin steak. It is made, according to Mr A. C. Moss, head chef at Simpson's in the Strand, by boning a sirloin steak, filling the slit with oysters, sewing it up, grilling it, unpicking the thread and serving at once.

Another dish making a welcome return will be planked steak. For this Mr Moss uses a full-sized rump steak and wooden plank. Cooked vegetables are arranged around the edge of the plank when the steak is nearly ready and the whole thing is popped back in the oven for a final few minutes before serving.

Down in the City at the George and Vulture, young stockbrokers, wool men, bank clerks and businessmen will have lunchtime 'classes' in the art of choosing meat for their grill. Chops, cutlets and steaks will be laid out on enormous plates in front of the 150-year-old frill with its glowing coke fire, and 'teacher', Mr H. Grady, will stand by to guide the choice.

The experts may argue about whether or not you should brush the meat over with oil or melted fat before grilling, or how thick a Châteaubriand steak should be. But they do agree on two things.

Only 'couture cuts' of meat – the primest, juiciest and tenderest steak, chops and cutlets – are good enough for grilling, and the grill itself should be thoroughly heated before you put your meat on it.

A grilled steak can be 'blue' (brown on the outside, raw inside), flaired (slightly burnt on the outside and underdone inside), underdone or well done. A minute steak is what its name suggests, grilled only half a minute each side. It must be cut thin, or beaten until thin.

Sprinkle the meat with pepper and salt and, if you wish, brush with melted marrow fat or oil. If it is a thin steak, put it under a hot grill; if it is thick, turn the grill down a little as soon as the meat has been sealed on both sides, and cook more slowly. Turn with tongs, a slice, or two spoons. Never stick a fork into the meat or the juices will run.

An expert griller can tell you whether steak is done to the required degree by testing the meat with the fingers. If it feels spongy when pressed gently, it is still rare, if it resists pressure, it is well done. A grilled steak should be pink and juicy and the blood should rise from the surface in beads.

Chop or cutlet? Can you distinguish between them? A cutlet has a bone that finishes in a right angle; the bone in a chop is shaped like a T. Cutlets should be trimmed of surplus fat and the meat flattened towards you with a kitchen knife. They do not need long cooking.

Do you know the difference between the undercut and the fillet? They are the same thing, the roll of meat beneath the sirloin from which most of the best grilling steaks are cut. In the case of mutton, the loin fillet is used for mignon steaks.

Porterhouse and T-bone steaks are confusing terms too. Here the experts differ about whether they are the same cut or not. Chef Moss is on the side that says they are. 'It is a sirloin steak (entrecôte) with the bone left in. The Americans call it a T-bone steak, we call it a Porterhouse and prefer it cut slightly thicker. There usually is enough on it to serve three.' Minute steaks are cut from the entrecôte also.

Do you know what is needed to make the perfect mixed grill? Another expert, M. René Lebègue, chef de cuisine at Grosvenor House, lists these ingredients and considers anything else superfluous: a lamb cutlet, pork sausage, lamb kidney, bacon, tomatoes, mushrooms, straw potatoes and watercress.

Suggestions by Bon Viveur for grilling or frying are:

Beef: Rump, fillet or undercut, eye of fillet (also called tournedos; it is cut from the undercut of sirloin).

Lamb: Loin chop (middle loin), chump chop, cutlet (neck end), crown cutlet (meat trimmed in cutlet with all bottom chine bone removed leaving neck bone only), noisette (cutlet with all bone removed and the meat rolled).

Mutton: Noisette (see lamb), 1-inch slices cut from middle leg.

Veal: Chop, cutlet, fillet, noisette (see lamb).

Pork: Chump, chop, loin chop, leg cutlet, noisette (see lamb).

11 August 1913
COOKING AND SERVING GROUSE
Elsie Wetherell

Grouse will fly from the moors to London on Monday – by aeroplane. There is no 'Glorious Twelfth' this year, as that day falls on a Sabbath. So the date upon which protection for the birds expires this year is the thirteenth – and it appears to be an unlucky day upon which to open the season, prospects being poor for reasons set out in a special article in the *Daily Telegraph* on Tuesday. Grouse has appeared on the menu during the close season, but this is really imported ptarmigan, or white grouse. It must not be concluded, however, that all white grouse on sale from Monday onwards is ptarmigan, because there will be some real white grouse from Scotland.

The grouse, which delights both sportsmen and gourmets, is said to be peculiar to the British Isles, and while there are several species of grouse, it is the beautiful and delicious red grouse, or moor fowl, that is so much appreciated by the epicure. It is supposed to derive its delicious flavour from the heather on which it feeds.

Grouse, like other kinds of game, must be kept a certain length of time before it develops its full flavour. In France this is described as the 'fumet'; it is really a natural principle which not only increases the flavour of game, but softens the fibres and acts as an aid to digestion as well. If game is cooked too soon it will be found lacking in this flavour; on the other hand, it must not be kept too long or it will become tainted and unwholesome.

The length of time for hanging depends on the age of the bird and also on the weather. An old bird must be kept a longer time than a young one, and a dry, cold climate is decidedly better for hanging than a muggy, damp one.

Grouse should hang at least forty-eight hours before cooking, leaving them unplucked and undrawn as long as possible. Hang in a current of air in a dry, cool place. If the birds are wet they should be carefully wiped and then hung in a warm kitchen, or, better still, in the sun, before being hung in the larder. When there has been an injury to the skin the part should be well dusted with pepper to keep the flies away. The birds may be hung in muslin bags.

Examine them each day, and at the slightest evidence of taint the birds should be plucked, drawn, and cooked as soon as possible. If there should be any taint this may often be removed by soaking the plucked bird in milk, or by washing it in water with plenty of salt and a little vinegar. Dry thoroughly before cooking.

Again, if a plucked bird is not required for immediate use, it can be kept a few hours longer by plunging it into boiling water and allowing it to remain for five minutes or so before drying and dusting with pepper.

There are several recognised ways of determining the age of a bird. In a young one the breast is plump and firm and the legs are smooth and supple, with a short-rounded spur; whereas in an old bird the legs are rough and scaly, and the spur much more fully developed. The plumage, too, of a young grouse is brighter and more glossy, and the wing feathers softer and not fixed so firmly.

Still the most popular way of cooking a grouse is to roast it, unless it happens to be old. Then some other method is best adopted. To roast a grouse, first pluck and single-end truss, after wiping both inside and out with a damp cloth, but do not wash it. Mix a small piece of butter with pepper and salt and a squeeze of lemon juice, and put this inside the body – it should be trussed like a fowl – and tie a nice piece of fat bacon over the breast. Cook in a good oven, basting frequently with butter or bacon fat; basting is most important as the flesh of grouse is inclined to dry; twenty to twenty-five minutes should be sufficient time for cooking.

The bird must not be over-cooked, or it will lose its delicious juicy and delicate flavour, for which it is noted. A few minutes before the bird is ready, remove the bacon fat from the breast, dredge it well with flour, and return to oven to brown. It is fashionable now to serve grouse with a garnish of watercress, and a fruit sauce, such as orange or lemon, is generally liked; or a tart fruit jelly or compote may be served. The toast underneath the bird, together with the fried bread crumbs and bread sauce, are no longer necessities. If a brown sauce is liked, no strong flavourings must obtrude and so spoil the bird's delicate flavour. Potato chips or straws are still in favour.

Here is an orange sauce, for which you will require: ½ pint light stock, ½oz butter and of flour, grated rind of one and juice of two oranges, one yolk of egg. Melt butter in pan, add the flour, mix well, then pour in the stock and stir until boiling; add the rind and juice of the oranges, and simmer ten minutes, stir in the egg yolk and strain before serving.

Of salads to be served with grouse there is a wide choice. They may be given a touch of orange, or of banana, shredded pineapple or apple and benefit accordingly; and some people like the American fashion of serving heaped tablespoons of boiled sultanas with grouse, as with chicken – and very good it is.

Réchauffé For Grouse

Here is rather a nice *réchauffé* for grouse. Remove skin and bone and mince the meat finely; chop one or two shallots and fry them in butter; add the minced grouse and stir until well beaten; season well and moisten with some very good brown gravy; keep warm. Then make an omelette with four eggs, and when just set put the grouse in centre; fold over and serve at once in a very hot dish. This makes a nice luncheon dish.

Grouse Salad

Mince two shallots and mix with seven teaspoonfuls of chopped tarragon
and chervil, 2 tablespoonfuls castor sugar, 2 yolks of eggs, salt and pepper
and pinch cayenne; mix with 12 tablespoonfuls oil and 3 tablespoonfuls
chilli vinegar and finally 1 gill whipped cream. Make a border of hard-
boiled eggs in quarters; put pieces of grouse in centre and decorate with
beetroot and pieces of anchovy, or sardine, and pour sauce over the grouse.

4 October 1913
COOKING IN SEASON –
OCTOBER FARE

October brings the pheasants, and it is probable that on this very day there
will be no more popular dish in England than the little brown birds, which
are perfect when roasted and served with the meal accompaniments. In
these days of autumn food supplies are abundant. Winter fruit is beginning
to make its appearance, nuts are golden brown and ready for use, plums,
pears, quinces, and apples are all ripening. Poultry is in good condition,
and fish abundant, including mackerel and herrings.

In this first day of pheasants the housekeeper will remember that the
hen bird is more tender than the cock, and that the flesh should be juicy.
If the weather is in the least foggy great care must be taken in hanging
all game. The larder must be airy, preferably having a good current
passing through it. Carelessness both in choice and in methods of hanging is often the cause of a lack of savour in a meat course that ought to
be delicious.

After the first novelty has worn off, pheasants will, probably, be utilised
for other dishes than a special roast bird. Casserole cooking is not to be
forgotten under these circumstances, and a braised bird is both succulent
and appetising. In arranging menus this week, specially for the *Daily
Telegraph*, Mr O Herman Senn gives a little-known method of braising,
which differs from the better-known recipe which has cabbage as seasoning. Naturally, every morsel of these delicate birds is utilised by the careful
housekeeper, and so curried pheasants will be found acceptable perhaps

for the menu of a dainty theatre supper. Boiled pheasant with oysters ought to be particularly good, but when oysters are not available a good white onion sauce makes an excellent substitute.

Braised Pheasant

Pick, draw and singe a good-sized pheasant, cut off the neck and part of the legs. Wipe the inside with a damp cloth and truss for roasting. Put the birds so prepared in a stewpan or fireproof braising-pan containing a small carrot, three slices of bacon, all cut up in slices; also about one dozen small, peeled button onions and an ounce of butter. Fry these a little. Season the pheasant with salt and pepper, spread about an ounce of butter or dripping on top of the pheasant, and cook in a hot oven for about twenty minutes; baste frequently. Next pour off the fat, add half a pint of demi-glacé or other good brown sauce, cover the pan, and cook gently for another twenty-five to thirty minutes. Take up the bird, place it on a hot dish, and garnish with the onions and bacon. Reduce the sauce, skim it, and pour over the pheasant. The dish is then ready to serve.

Medallions of Pheasant

Pick, singe, and draw two good-sized pheasants, truss them as for boiling, and braise the birds with mirepoix of sliced bacon, carrot, onion, and a bunch of herbs; moisten with seasoned stock, and cook the birds till tender.

When cold, remove the breast fillets and other parts of meat free from bone, cut these into neat round slices, not too thinly, and place them on a wire tray. Pound the trimmings of meat in a mortar, adding one to two tablespoons of white sauce, two or three ounces of cooked ham, and two yolks of hard-boiled eggs. Rub this through a fine sieve, and season with salt and pepper, add a little cream to make the mixture smooth enough for spreading. Spread over one side of the ground fillets of pheasant, then place them on thin rounds of cooked tongue or ham, the same size as the pheasant fillets. Have ready a white chaud-froid sauce, flavoured with the stock made from the pheasant bones, and containing, of course, enough aspic or gelatine to allow the sauce to just set when cold. Mask the prepared medallions with this sauce – they must be well coated – and place them on a wire tray till the sauce is set. Decorate each with a star-shaped slice of truffle, green peas, and points of chilli or pimento skin. Next mask or coat each with a thin layer of aspic jelly. Put a little mixed salad in as many

 241

soufflé cases as may be required, and upon this place the medallions. Dish up neatly and serve.

Note – The salad used may consist of endive, small cress, and celery, all cut into fine shreds, and seasoned with a little mayonnaise, or else oil, vinegar, salt and pepper.

Curried Pheasant

Cut the remains of one or two cold pheasants into small joints, remove some of the bones, and season with salt. Next fry them in two ounces of butter, previously melted in a stewpan with half a peeled and finely-minced onion. Sprinkle over a dessertspoonful of mild curry powder and a large tablespoonful of flour; stir well, and moisten with about a pint of veal stock, stir, and let boil, then cook gently for about twenty minutes. Next add a dessertspoonful of redcurrant jelly, the grated rind of half an orange, and a dessertspoonful of lemon juice. Cook for another five minutes. Just before serving add a tablespoonful of coconut milk. Arrange a border of plain boiled rice on a hot dish, put the cooked pheasant in the centre of the dish, garnish with lemon (if liked), strain over the sauce, and serve with a small jar of chutney.

Boiled Pheasant with Oyster Sauce

Truss one or two pheasants for boiling and wrap the birds in well-buttered, thin white paper. Have ready a pan of boiling stock or well-seasoned water, including a bay leaf. Put in the pheasants; as soon as the water boils remove the scum, then allow to simmer gently until the birds are quite tender. Take up the pheasants, untruss, and place on a hot dish. Serve with oyster sauce made by using some of the pheasant liquor or stock.

To make the oyster sauce: Beard a dozen large sauce oysters, cut each in half or quarters. Put the beards and liquor from the oysters in a saucepan with half a pint of pheasant stock, and boil up with half a pint of milk. Melt in a saucepan 1oz of butter, add a generous ½oz of flour, and cook for a few minutes, stirring all the time. Then add gradually the strained stock, as above prepared; stir till it boils, then simmer for about fifteen minutes. Add the oysters, a little lemon juice, season to taste, reheat, and serve separately with the birds.

23 September 1949
'GO-SLOW' MAY HIT
MEAT RATION
Daily Telegraph Woman Reporter

The 'go-slow' methods by Smithfield porters, reported in the *Daily Telegraph* yesterday, may interrupt to some extent the supply of London's meat ration this week-end. Suburban shops will be in the most vulnerable position, and even in central London some of the English veal planned for a proportion of the ration has deteriorated because of the slow rate of clearance.

Beef and imported lamb make up the rest of the allocation. Rabbits are plentiful and are not restricted to registered customers. Many butchers also have poultry.

Fruit is in good supply. The first of the pineapples recently bought by the Ministry of Food from the Azores arrived in London yesterday. They are mostly large and will cost about £1 each.

English apples and pears of good quality and free of price control abound. For Cox's apples 1s 4d lb was asked, and 6d and 8d lb for other varieties of eating apples. Cookers were from 4d lb. Monarch and President are the main varieties of plums still being gathered – 8d lb is the usual retail price.

Large Spanish honeydew melons were 4s each and small, round French melons of excellent flavour 1s and 1s 6d each. English hothouse melons were from 5s 6d each. Brazil nuts were at prices ranging from 3s to 5s 6d lb. Kent cobs were 1s 9d and 2s lb.

Tomatoes have risen in price and were 10d and 1s lb. Yesterday, lettuces were cheaper at 4d and 6d each. Other vegetables remain dear.

Cranky Cradock

4 February 1971
DO YOU KNOW HOW TO HAND YOUR GUESTS THEIR ASPARAGUS ON A PLATE?
Bon Viveur

Etiquette crops up again, following your second lot of (pre-postal strike) problem postcards. Mrs Ellis, for instance, says: 'Please advise on up-to-the-minute, sophisticated eating customs.' For a start, she asks: 'How do you eat kebabs on large skewers laid on a bed of rice?'

The answer: Take a table fork in the right hand and the handle of the skewer in the left (almost certainly in a table napkin because it *should* be very hot!); put the prongs behind the end of the skewered items and withdraw the skewer gently.

Eat with fork only if pieces are small and tender enough to break down without strugglings and wigglings. Otherwise, use a knife as well.

'What is your counsel of perfection on eating asparagus?' is another query. It is almost as important to know what *not* to do in this context. Never in any circumstances use those dreadful Victorian *nouveau riche* innovated asparagus tongs. Just pick up the stems with your fingers.

Of course, in private houses, unless the cook/hostess does her job properly and provides a finger bowl, the guest is going to be very uncomfortable. The hostess who does not possess finger bowls can use any small glass, or even china, bowls instead.

She should also, when handing round hot plates of hot asparagus with melted butter poured over the tips, make sure guests know The Melted Butter Drill.

Pudding forks and spoons, together with everything else, are – as everyone knows – laid to the left and right of each cover, never at the top. If you take the pudding fork when (naturally) serving from the left and put this prongs-downwards in front of each person (parallel with the table's edge and two-thirds up the place setting) the asparagus plate can be set down with its furthest edge tipped up by the inverted fork. The edge nearest the diner will then be lowered to form a 'pocket' for the butter into which the asparagus can be dipped. Asparagus should be set with the stems to the right of the diner. Should the diner be left-handed, simply turn the plate round.

Fish, too, has its problems. We have yet to find the fish that suffers on the palate through being eaten with an ordinary table knife and fork. So, an ordinary knife and fork is quite correct; only those terrible Victorian-instigated fish knives and forks are frowned upon.

Mrs B. White writes: 'The rind and juice of a lemon or orange in a recipe may be taken by the reader to signify a large, medium or small fruit with varying amounts of juice and grated ring. Could this not be simplified?'

We ourselves do try very hard to ensure that our published recipes specify large, medium or small. We have just taken three such lemons, weighing 5oz, 4½oz and 4oz respectively; yield of finely-grated rind, without pith was: large, ¾oz; medium, a fraction under ¼oz, and small, 15oz.

We then extracted and strained the juice from each lemon and obtained 3 fl oz; 2¼ fl oz and 2 fl oz. We hope that this will help!

25 September 1969
FONDUE IS A FEAST BY ITSELF
Bon Viveur

To cheer up the first really chilly autumn evening, we suggest you give a Swiss supper party. The highlight of this party would, of course, be as

Swiss Cheese Fondue, which is so much more to the Swiss than simply the most succulent of all cheese dishes. It is well to remember that these fondues, no matter from which Swiss *canton*, need only be accompanied by light, simple dishes.

The Swiss themselves restrict the meal to fondue with coffee and cake served after a decent interval. Alternatively, for stout trenchermen, they would offer a platter of assorted cold meats before the fondue.

The platter would, in this instance, comprise leaf-thin slices of Parma ham, the Italian salami called *Chiterio* arranged with great neatness as individual servings on meat plates or platters with gherkins, a scattering of black olives, a few heart-of-lettuce leaves and a fine dice of a frothy forked-up little mound of good meat jelly.

With it serve black bread, very thinly sliced and very thickly buttered and reverse your classic thinking when it comes to wines.

Serve a red Swiss table wine with the meat platter and a white wine with the fondue, unless you are going to risk costly and potent 'chasers' of kirsch.

It might be better to omit these, actually, because there is already a little kirsch in the fondue we have chosen for you and in the 'cake', which is called a *Zuger Kirschetorte*.

Whichever you choose, this is a meal which you and your guests can eat informally grouped around your sitting-room – if, of course, it has a table large enough for all to cluster around, for the fondue.

If you have a complete Swiss fondue set you merely follow the recipe for *Fondue à la Fribourg*.

But if you are forced to improvise with either a hot-plate or a keep-warm-only nightlight table heater, make the fondue in the kitchen on your cooker with an asbestos mat between top-burner heat and base of chosen pot.

This enables you to melt the cheese with the wine very slowly indeed, which we regard as essential in such circumstances.

When completed, carry it through to the table. Pile a napkin-lined basket high with ¾in to 1in bread cubes, and then all grab forks, spear cubes, swirl in the mixture and convey at speed to inelegantly wide-open mouths.

25 April 1960
THE SECRETS OF BON VIVEUR
Sheila Hollis

Fanny and John Cradock probably did more than anyone else to restore our regard for food after the war, and, in the *Daily Telegraph* under the pseudonym of Bon Viveur, they certainly helped raise the standard of hotel and restaurant catering.

If all those thousands of readers who watched their magical cookery shows at our many food and Cookery Brains Trusts ever wondered where Fanny learned to cook, her new book, *Something's Burning – an autobiography of two cooks*, provides the answer.

It describes her childhood, when a love of good food and wines was instilled in her by a grandmother who adored cooking, a mother who would breakfast in bed at 11 a.m. on oysters and dry champagne, and a grandfather who began her gastronomic education with game, Stilton and port.

She has never had a cookery lesson in her life. She learned by assimilation, by instinct and by an inborn talent, for cooks of her calibre are born, not made.

11 January 1973
CATCHING UP WITH THE CONTINENTAL COOKS...
Bon Viveur

Inevitably we have been speculating on what will be the effects of joining the European Economic Community on this reserved and highly individual island people.

We also reflect, rather sadly, that overnight the British have become the only member nation of the Common Market to buy bottled mayonnaise, cook with malt vinegar and depend very largely upon meat cubes for stock and tins for soups.

Against these shortcomings and heavily on the credit side, we are incessantly reminding our many new European 'cousins' how the standard for cooking has soared in our private homes.

For the British, the legend persists that the French in particular have a miraculous gift for conjuring up a feast from a few scraps. This is sheer nonsense!

They do, however, have a profoundly practical approach, especially in the lower-income groups, to making their housekeeping money go a very long way and for wasting absolutely nothing.

So let us be practical and acknowledge a few ways in which we can still improve, despite the fact that more Englishwomen run homes and go out to work than in any other Common Market nation, save only the enormously prosperous and hard-working Germans.

It is still a waste of money and a tremendous sacrifice of flavour to buy those bottled substitutes for mayonnaise when a batch can be made, in seven minutes, which will last for a month in ordinary domestic refrigeration. It will take up little room in its basic form, be covered with witted greaseproof to exclude crusting and be ready for drawing upon for many variations on the real mayonnaise theme.

Anyone can make it, by our method, without the slightest fear of curdling, since you lock the door on this before adding a single drip of oil!

For Mistake-proof Basic Mayonnaise, put four separated egg yolks into a bowl with a flat eggspoon of salt and a flat saltspoon of black pepper. Whisk and whisk until these become a thick, creamy batter, allowing three minutes with a hand rotary whisk at full speed.

Then add three-quarters of a pint of olive oil – still electric whipping, or co-opt a slow pourer while you work the hand whisk. If you can get in a pint of oil so much the better.

The mixture should be far too thick by the time you have finished. Then a dollop at a time as needed, take some of this basic, beat in wine vinegar or grape or lemon or orange juice to taste and finish with either single cream or top of the milk.

For a further variant whip in one stiffly-whipped egg white to every quarter pint of basic mayonnaise just before serving. This does the double chore of reducing cost and gentling off the oil content for delicate tums.

It is also wasting money and flavour to use meat cubes and tap water instead of bone or vegetable stock when both can be made as well, if not better, in a lidded casserole or foil-covered stockpot or big saucepan.

In it goes from bed-time to breakfast or from the moment of morning departure to work until the evening return. Even the hold-up engendered by waiting for the stock to become cold so as to cut the fatty top crust away, can be dismissed entirely. Just use scraps of absorbent kitchen paper or tissue to tow through and thus absorb the hot liquid grease until only clear stock remains.

If you are one of the increasing number of folk pushing up the annual wine-consumption in Britain you can abstain from buying any vinegar, real or malt: just make your own from the lees of the bottles. (We are assuming these to be mainly 'plonk' wines.)

Vinegar is simply soured wine, so just invest in the smallest available barrel from one of the many home-made wine equipment shops sprouting up everywhere, pour in the accumulated lees and (for city dwellers) stick out on a south-facing windowsill.

Being country dwellers we keep our little barrel on a south terrace which takes the greatest load of traffic: everyone who passes on their lawful occasions gives the little barrels a vigorous shake. When they have had a few weeks of sunny weather just strain the contents through several folds of butter muslin and that's wine vinegar.

21 December 1969
HERE'S OUR PLAN FOR THE YEAR'S MOST INDIGESTIBLE MEAL
Fanny and Johnnie Cradock

We have a grandson now, so more than ever we safeguard the three Christmas days as family days – not ones to be spent in the kitchen.

Even for a couple of passionate cooks like us, it seems more important to help fill minute socks and gigantic pillow cases, play trains, produce shining new shillings for church and slow our pace to match elderly relatives and small feet in very new shoes.

But This Calls For Very Careful Planning, lest our advance labour-saving preparations prune away all glitter and colour.

We have ensured 'no mess' in our newly-decorated home by settling for white and gold Christmas decorations. House-grown white bulbs and seed-raised mimosa trees have been teamed with set piece decorations... white-painted, spangled tree roots blitzed from this neglected garden, now bauble-hung and tinsel-twined with white and gold junk violins, trumpets and tambourines slung from gilded hoops.

On the food side, too, we have made extensive advance preparations. Here is our list to date: chocolate log cake, yeast dough for holiday croissants, set out pickles, plum cake, plum pudding, mincemeat, sweet short pastry, potted shrimps, French dressing, mayonnaise, paper water-lily napkins, chocolate clowns, nest for sugar mice, sweetbread pâté, salted snail trays, potted shrimps, cheese board with straw and labels, chocolate trifle boxes, trifle macaroons, confectioners' custard, strawberries for *bavaroise*, sorbet, brandy butter, gilded nuts, royal icing candlesticks and a jam tray assortment. (Set twelve varieties out on long narrow tray, store on shelf – and only spoons need washing and replacing after each breakfast!)

And now to menus we have planned for the three days.

Christmas Day

Breakfast
Fruit bowl
Croissants (sections taken from thawed yeast dough, rolled and baked
    in time it takes to prepare and lay remainder of breakfast)
Coffee
Home-made preserves

Buffet Lunch
Potted shrimps
Assiette de crudités
French dressing
Mayonnaise
Boeuf en daube (cooked with beer)
Large mincepie

Board of English cheeses
Celery
Assorted crispbreads and biscuits
Drinks: Hot spiced wine; tawny port for the chesses

Tea
China tea with orange (for replete grown-ups)
The cake
Log cake (chocolate sponge mixture coated in softened chocolate
    keeps for a minimum of 10 days)
Victorian sand cake
Sponge rabbit
Tray of chocolate clowns
Nest of sugar mice
Jelly fishpond

Christmas Dinner
Germiny (rich soup with sorrel from garden or adaption with spinach)
Larded and barded turkey (otherwise flesh too dry for our palates)
Pommes amandines (potato cakes rolled in flaked almonds and fried)
Sou-fassum (Escoffier's cabbage ball)
Sausage baskets (stuffed chestnuts)
Forcemeat balls
Ham in puff pastry
Mushroom and pistachio stuffing
Madeira sauce
Lemon sorbet (to clear palates)
Round plum pudding with brandy butter
Edible chocolate boxes
French chocolate specialties
Traditional crystallised fruits, dessert and nuts
Coffee
Drinks: Champagne throughout dinner. This we regard as being the
only drink capable of standing up to the year's most indigestible meal.
Vintage port.

Boxing Day

Breakfast
Same as before – probably more black coffee!

Lunch
Terrine de ris de veau (gently reheated under foil in outer pan of water)
Jambon au cidre (slices in sauce from cider stock)
Riz au safran
Jacket potatoes
Salad
Board of English cheese
Beignets de Noël (small portions of cold Christmas pudding shaped into balls, dipped in raw egg, rolled in ground almonds, deep-fried, served dredged with sifted icing sugar and accompanied by brandy butter)

Buffet Supper
Burgundian snails
Turkey sliced and layered with pâté (treat portions as sandwiches and garnish on flat dish)
Cold spit-roasted sirloin with home-made chutney and pickles
La raclette
Chocolate box trifles and strawberry bavaroises

The Sunday

Breakfast
As before

Lunch
Whatever is left from the two buffets freshened and re-garnished

Supper
The end to messes – our family will be wanting plainer food so:
Stockpot soup
Cheesy-eggy-hammy topside
Grapefruit and orange salad

Our Chores

Here are the holiday cooking chores:

December 23: Scrape vegetables and set up basket of *crudités*. Make *boeuf en daube* to store in refrigerator. Bake mincepie in Victorian sponge tin. Sponge rabbit. Weigh out rice and saffron. Scrub potatoes for jacket roasting. Prepare forcemeat balls, dry ingredients. Start family stockpot with batch of beef bones. Cook ham in cider with sultanas and prunes, simmer liquor for ham sauce.

December 24: Bring stock to the boil and simmer for 20 minutes (adding turkey giblets). Grind coffee for all three days using fresh beans. Make and store in refrigerator grapefruit salads. Prepare celery. Set cheese on board, cover with foil and keep out of refrigerator.

Set out all ingredients for hot spiced wine. Make jelly fishpond. Make germiny and set in double pan for reheating. Stuff, bard and lard turkey, wrap in foil for roasting and make all trimmings for turkey.

Pudding into steamer with *sou-fassum*. Make Boxing Day cider sauce for ham and Christmas dinner Madeira sauce. Spit or oven roast sirloin. Assemble trifle.

December 25: Make breakfast croissants. Bring stock to the boil and simmer for 20 minutes. Steam pudding and *sou-fassum*.

Turkey, in foil, into oven, it takes care of itself. In last half hour before Christmas dinner when turkey is cooked and ready, rest it in foil out of oven so that flesh can settle. Slip in ham wrapped in leaf-think yeast dough brushed with egg wash.

Sauce over steamer to reheat gradually. Reheat all pre-pared turkey accompaniments in oven warming drawer.

December 26: Make breakfast croissants. Bring stock to the boil and simmer for 20 minutes. Slice ham and pour over sauce, cover with foil and reheat on oven for at half-time of baking jacket potatoes.

Make saffron rice and *beignets de Noël*. Slice up turkey with pâté, carcass into stock pot. Remove bone from remaining sirloin and put into stock pot. Set Swiss Tilsit to slow-melt for *la raclette*. Strain stock and leave to chill.

December 27: Make breakfast croissants. Make cheesy-eggy-hammy topsides. Remove fat crust from top of strained stock, reduce to half quantity by simmering, add a teacupful of medium dry sherry and serve piping hot.

1 September 1977
AUNT MEG'S CRUSTY FLOWER-POT LOAVES ARE A DELIGHT
Bon Viveur

Aunt Meg is so-called by adopted nephews, nieces by the score, a collection of young couples to whom like us she is no relation whatever. The young married perch on her kitchen units or lean on over the stable door through which the sun pours on to her big scrubbed wooden table.

Aunt Meg's concessions to modern cookery are an electric mixer which she bought after five years' persuasion. Already it is nose-out-of-joint by a French machine which she boasts chops, slices, shreds, minces, purees and also does all the mixer's job.

She also cherishes a collection of French knives and a freezer.

She stands four square at that kitchen table producing pies and flower pot loaves.

She regards pies as the prime answer to economy cooking. She cares nothing for their fattening qualities and is the shape of a cottage loaf herself. She insists that with assorted pies, a proper stockpot and a well stocked kitchen garden, she can cope with any price increases.

We were with her when the village fete was imminent and she had a dozen coming for luncheon and it was also bread-baking day.

We hitched up on to a spare unit space and were supplied with wedges of Aunt Meg's Treacle Tart and cups of her special Hot Drinking Chocolate.

We claim to have introduced her to the frozen puff paste she now uses but what she makes with it are her own. The results are special and based on a trip we took together into Gascony some years ago.

A Gascon specialty was Aunt Meg's inspiration for the Pâté Pie but her Country Pie is made with dripping paste using only vegetables and mousetrap cheese. She used Gruyère and Parmesan but now these are priced out of reach so she substitutes.

She is a great adapter of other folks' ideas. Hence Flower Pot Loaves baked in well-scoured earthenware flower pots and wonderfully crusty whether as Wholemeal Herby Loaves with garlic butter or, our favourite, Mixed Fruit Loaves with Aunt Meg's Spiced Butter.

For flower-pot cookery, choose earthenware pots 5in high, with base and top diameters 3½in and 5in. Scour, scrub, rinse and dry out in oven at 225°F, Gas ¼. Line each base to cover the hole with a double fold of aluminium foil cut to fit. Press in more foil completely to line out bringing the edges up over the rim and smoothing carefully. Brush with melted lard.

The Recipes

Flower-pot Bread

Use 21oz wholemeal flour, 3oz strong white flour, ½oz baker's yeast, ½oz soft brown sugar, 8 fl oz each of lukewarm milk and blood-heat water, 1.2oz salt, 1 rounded tbsp black treacle, 1 heaped tbsp milled fresh parsley, 1 rounded tbsp milled fresh thyme leaves, 1 flat dessert sp milled tarragon tips and 1 finely crushed garlic clove.

Method: Stir yeast with sugar until liquefied. Mix water and milk, then stir in warmed treacle and garlic paste. Put half the wholemeal and half the white flours into warmed earthenware crock, work in all herbs, make a well in centre, pour in yeast mix and all the mixed fluids.

Work up to obtain a very loose paste, then work in salt. Cover and prove in warm place for 15 minutes. Add remaining flours, mix thoroughly, turn on a floured surface and knead with heel of one hand for a minimum of 10 minutes.

Divide, and use to two-thirds fill each prepared pot. Cover and prove again until mixture is sufficiently risen to dome over pot tops.

Bake mid-shelf 425°F (Gas 7) for 5 minutes, then brush tops with milk and bake until breads give off hollow sound when rapped with knuckles. (Time approx. 18 minutes.)

To refresh your memory. Garlic butter is 4oz butter, 2 large peeled, or crushed garlic cloves and 1 flat tablespoon milled parley heads, all whipped together in an electric mixer.

Spiced Butter
Use 2oz butter, 3oz soft brown sugar, 1 flat eggspoon each of powdered cinnamon, cloves, nutmeg and ginger. Whip as for Garlic Butter.

Hot Drinking Chocolate
Use 1 heaped tablespoon sweetened drinking chocolate, 1 flat tablespoon ordinary cocoa, 1oz vanilla sugar or 1 split vanilla pod, 1 standard separated egg, 1 pint milk.

Method: Mix cocoa, chocolate, vanilla sugar and egg yolk with a very little of the cold milk. Heat remainder very slowly with vanilla pod, if used, bring to boil and pour on paste, stir well, then pour back and forth three times. Reheat to boiling, remove from heat and whisk in stiffly whipped egg white.

Taste and add more sugar if required. Stir well then pour into cups and run single cream or top of milk over back of a dessertspoon into each cup to form a cold 'lid' through which the hot chocolate is sipped.

Aunt Meg's Treacle Tart
Use 14oz bought frozen puff paste, 1 small tart apple, 2 generous tablespoons golden syrup, the grated rind and strained juice of 1 lemon, 1 dessertspoon soft brown sugar, 1 flat teaspoon each of ginger and cinnamon, 3oz sultanas, 3½oz roughly crumbled crustless bread, 1 tablespoon black treacle.

Method: Roll out puff paste until paper thin. Cut a 10½in circle and fit into a standard 9in flan dish or ring. Cut three 9in circles. Gather up the remnants and roll out to a fourth 9in circle. Brush base paste with melted butter, sift with icing sugar, cover with paste trimmings circle. Grate the unpeeled apple, mix with all remaining ingredients.

Fill into flan container. Cover with one of the three remaining 9in circles. Brush with melted butter, dust with sifted icing sugar, cover and repeat twice more.

Bake at 375°F (Gas 5) one shelf above centre until paste is risen in richly brown layers (approx. 30 minutes). Turn heat to 300°F (Gas 2) and allow a further 8–10 minutes. Serve hot or cold.

28 August 1963
FOR THE HOUSEWIFE WHO WANTS TO KNOW HOW TO COOK
Fanny and Johnnie Cradock

A great cap still exists between the recipes published in domestic cook books and the instruction on how to interpret them correctly. So many recipes, which have become standard usage more through endless repetition than genuine worth, are without benefit of the practical cookery tips and tricks which make work easy for beginners.

Consider this statement: Fried chicken should be crisp and dry outside but the sealed-in flesh must be moist, tender and only just cooked.

Guesswork won't help. Only a clairvoyant with an in-built X-ray equipment can *look* and know! Yet there is a simple way of achieving perfect results every time. Cook large chicken portions for two minutes in very hot olive oil which seethes violently when tested with a strip of raw potato. Turn off the heat and finish the cooking for a further 6½ minutes in the oil's diminishing heat.

For half portions (divided leg and thigh, or divided wing and breast) allow 1½ minutes with heat on and a further six minutes with heat off. This way the complex becomes absurdly simple, yet it is conspicuously absent from all the 2,000 cook books on our shelves.

When the bachelor in his flatlet fries himself some sausages, he obeys the dictum that does appear with monotonous regularity: 'Prick all over with a fork and grill or fry'. If the poor soul were told instead to sling the sausages (unpricked) into a greased baking tin and cook till browned at 358°F, gas mark 4 (turning them over after the first 12 minutes) he would be able to enjoy sausages which never burst.

The Englishman's favourite – a mixed grill – could include kidneys which were not leathery outside and bloody within if his cook book told him how the highly discriminating butchers of Les Halles laid down that the job must be done in the suet jackets they are tucked inside when taken from the carcass of the beast.

Set them in a dry, covered, heat-resistant container and cook in the oven at 379°F, gas mark 5, for 15–20 minutes for the lover of underdone flesh, 25–30 for the well-cooked meat brigade. Then either slice them

– the crisp fat is delicious – or detach them from their crispy envelopes.

Explosively crisp pork cracking is equally easy to come by – but we've courted astigmatism searching for the method between the covers of any book. Score the pork with a very sharp knife – far more closely and deeply than the average British butcher does, season liberally with salt and roast at a high temperature alongside the meat.

10 May 1973
PUTTING A 'WRONGED' CASSEROLE TO RIGHTS
Bon Viveur

Some years ago we were cooking on stage to an audience of about two thousand people, and Johnnie wore dark glasses because he had eye trouble at the time.

He slipped an omelette masked with meringue under the grill to brown and suddenly the audience began to laugh.

'It's beginning to brown nicely and won't be long now,' said the grill cook, blissfully unaware of the clouds of smoke, or the fact that the topping was already soot black! In moments, and by sliding a sharp knife under the blackened top crust (deposited in a waste bucket) and dusting the exposed, raw meringue thickly with sifted icing sugar, it was back re-grilling to a light golden brown – without benefit of dark glasses!

There are, in fact, quite a few ways in which disaster can be turned into success at speed.

Suppose everyone is waiting for a ready-to-serve casserole. On taking it from the oven, you find it looks more like a pond with submerged flotsam and jetsam than a thickly sauced pot of tender meat, game or poultry.

This can be put right faster than it takes to explain. Always keep a packet of potato flour on your dry goods shelf. Put one rounded dessertspoonful of this into a little bowl, stir to a paste with cold water and stir in gradually to the too-thin sauce. In seconds this will thicken without taste, and without density or lumps.

The packets are labelled 'Potato Flour' and you should be able to obtain some at any good old-fashioned grocer.

Curdled mayonnaise is another familiar disaster if one can judge from the letters we have received.

If it ever happens to you, turn the separated wreck into a jug. Put an egg yolk into a small bowl and whip it like mad until it is thick and creamy. Beat in drips of the ruined mayonnaise very gradually: you will find that if you begin very slowly the mixture will 'take' and begin to thicken. After this you can increase the flow – whipping all the time.

Then there is the equally familiar 'accident' which arises about this time of year when you are fishing out the last bottle or two of some kind of preserved fruit. You open it up, turn the contents into a dish and look depressingly at the pieces of fruit floating in a lot of slightly sweet, slightly fruit-flavoured liquid. The fruit has over-contracted, of course, and you have not packed your jars tightly enough with it, so have added too much under-sweetened fluid.

Take a much larger pan than is necessary and strain the fruit fluid into it. Put it on over full heat so that it boils high without boiling over, and let it go on boiling until the large quantity of mediocre fluid has reduced sufficiently (by bubbling) to turn itself into a smaller, proportional to fruit, amount of well-flavoured syrup. (Add more sugar if still needed.)

Then there is the 'friends-to-tea' disaster. You have baked a cake – you have, of course, used the recipe before, so you know it works. But unaccountably, and with little time left, you find your cooled-on-a-rack cake has sunk right down the middle!

Cut out the soggy centre completely taking a little more than you really need so that you can crumble up the outside of the removed centre and mix the crumbs with coffee syrup and coffee butter cream for a coffee cake: chocolate for a chocolate one; desiccated coconut, cake crumbs and a little jam (to a really firm paste) for a plain cake mixture; or, if you can run to it, a quickly-made bit of almond paste with a few glace cherries and snippings of nuts or angelica folded in. Pile chosen mixture into the centre.

Finally, to disguise all, dust cake top with sifted icing sugar, or ice it if this is what you intended in the first place.

Next time you find yourself landed with those very floury old potatoes which collapse into a sad mush because you have inadvertently boiled instead of steaming them, grin and turn the mess into a sieve and drain. Then run the end (floppy) product through the sieve into a saucepan. Put this over a low heat and stir with a wooden spoon. The heat will dry out the moisture and after a time you will find the mixture becomes stiff and pasty. Season with salt and pepper to taste, stir in a nut of butter and give a thorough beating.

You will thus obtain some very nice, creamy, poor man's Duchess Potatoes. If you can spare an egg yolk and beat that in too – off the heat – you will achieve the real thing.

Now let us pretend you have made a beef steak and kidney, pastry-covered meat pie in a pie dish. You open the oven door and see that to your horror you have put in too much sloppy fluid and this has oozed under and is steadily sogging the only partially cooked pastry.

Take the pie out and stand it on a working surface. Run a sharp knife all round the pastry lid and then, with the aid of two metal slices, lift off on to a baking sheet.

Then put it back in the oven to finish cooking, dry out and become a crisp, baked pastry crust, whereby you give the pond-fluid surrounding the meat the potato-flour treatment we explained.

Make-Believe Menus

19 February 1961
DON'T LET THE WAITERS BULLY YOU
Egon Ronay

It is preposterous that so many headwaiters and waiters in this county should be such bullies to the unknown diner.

Whether they are Greek, Italian, French or English, I, for one, do not intend to let them get away with it. As you will see in this column from time to time.

Take the case of an otherwise excellent Chelsea restaurant, which a colleague of mine and his wife visited for dinner recently. There were numerous unoccupied tables but he was shown to the worst table near the lift. Not being one to stand for any nonsense, he insisted on, and got, 'a wall table'. (He has an excellent dinner, and, from then on, extremely efficient service.)

The lesson is simple: don't be hoodwinked by the excuse of 'reservations', but insist, imperturbably, on the table you want. They invariably find a way.

This sort of treatment will not occur if you are well known, as are members of eating clubs. Many such clubs have been brought about by our present licensing laws; a few good ones prefer to stay clubs to keep their clientele homogenous. You have to sign a membership application

48 hours before your first visit to the club, but there should be no difficult in joining the three I suggest here.

It is not just because of the exceptionally likeable personality of Eddie Clark, ex-king of bartenders, that I recommend his Albermarle Club (25, Albermarle Street, W.1). He has a knack of making people feel at home in his well kept, pleasant bar and restaurant which – like the owner himself – strike a happy balance between informality and respectability.

Both are English and more elaborate dishes are prepared with a feeling for flavour, but I would prefer to see more red Bordeaux and Burgundies older than 1955 on the medium-priced list. A useful address for after-theatre suppers.

One gn p.a. Noon–3.30 p.m., 6 p.m.–midnight: closed Sat. and Sun. 30–35s with wine.

Six guineas will seem a very high membership fee at the Walbrook River Club (Cousin Lane, City, E.C.4). But there is no eating place more typical of London. (Country membership is 2 gns.) There is a paradoxical feeling of romance about the proximity of the Cannon Street railway bridge, and you can almost touch the river from the wall-size windows. A pity it is only open for lunch. The food, mainly of grills and roasts, is very good and not too highly priced.

I cannot say the same of the wines. No one is justified in charging 29s 6d for a fresh *Niersteiner*, and carafe wines could easily be less than 21s. Lunch only, noon–3.30 p.m. Closed Saturday and Sunday. Approx. 25s without wine.

One wines and dines in the lap of luxury at the ornate and comfortable White Elephant Club (28 Curzon Street, W.1), a blend of New York's '21 Room', Maxim's of Paris and the Café Royal of Oscar Wilde's day. The Franco-Italian cuisine and service excels and you can order supper up to 1 a.m. I am only sorry that the wine list isn't more elaborate in selection and presentation.

Londoners 3 gns, country members 2gns p.a. noon–12.45 p.m., 7 p.m.–2 a.m.; closed lunch Saturday, whole day Sunday. Set lunch 15s 6d, à la carte meal 30s.

15 January 1929
HOW TO READ THE
RESTAURANT MENU
Mary Evelyn

Of late years French menus have become more and more difficult to understand on account of the fanciful and far-fetched names given to dishes by many chefs. It is only fair to add that master chefs who combine scholarly learning with super-excellent technique disapprove of this practice. They argue that the object of a menu is to let people know what to expect, and that it fails when this is not achieved.

As a matter of fact, it requires a certain culinary, literary, and social sophistication to understand even the names of some dishes included in classic cookery. A dish may be named after its method of preparation, its principal ingredient, the particular sauce or garnish used, a place, person, dynasty, or occasion, or after some leading characteristic.

A study of the names of French dishes is interesting and worth while in these days when the French cuisine (or at least the menu written in French) is met with so frequently at home and abroad. Most of us know that Béchamel is a white sauce named after the maître d'hôtel (Lord Steward of the Household) of Louis XIV, but how many of us would understand all the following menu?

Potage à la Mèdicis
Filets de Sole Vénitienne
Noistettés de Veau à la Villeroi
Faisan à la Périgueux
Salada Chicorée
Soufflé à la Royale

All these are classic dishes, and have a certain family resemblance throughout the ages, although their details may vary slightly according to the fashion of the moment or the genius of a Dubois, Escoffier, or Cédard.

Potage à la Mèdicis is always a game and tomato soup, with macaroni frequently served with grated Parmesan.

 263

Sole Vénitienne has its name because it is finished with Sauce Vénitienne, and this according to Dubois and Escoffier is made of white wine and vinegar in equal quantities, and herbs, with, of course, a few other ingredients. For the rest, the fish is poached, and as a rule garnished with potatoes.

Noistettés de Veau à la Villeroi – Escoffier tells us noisettes cut from the fillet, especially those of mutton or lamb, make one of the choicest entrées. They differ from cutlets in being served on a croûte, and in the case of Noisettes de Veau à la Villeroi included by Dubois in his Cuisine Classique they are first braised, and masked with a sauce Villeroi, allowed to get cold, then egged and breadcrumbed, fried, garnished with petits pois à l'Anglaise, and accompanied by a Sauce Allemande.

Faisan à *la Périgueux* obviously a truffled dish, easily recognised because everyone knows the association between Périgord and truffles. The pheasant, as a matter of fact, is not only stuffed with truffles, it is accompanied by a Périgueux sauce made of truffles cooked in sauterne, blended with a brown or Epagnole sauce.

The *chicorée*, of which the salad is composed, it is well to remember, is the blanched green salading we call endive, not the white Belgian chicory that resembles seakale in appearance.

Soufflé à la Royale sometimes appears as a baked and sometimes as a steamed soufflé. Escoffier bakes it in a proper dish, and makes it of layers of soufflé mixture and crushed ladies' fingers soaked in kirsch sprinkled with chopped fruit, also soaked in kirsch. Dubois steams it, garnishes it in his own special way, and turns it out.

22 September 1966
WHY CAN'T A MENU SAY WHAT IT MEANS?
Gretel Beer

'Fresh butter beans in cream sauce,' said the menu. The restaurant was fairly small and surrounded by deep country. The season was right and I was mentally praising the owner for growing and serving country-fresh vegetables.

Alas, too soon. The butter beans were quick-frozen (could it be that 'fresh' really meant 'fresh from the packet'?) and 'cream sauce' was but another name for the well known paperhanger's concoction tasting faintly of margarine.

It seems strange that when the laws concerning the labelling of packet and canned food are getting stricter all the time, the 'poetic licence' granted restaurant owners appears to be unlimited. A swift survey of menu descriptions generally has convinced me that new thinking and possibly new laws are more than somewhat overdue.

Firstly, there are the totally misleading descriptions such as the word 'fresh'. I have nothing against quick-frozen foods, but I do object to them being described as 'fresh' on the menu.

The description of peas on a menu practically requires an interpreter. 'Fresh garden peas' usually means quick-frozen peas. 'Garden peas' means tinned but not processed peas. Just 'peas' more often than not refers to processed tinned peas.

Until such time when restaurants either supply an interpreter with their menus or print an explanation note on the side, I think 'fresh' should mean exactly that. And since 'garden' in connection with peas makes little sense – perhaps it could be dropped altogether?

More or less the same applies to the words 'home-made', 'country-style' or 'Auntie X's' when applied to similar brands of dehydrated soup. 'Home-made' (to me at least) means *cooked* not *reconstituted* in a kitchen and until I'm introduced to 'Auntie X' I'll doubt her existence.

Secondly, I think that a revision of certain terms which have now become obsolete is more than overdue. I'm referring to items like 'surrey chicken', 'Norfolk turkey' and 'Aylesbury duckling'.

Most of them are down-right untrue anyhow – if all the chickens described as Surrey actually came from there, traffic in Surrey would be at a standstill.

Under present conditions surely it is far more important to know whether a chicken is battery bred or free-run? Who cares where it comes from?

Thirdly, there is the 'poetic' language employed by some menu writers. 'A rich profusion of delectable cold cut meats' turned out to be a platter piled high with masses of greenery (which kept slipping on to my lap) covering one slice of pressed ham, a slice of very dry salami, a small piece of chicken, smoked cod's roe and a slice of tongue.

I discussed this with Peter Evans of Easting House fame, whose restaurants supply whatever the menus promise (I'll forgive him his one and only lapse of 'morning-gathered mushrooms').

'On the whole I agree with you,' he said, adding a few salient points about the mis-use of the term Scotch beef, 'but would you mind over-elaborated descriptions if the food lived up to them?'

No, but I still do not like the feeling that someone has spent a lot of time, money or thought on dreaming up these descriptions. I'd rather see it spent on ingredients or staff, or simply thinking beautiful thoughts about improving the food.

'You're wrong,' said Anthony Petty, editor of *Hotel and Restaurant Management*. 'A menu is a sales vehicle and as such it should have drama.'

Sad as it is, I've found that if there is drama in the menu there is always, but always, tragedy in the food.

22 January 1916
WAITERS AND COOKS

In the day-dreams that even the most practical woman sometimes permits herself, she sees that ideal domestic staff she would like to have. It may include the replica of someone's perfect nurse for the children, of the peerless housemaid of another, and the dignified personality of the butler of some great house. For the footman and butler of the county family, for instance, are types of a branch of service essentially English. They fulfil their duties with the assurance that they are doing them in the right way, and there is nothing of the servile and obsequious characteristic of the Austrian, for example, who, up to a year and a half ago, loomed so large in our hotels.

But the opportunities for the English lad to train himself for private or hotel service were up to about three years ago, not easy to find. On the large country estate a boy generally was able to enter the house, the stables, or the gardens as his tastes suggested. The outsider, however, had few such possibilities before him, and the hotel in the market town was almost the only door by which he could hope to earn a useful and a well-paid vocation. For the London lad there might once in a way be some chance in a restaurant, but the foreign manager preferred his own people, and the youthful British might serve for the dirty drudging work, without any encouragement to rise to better things.

There is a pleasant experience before anyone who is fortunate enough to receive an invitation to lunch at the Westminster Technical Institute, Vincent-square. For there you may realise how the London County Council has been able to utilise three classes of their students to the mutual advantage of all. If boys are being trained as the future chefs of hotels, restaurants, and clubs the value of their instruction is enhanced enormously if the dishes they are preparing are those that might appear in any well-planned menu. The lads who are learning to be waiters get a far more practical insight into the work they will have to perform when they move between the kitchen and the guests actually ordering what they want. And the students who are the equivalents of the latter at hotel or private house are the young ladies who are having their art education under the same roof, and who are able thus to enjoy far more dainty meals at nominal cost than falls to the lot of the majority. Thus, there is a co-ordination of interests of very exceptional order.

The school is directed by a very practical committee, appointed by the County Council, while Mr Iwan Kriens is the chief instructor in cooking. It takes three years' training to turn out a young fellow as a proficient cook. The roll of honour claims the names of at least two past students, while others are rendering good services at the front in cooking for staff and officers' recesses. In the perfectly-appointed kitchens are the three groups, each representing its stage of training. 'What is the first lesson to which you put your chef-in-embryo?' is an obvious question, and the rather unexpected reply is, 'To peel a potato.' There are right ways and wrong ways to perform this elementary task, and it is, perhaps, a new idea of the importance of detail that dawns upon you when the information is vouchsafed that, for the first three months of their training, the lads touch nothing except vegetables, until they can present every item as it will be wanted as any accessory to a casserole stew, as garnishing, or for some special dish.

Then onwards are the simpler soups, the boiled fish and meat, the elements of frying and the making of pastry. Each term should see the lad advancing, but some of course show a much greater aptitude for learning than others. Indeed, if five out of the fifteen who come in every term prove to have the instincts which will make a good cook, it is considered a good proportion. Those who manifest this ability are taught in the last year the difficult arts of the calling which will help them when they enter upon high-class work. As most of them will go to hotels or restaurants, great emphasis is also placed on the accurate keeping of their lists of stores and supplied, as well as of exercising rigid economy.

A bright and intelligent company of lads in black coats with the ortho-dox shirt-front and tie and the white apron of the French garçon are learning how to wait. They come forward to take the umbrella of the lady guest or the stick and hat of the man alertly, and offer the menu for selec-tion in excellent style. You choose your fish, your meat, and your sweet, and in a very short time the first, with its accompanying sauce, is brought up. But meantime at the service table below the order has been checked and the lad given his slip of paper exactly as he would have it at a well-ordered restaurant. The habit will be learned before he seeks a situation in such an establishment, and will give him a repute for quickness that will stand him in good stead. He will also learn how to make out and present the bill.

But the duties of restaurant waiter or private footman are not confined to the serving of the meals. There is the cleaning of the silver, the care of the tablecloths and serviettes, the laying of the tables, and all this is equally thoroughly taught. The school attends to all these matters, and its pantry, china cupboards, and linen presses are important features of its equipment. All this has been, in the past, knowledge picked up at haphazard, and the only wonder is that it has been acquired at all.

That there will be a greater demand for such qualified service after the way no one at all competent to speak had any doubt whatever. We shall have to economise in the matter of personal attendance, and the flat, with its central kitchen and organised staff intelligently directed, will supersede many of our more antiquated domestic methods. Women are recognising this fact, and are preparing themselves to meet new condi-tions. But in men's clubs and blocks of bachelors' chambers, as well as in hotels and even large private houses, there will still be place for a percent-age of male direction. It is well, therefore, that English boys should be efficiently trained to secure the good posts and the good wages that special qualifications can always command.

3 May 1957
WHY NO BRITISH MICHELIN?
Egon Ronay

At the Michelin headquarters, an unpretentious grey building in a prosaic part of Paris, I was shown the files of 10,000 hotels and restaurants. From these I soon learnt that it is easier for a camel to go through a needle's eye than for a restaurant to be included in the illustrious company of the 11 three-star, 55 two-star and 600 one-star establishments in France.

The methods of the secret police of gastronomy interested me. Twelve inspectors, called 'tourist attachés', have to be men of general good taste with a liking and knowledge of good food and wine, judgment perfected by years of training and they must, above all, have absolute integrity. They are not chosen from among chefs.

The ones I met, intelligent, alert men, had formed interesting conclusions on the French travelling public and tourists. They find that as car-ownership spreads among all classes, SAUCES become less important, SOLID MEAT dishes more so, LESS TIME is spent on eating and GRILLS are consequently popular. Young French people are more interested in food and wine than their parents were at their age. This is true in Britain, too.

I handled the first *Michelin Guide*, a thin little book published in 1900. This year's plump edition is called the 'guide to reasonable bills' and has a separate section of maps of places where the bill will not exceed 750 francs (about 15s) including wine, coffee and tips.

Apparently 70,000 pieces of information are sent in yearly by guide-holders. These are expertly checked. British tourists, I learnt, show accuracy and understanding in their assessments (which doesn't strengthen the anti-guide case of big British organisations).

The next day I accompanied Monsieur T..., one of the 12 Michelin inspectors in search of a star. The restaurant in question (he asked me not to divulge the name) has been asking to be awarded a star for a long time. Its chef-owner is a member of a well-known family of caterers. Reports were not convincing enough, so we lunched there.

As we walked in, without booking, my restaurateur's heart wished the proprietor knew how important the next two hours were to be.

The room was pleasant and the waitresses wore regional costume. The menu offered a wide choice though no wine list was presented, just offered verbally, in spite of the interest we had shown. A bad point we thought.

My eggs in aspic were quite good, but did not show finesse and my companion was understandably not impressed with his hors d'oeuvre. It was much tastier (we both tasted each dish), but less varied than an average one in Britain. Alas, one of our main dishes, though the specialty of the house, was the restaurant's downfall: it was judged too rich and heavy for my French friend and its showy (flambé) presentation made him think that the show, not the cooking, had preference.

The wines recommended by the maître d'hôtel were too ordinary. The coffee was good but it couldn't change our minds. Our impression was confirmed by 'tired' silver ('ça a l'*air fatigue*' he said of the fork) and by a certain lack of ventilation. (Some of our official guide-book compilers please note that we had not examined the plumbing before forming our judgment on the cuisine.) Monsieur T . . . did his best, by 'ça manquait quelquechose', he said, with a typical Gallic shrug of his shoulders, as we parted. The restaurant proved unworthy of the coveted star.

The British public wants reliable guidance for Britain. Why is it then that the motoring organisations (though this year they show a little more promise), the Tourist Board, and the big public companies concerned are doing nothing about this question? Is it because their very able executives, reared on public school food, care little about good food themselves? So the British public gets blamed for their own lack of interest. This saves them taking the plunge.

Is there really no interest in Britain? Aren't there good restaurants to discover? Is the anaemic collection of books on restaurants adequate? In my second report the scene moves to Britain.

17 November 1965

THE HILTON HOTEL

I entered that great Aunt Sally of the catering world – The Hilton Hotel – with my breast bursting with tidings, if you follow my meaning.

Do you know, said I, that Mr Egon Ronay has demoted you in his latest hotels guide?

You are out of the First Division. Out of the De Luxe class.

Into Grade I, rubbing shoulders with mere places like the Ritz.

It is all there in the *Egon Ronay-BMC 1966 Guide*, out tomorrow. 'Service, particularly at the reception desk, is haphazard and unworthy of such a place,' it says.

('It is in fact diabolical,' Mr Ronay told me personally. 'I twice asked for someone I knew who was staying at the hotel and was told they weren't there. And I once delivered a parcel for someone staying there which never got to them. He had to ring up and ask for it before it arrived.')

And how did the Hilton react? 'I am afraid I have no comment to make,' said Mr Nicholas Behard, of their front office management, 'Everyone can form their own opinions about an hotel. We think we are in the top class.

'We started a new concept in the hotel business in Europe. We have difficulties. So did the people who opened the Savoy. Now it's a institution...'

For a man with no comment he was doing all right.

In fact, the poor old Hilton is fairly upset about it. It's not so much being put down that hurts it's the fact that it is now junior to that upstart Carlton Tower and that old Granny Grosvenor House.

The Hilton people feel they have got a friendly hotel which isn't so stuffy that it frightens every guest out of his wits and which offers every comfort anyone could wish (at prices ranging from 252s for a double a night upwards – a long way upwards).

'The rooms, too are not up to standard. Not tatty. But the newness is wearing off,' adds Mr Ronay.

'We are due for our end-of-season clean-up,' said the hotel.

If it is any comfort to Conrad Hilton and his boys, Mr Ronay's 25s Four Square Book (published in association with The New English Library – came apart from its binding after it had been in my gentle hands for two hours 35 minutes.

Spam and Fake Eggs

HOME COOK MOCK FOIE GRAS
Recipe from *Good Eating* (1944)
The *Daily Telegraph* Home Cook

4 oz cooked liver (ox liver will do if well cooked, or liver sausage);
2 rashers fat bacon;
1 dessertspoonful grated onion;
1½oz margarine or beef dripping;
Few sliced dates or raisins;
Sprinkling of cayenne;
Dry mustard, salt

Mince liver and bacon twice. Cook onion in fat, add minced mixture and sliced fruit, sprinkling with seasoning. Bring gently to boiling point and pot.

Ann Gore Davids, 27 Upper Montagu Street, W.1.

4 December 1944
WHERE THE FOOD GOES

To the Editor of the *Daily Telegraph*

SIR – I was proud to read the statistics just published relating to the splendid war effort of the people of the United Kingdom, but as a housewife I have to smile at the figures in Table 25 of the White Paper 'Civilian Consumption of Principal Foodstuffs'.

Even taking into consideration the footnote that 'the figures include food used in catering establishments and quantities for food manufacture...and for this reason are greater than the domestic ration' – I am amazed to learn that in 1943, according to this report, I consumed 4.32 pints of liquid milk per week and 20oz of sugar! An average of 2–3 pints of milk per week and 8oz sugar are the cold facts!

In view of the fact that we cannot all take our meals away from home, one is tempted to ask, 'Could a little less go to catering establishments and a little more to the housewife?'

Yours truly,

Housewife, Sevenoaks

3 July 1955

MISTRESS, WHAT D'YE LACK?
Rt Hon. Walter Elliot M.P.

The end of rationing tomorrow is a fade-out, not a black-out. It is a decisive but not a dramatic event. It is, in fact, the culmination of a process which has now continued over many months, indeed over years. That is exactly what makes it important.

This is not a step which is going to be reversed. The huge machine of rationing has now been dismantled. It can scarcely be set up again in our time, short of another war.

This is an event of both national and international importance. One of the great markets of the world has reopened its gates.

There are risks, of course, as well as advantage in such an operation. But our economy lives by risk. When we move away from the meticulous measurements and apportionments of the war and the post-war years we move towards our own tradition.

That is why, paradoxically, all these red-tape entanglements will be so soon forgotten. Do not let us expect gratitude for this act. Within a few months, rationing will seem as though it had never been.

 273

The end of rationing now had come about from two causes. First there is the improvement in supplies throughout the world. Secondly there is the renewed strength of our currency making it possible for us to draw on these supplies.

Each of these causes has developed more rapidly in recent months than seemed at one time possible. The combination of both has brought about a situation in which the difficulty would be not to take rationing off but to keep it on.

The recovery of the world's supplies has been spectacular. We are, of course, well acquainted with the enormous crops of grain which have been and are being won in the United States and Canada – so great that the stores are bulging and running over, and men are beginning to stack wheat in the streets.

But the Old World is also bringing forward massive food contributions. The skilled and industrious populations of Europe were expected to recover and surpass their pre-war productions, given a few years to make up for the wastage of war. But the Asian countries are also making a great and unlooked for effort.

India, for example, is a land where famine is, if not chronic, at any rate recurrent. Her last famine was as recent as 1951. Yet she has now completely abolished the rationing of rice and wheat.

India is even considering the resumption of her pre-war export of high quality rice. She is still importing rice from Burma, but only to build up a reserve, and not for immediate needs.

Her production picture shows a sound position. Rice tonnage in 1952–3 was 22½m tons. In 1953–4 it is estimated at 27m tons. Wheat, which was 6,380,000 tons in 1952–3, is estimated at 6,890,000 tons for 1953–4.

There is behind this, of course, the spectre of India's extra 4m mouths a year. But, for the time being, this has been conjured away.

These are not in any way academic figures so far as we in Britain are concerned. In 1951 India imported 3m tons of wheat. This year, so far, less than 10,000 tons of wheat has been imported by her. The repercussion of this rapid drop in demand, upon the world market, may be seen in the spectacular fall of North American export wheat prices, and the immediate journey across the world of the Australian wheat representatives.

It is impossible to circumscribe and limit the access of the British housewife to markets which are being supplied on such a scale. For remember, behind the world's wheat crop stands the world's maize crop. A surplus of bread grains means, at no great remove, a surplus of coarse grains.

Coarse grains are stock-feed. A lavish supply of coarse grains means, sooner or later, and sooner rather than later, an increased supply of live-stock and live-stock products, into which they are converted.

It might be thought incredible, but it is true, that even in the face of such a situation some still hanker after the days of ration-books and scarcity. Socialist ex-Ministers of Food, such as Mr Maurice Webb and Mr Strachey, have deplored the steps towards de-control which were being taken, and have prophesied the rapid re-establishment of controls if Socialism were again returned to power.

'Drastic economic controls' would again be necessary, said Mr Strachey. One can scarcely avoid the conclusion that, to the Socialist, controls are not the means to an end. They are themselves an end, a good thing.

As with the ending of the Defence of the Realm regulations, this step cannot simply be cancelled. A whole cycle of legislation, organisa-tion, administration would need to be gone through before it could be begun again. Here is a strong guarantee against the march inland of the restrictionists.

Meanwhile, let us remember, and marvel at, the great risks that were run, the hardships that were undergone, the narrow margins by which we won past. Rationing was imposed in the Second World War; not towards the very end of the war, a last resort, as in 1917, but right at the start, by a sadder and a wiser nation, knowing that long tough struggle was ahead, and determined to see the thing through.

The coupons began with sugar; but before we saw the last of them they had extended even to our daily bread. Rationing was a necessary evil. But for all that, an evil.

We saw it all through together, in a country which, on the whole used the black market less, and accepted evils more cheerily, than any country in Europe.

But not for worlds – certainly not for Socialist worlds – would we go that way again. 'Skin for skin,' say the Scriptures, 'all that a man hath he will give for his life.'

For his life, yes. But to start open-eyed down that path, for the whim of some bureaucrat, or in pursuit of some shadow of social reform – perish the thought!

The housewife of Britain swings her shopping basket across her arm. In its time, it has bridged seas and moved mountains. Let the world attend. She is going out to fill it again.

8 May 1915
FARE FOR CONVALESCENTS

Feeding is of first importance when the sick reach the convalescent stage. Proper food has as much to do with the return to normal health, as careful nursing. There are so many different types of patient that the fare required must be specified by the doctors in charge. Common sense, however, and a knowledge of methods of handling ingredients go a long way towards providing the actual dishes from amongst the materials broadly indicated. Where there is question, for instance, of milk fare it is strange, but true, that there are people who cannot make an appetising dish of milk porridge, a rice pudding, or a bowl of arrowroot, smooth and of the right consistency.

Patients recovering from enteric or typhoid are most difficult to feed up. Surgical cases and instances of men suffering from shock require different treatment. A man getting over a mere wound or an amputation and progressing favourably can eat almost anything, and makes a healthy demand for good food. Undue haste in meeting these demands must be guarded against, but, even with strict adherence to the doctor's instructions, there is reasonable choice that will permit of a varied, attractive, and nourishing diet. Patients who have got over the fever stage may, probably, have bread and milk, arrowroot, or corn-flour, with milk, rice, tapioca, or semolina sometimes in the form of a pudding. All these must be daintily served as well as properly made. When convalescence has definitely set in almost any easily digested food is allowed, and here intelligence is wanted for the proper selection from such delicacies as raw or cooked, fish boiled, steamed, or chickens boiled or roasted, sweetbreads, eggs as omelets, scrambled or served with minced chicken, or boiled soft and eaten with thin bread and butter.

At a later stage calves' brains and feet are suitable, then sheep's tongue cooked fresh, and tripe. With these may be given milk puddings and stewed fruit with custards boiled or baked. Vegetables require due selection. The most delicate are asparagus, cauliflower, and marrow. Mashed potatoes may be eaten when the early variety would be disastrous. French beans come on in due course; then braised celery.

The suggested day's regimen and the recipes are from Mr C. Herman Senn.

Regimen for Convalescent

Breakfast – Grilled fish, a slice of buttered toast, a small cup of coffee or cocoa with plenty of hot milk.

During the morning – A cup of beef tea or an egg beaten up with milk.

Luncheon – A plate of vegetable purée, chicken omelet, bread, butter, and small piece of cream cheese.

Afternoon – A cup of hot milk diluted with a little hot water, a few crisp biscuits.

Evening meal – Minced beef or chicken with vermicelli, or a grilled cutlet, underdone; stewed prunes, boiled or baked custard, a cup of weak tea or coffee with milk.

Grilled Sole

Procure a fairly thick sole, weighing about 10oz or 12oz, trim off the fins and head, and remove both skins (the black and the white); then wipe the fish with a clean damp cloth. Next, season sparingly with salt and very little pepper, brush over both sides with melted butter, or, better still, with pure olive oil. Place the fish on a preciously cleaned and greased grill and broil over or in front of a clear fire. Allow about five or six minutes for each side to cook. When done place the sole on a hot dish, put a small pat of parsley butter or plain butter on top. Garnish with slices of lemon and a few springs of fresh parsley, and serve hot. Note: Whiting, a slice of cod, or salmon can be cooked in the same way. The time required for grilling depends largely upon the thickness of the fish. Parsley butter is made by mixing a pat of fresh butter with a small teaspoonful of finely-chopped parsley and a little lemon juice. Knead it well, and make up into an oblong roll, then place it on top of the grilled fish.

Chicken Omelet

Take about 4oz of cold chicken (boiled or roast), free from skin, bones and gristle, and cut the meat into very fine shreds or dice; put this into a saucepan with a tablespoonful of white sauce, season to taste with salt, pepper and a grate of nutmeg, then heat up the mixture and keep hot till required. Next make a plain omelet. Break three fresh eggs into a basin, add a small pinch of salt, a tiny pinch of white pepper, a small tablespoonful of cream or milk, and beat up thoroughly. Melt rather more than half an ounce of butter in a clean omelet pan, when hot pour in the egg mixture, then stir over the fire with a fork or spoon, shaking the contents of the pan at the same time. As the mixture begins to set, shape the omelet on the outward side of the pan, put the chicken mixture in the centre of the omelet, fold in the ends and let the omelet take colour; then turn it out quickly on to a hot dish or plate, and serve at once. Note: A finely-chopped, peeled shallot may be added if liked, but this should be fried a little with the butter before the egg mixture is put in the pan. Onion or shallot is generally allowed to a convalescent patient.

Minced Beef With Vermicelli

Mince finely by chopping or pass through a mincing machine about half a pound of cold beef. Cook 2oz of vermicelli in boiling salted water for about five minutes, drain, put in a saucepan with a little butter and gravy, and keep hot. Heat up a quarter of a pint of well-flavoured and seasoned tomato sauce in a stewpan, put in the minced beef, season carefully with salt and pepper, and heat up thoroughly. Range the vermicelli in the form of a border on a round dish, and put the cooked meat neatly in the centre. Garnish the dish with snippets of toasted or fried bread, and serve hot.

26 February 1916

SUBSTITUTES FOR SUGAR

Sugar has been a cheap commodity in the household for so many years that the housewife has never had to realise that it is not the only sweetening she can use in the cooking process. Prices have risen now and there is the possibility of a shortage in supplies, so a modification, at least, in the expenditure on sweets must be made, and the free hand with the sugar bowl must be controlled. Sweetening is best done during the cooking of food.

Children will undoubtedly get less in the way of cheap sweetmeats now that prices are likely to be much higher, and as a mere matter of diet they will require more food that appeals to the palate and yields the regulation amount of heat. There are many alternatives, such as honey, syrups, glucose, starch sugar, and saccharine, which is 100 times as sweet as sugar. Many know the value of dried fruit – figs, apricots, prunes, and dates, and they are often introduced into puddings or cakes when, as a matter of course, less sugar is added. The value of bananas must also be noted. Few, however, understand the properties of malted wheat, rye, and some vegetables, including parsnips, yams, onions, Jerusalem artichokes, and beetroots. There was a demand in the household at one time for glucose for jam making, and it was useful when mixed with sucrose. It will not crystallise, and it does not ferment.

Sweet potatoes made into scones do not require to be treated with sugar, and a very appetising tart can be made with Jerusalem artichokes, into which only a little sugar need be introduced. Dates shredded and cooked in a rice pudding reduce the amount of sugar by half, and similar results are got by any dried fruit. This suggestion may not look like strict economy at the first glance, but a reduction of an expensive and scarce commodity is essential, while the palatable and nourishing value of the dish is increased.

Parsnip Cake
Cakes are quickly coming to be looked upon as luxurious fare, but a simple little recipe for a parsnip cake might be tried:

Take 8oz of prepared flour, 8oz to 4oz of fat, 1oz of syrup, 5oz to 6oz of finely-grated parsnips, and one banana cut into small dice, a pinch of salt, and a little ginger or other spice, and treat in the usual way, when a palatable and nourishing cake will turn out.

Onion Cake
This vegetable is not so acceptable in England as it is in many other countries, and a cake made of it will, perhaps, not be met with the same enthusiasm as in Switzerland. Experts declare that when an onion has been boiled and the water drained off it loses just the properties frequently

looked upon as objectionable, and a very decided sweet taste remains. The recipe is as follows:

Line a tin plate with short crust, prick the bottom. Boil two shredded onions in water for five minutes, drain the water off, and stew in 2oz of fat till tender; add an equal amount of breadcrumbs and half a pint of milk, a pinch of salt and sugar, and one or two eggs well beaten. Mix all together, fill the crust with the mixture, and bake. Any flavouring can be added according to taste, such as cinnamon, vanilla, lemon, or ginger.

A sudden change to cold weather brings the need for a few little dishes made of simple materials, but tasty and heat producing. The recipe for mulligatawny soup is easily managed:

Fry ½lb onion in 2oz fat, when brown add ¼oz curry powder, fry; then add 1oz curry paste and 2oz rice, cover with stock, and cook till done (one hour). Strain the soup, season to taste, and serve with ½oz of rice cooked in water or stock, and, if available, a few pieces of rabbit cut in dice.

Sugar and Spice

29 September 1992
A SLIVER OF EDAM WITH YOUR DUCHY?
Oliver Pritchett

I can't wait to get my teeth into a Duchy Original biscuit. These, as reported in this newspaper yesterday, are made from oats harvested on the Duchy of Cornwall Home Farm next to Highgrove, and are shortly to be marketed as part of a scheme instigated by the Prince of Wales. These biscuits will be sold through selected outlets and will come in discreetly designed packaging made of recycled paper. Profits from this admirable operation will go to charity.

Having taken soundings among Royal-watchers and palace insiders, I gather that people will not be required to remain standing while eating the Royal biscuit. All the same, we will be expected to exercise good judgment; it wouldn't do for an architect to enjoy a Duchy Original bicky with his mug of Gold Blend for elevenses at his drawing board while he takes a short break from designing an unsightly multi-storey car park. Equally, it would hardly be appropriate to eat one of these biscuits after scoffing a sandwich made with white bread, incorrect netted tuna and non-organic lettuce.

I imagine them being served at refined coffee mornings.

'Oh Mrs Fanshawe, I'm afraid this Duchy Original biscuit is broken.'

'Never mind, Mr Trumpworthy, I expect the Prince of Wales was distracted the moment while placing it in the discreetly designed packet.'

While nibbling on a thoughtful Hob-nob yesterday, I got to wondering what 'suitable outlets' would be selected for this biscuit. I imagine they will be found in those shops that have homely names like 'Molly's Pantry', where you are served by Benenden old girls in red gingham pinafores.

It is in these shops that you suddenly realise that, in spite of all talk of a classless society, the old-fashioned British social structure is actually preserved in the form of groceries. All in discreetly designed packaging with elegant lettering. We shall have not only the Duchy Original biscuits, but also the Duchess of Somewhere's Special Recipe Fruit Cake, Lady So-and-So's Treacle Toffee, the Laird of Lucknoo's Tartan Shortbread and, of course, The Gentleman's Relish.

Then, somewhere on the shelves, we are likely to find Parson Parkinson's Extra Strong Mints, before moving on to the servants' quarters and to the peasant classes with Mrs Bulstrode's Home Made Quince Jelly (with the nice frilly cloth cap on the jar) and Old Seth Slummock's Potent Pickled Onions.

It is here that we begin to suffer those delicious agonies of snobbery. Will we be found guilty of social climbing if we ask for The Gentleman's Relish? Do we need a minimum of three A grades and one B before they will sell us a jar of Oxford Marmalade? Perhaps the young lady in the gingham pinafore will say: 'I'm sorry, but we can sell the Duchess of Somewhere's Special Recipe Fruit Cake only to personal friends of hers.'

And what about that handsome and dignified bottle of Olde Runcorn Cordial? The label, in beautifully embellished italic script, says it is made by monks at Runcorn Abbey from a blend of herbs and wild flowers and spring water from a secret formula handed down by the 14th-century Abbots of Runcorn. Is it all right to ask for it if you are lapsed C of E?

When you visit Molly's Pantry you cannot help marvelling at the number of natural products that can be turned just as easily into jam or chutney or soap. And they are all put together and neatly labelled under names like Miss Trimble or Mrs Wilkinson or Pansy Poppet, who all sound like the principal suspects in a Miss Marple murder mystery.

Perhaps, with his Duchy Original biscuits, the Prince of Wales has not just shown the way to British agriculture, but also to other members of the Royal Family. With all these unseemly calls for cuts in the Civil List and for Royals to go out and get a job, the answer may lie in grocers. Pop into Molly's Pantry for Prince Michael of Kent's Low Calorie Mayonnaise, Princess Margaret's Tangy Savoury Snacks, or even a bag of Prince Edward Potatoes.

23 March 1955
BAKED HUMBLE PIE

You can actually eat humble pie. We never knew it until a reader wrote for the recipe. The request – from a man – started a search among the old cookery books. And this is what we found:

To make lumber, umbles or humble pie, cut the umbles of deer (the edible entrails) in thin slices, season with pepper, salt, nutmeg and ginger. Place in a dish in layers, with bacon between, sliced dates, raisins and currants.

When ready for the oven, pour in gravy, claret and butter beaten up together.

Pepys, in his Diary, twice refers to umble pie, which he apparently ate with great gusto.

6 March 1986
MAKING LIGHT WORK OF PERFECT PASTRY
Janet Laurence

I used to make terrible pastry. Then I consulted the best cooks I knew and gradually uncovered the secrets of successful shortcrust.

Light handling is one. Fat needs to be blended into flour by rubbing so lightly it does not become at all greasy. Solve the problem of hot hands by using a pastry cutter or food processor; pulse just long enough to cut fat into flour, add liquid whilst processing and stop as soon as pastry starts to come together.

The liquid amount is critical. Use just enough to bring pastry together nicely when pressed firmly. Too little makes it too short; too much, too tough.

Resting for at least 20 minutes after mixing enables flour to absorb liquid, making handling easier. Also, gluten relaxes, avoiding excess shrinkage.

As for ingredients, wholewheat or high extraction flour will give good flavour and nutritional qualities but require a few drops more liquid than ordinary plain. A mixture of butter or margarine and lard gives both good flavour and shortness. Water should be ice-cold and an egg yolk used as part of the liquid gives extra richness and flavour.

When rolling out, use a well-floured board, flour pin rather than the pastry surface, and use short strokes in one direction. Move pastry round to achieve good shape and prevent sticking. Always use first rolling, even if patching is necessary. Pile trimmings neatly on top of each other for a reasonable second rolling.

My favourite shortcrust is the one below. Endlessly versatile, it is ideal for flans. When lining a flan case, push in a little ledge of pastry before cutting off surplus. Then raise the ledge, pinching it even, to double the depth of the case.

For crisp flan pastry, bake blind by lining with greaseproof paper and adding dried beans. Remove these after 15 minutes to finish cooking pastry. Ballooning bottoms mean trapped air, prick with a fork to release.

Shortcrust Pastry
Ingredients:
8oz plain flour sifted with pinch of salt;
3oz butter or margarine and 2oz lard, cut into small cubes;
3 to 4 tablespoons ice-cold water

Method: add fat to flour. Scoop up handfuls of fat and flour from bottom to above level of bowl then flick thumbs repeatedly over fingers, giving fat and flour a brief rub before mixture drops back into bowl. Repeat until mixture looks like crumbs. If it starts looking greasy, stop and use a knife to cut any remaining lumps into small bits. Sprinkle over 3 tablespoons water, stirring with knife to incorporate, then use hands to bring pastry together with gentle pressure. If mixture is too dry, add a few drops more water. Remove pastry from bowl and gently work with hands for a few seconds until it forms a reasonable cohesive ball. Cover with upturned bowl for 20 minutes, or wrap for longer storage. (If freezing, flatten ball for quicker defrosting). Pastry is now ready for use.

Baking: bake at 375°F / 190°C (Gas 5). If time isn't available for baking blind, place flan cases on a preheated baking sheet to help crisp bottom.

7 February 1934
'CLOTILDE' SUGGESTS FRITTERS BY WAY OF A CHANGE
Clotilde

Beignets du Mardi-Gras, or puffy fritters, make an interesting change for the sweet course. For six people, boil half a pint of water in a saucepan, add a little sugar, a pinch of salt, some butter as big as a walnut; add to this liquid half a pound of sifted flour, beat it over the fire. When the paste leaves the sides of the saucepan and does not stick to the fingers, turn it out into a bowl. Then work it with the palm of the hand to make it more supple; work in some eggs one at a time alternately with a portion of half a glass of rum, till the paste is a batter neither too thin nor too thick.

To make sure that the mixture is just right, pour a teaspoonful of it into the hot deep fat in which the fritters are to be fried. If it puffs up and is very light the mixture is ready for use. If it does not, add some more egg until it is.

These fritters ought to be put into the hot fat over a low heat at first, and about six may be put in at the same time, leaving a second for the fat to recover its temperature when each is put in. When they begin to colour and turn by themselves in the fat quicken up the fire. Drain them, dust with sugar and pile them up in a pyramid

For *beignets de peches molles*, first make a batter with 10 teaspoonfuls of flour, 3 yolks of eggs, 1 tablespoon of fine olive oil, a wineglassful of dry white wine, and a pinch of salt. Mix well with a wooden spoon to a smooth, thick batter, adding a little more or less wine as required; the size of a wineglass varies. Whisk the white of three or four eggs to a stiff dry froth and fold lightly into batter.

Ripe, luscious peaches are the best to use for beignets. Peel them, take out the stones, cut in quarters, sprinkle them with rum, powder with sugar, add the grated rind of a lemon, and let rest for one hour. Lift out and drain each piece, dip it in the batter, and plunge at once into the deep frying fat. Leave until they take a good colour, drain, and dust with castor sugar.

The batter must be thick or it will run off the fruit, and the white of egg must not be whisked and folded in until the last minute.

The prunes that come from South Africa in the spring make very good beignets if the above directions are followed.

29 January 1927
TEA-TIME DAINTIES
Elsie Wetherell

I make no apology for giving more recipes for hot cakes for tea, as for some time yet most of us will enjoy them on cold days. Next week recipes for orange marmalades will be given.

North Country Scones

¾ lb flour;	½ oz yeast;
1 egg;	1 teaspoonful castor sugar;
1 ½ gill milk;	1 oz butter

Cream the sugar and yeast together. Melt the butter in a pan, add the milk to it, make lukewarm, and add the yeast and sugar to it. Strain into the flour in a basin. Add the well-beaten egg, and mix all thoroughly well together. Then turn the dough on to a floured board and knead well. Cut into rounds, and put these into small round tins. Stand in a warm place to rise for an hour. Then bake in a moderate oven fifteen minutes.

Tea Scones

1 lb flour;
Pinch salt;
1 dessertspoonful baking-powder;
2oz sugar;

2oz butter;
2oz seedless raisins;
A little milk and water

Sieve flour, baking-powder, and salt together. Rub butter in lightly. Add the raisins and sugar. Mix to a light dough with half milk and water. Roll out, cut into rounds, and mark across in four with back of knife. Bake in hot oven ten minutes.

Soda Scones

½lb flour;
1 dessertspoonful sugar;
1oz butter;
1 teaspoonful cream of tartar;

½ teaspoonful bicarbonate of soda;
½ teaspoonful salt;
1 egg;
1 gill milk

Mix the soda and tartar together well so that there are no lumps. Then sieve them with the flour, salt, and sugar. Rub in the butter lightly. Beat the egg well, add the milk to it, and form all into a light dough, using a knife. Turn half the dough on to a floured board, and lightly form by patting with the hand into a round, and cut into four or eight pieces. Do the same with the other half of the dough, and put all on to a greased tin. Dust scones over with flour and bake in a really hot oven for ten minutes. They should be half an inch thick when placed in the oven. The oven must be hot or they will not rise well.

Gingerbread

1 lb flour;
¼ lb brown sugar;
¼ lb lard;
½ lb treacle;
1 teaspoonful baking powder;

1 teaspoonful carbonate of soda;
2 teaspoonfuls ground ginger;
1 egg;
A little milk;
Pinch salt

Melt treacle, sugar, and lard. Mix the dry ingredients well and add the melted treacle to them, also the egg well beaten and enough milk to form a stiff batter. Turn into flat round greased tins, and bake in a moderate oven about three-quarters to one hour.

School-Room Cake

1 lb flour;

6oz lard;

8oz currants;

1oz candied peel;

1 teaspoonful each of mixed spice
    and baking-powder;

½ teacupful milk;

9oz brown sugar;

5oz sultanas;

2 eggs

Rub the lard (or half lard and half good beef dripping) into flour, and add sugar, baking powder, and spice; then the fruit and chopped peel. Beat the eggs with two tablespoonfuls of water. Stir into dry ingredients, adding the milk. Beat all well together, and turn into a well-greased 2 lb cake tin. Bake in a steady oven 1½ hours.

How to Cheat on the Mincemeat

22 October 1970
NOW'S THE TIME TO BAKE YOURSELF A WHITE CHRISTMAS
Bon Viveur

During the leanest period of the last world war we lived in a 16th-century house in Warwickshire, which had once been an alehouse. Bits had been added, the house spread out in an L, so long in the stem that a visiting friend christened the upper corridors 'the penny tram rides'.

There was so much room in the stables after we had garaged our battered 1936 saloon that we bought a pig and housed it there, obtaining feed legitimately by handing over half the pig to the Government. Then we won a goose in a raffle, and on these somewhat limited items we had twelve to stay over Christmas.

On Christmas morning our sole American guest produced a large round tin with inside it a crystalised fruits-topped cake wrapped in layers and layers of waxed papers. Our friend was a Southerner and the cake had been baked by the family's cook six months before.

It was gorgeous, white inside . . . and to us at that time, the absolute peak of luxury.

When it comes to Christmas there are three different ways of presenting this cake. You can simply rough-cut a mixture of crystalised fruits – say peach, apricot, pear, fig and greengage; add a few matchstick-width link-long strips of softened angelica, half a dozen rough-cut walnut halves and about 3oz of halved, glace cherries.

Mix them all together. Brush the top of the cake lightly with sugar syrup and press the well-mixed assembly on top, bringing it to a slight peak at centre and pressing a whole crystalised apricot into the top centre.

You can also, of course, ice this cake traditionally, giving it the standard top and side covering of almond paste and, when this is dry, icing with classic royal icing.

Best of all, we think, is to leave out the almond paste and by-pass the royal icing in favour of our Fondant Icing.

Instead of rolling out a circular piece large enough to envelop the cake sides and top in one, do the job in two stages and thus eliminate any possible fear of little cracks appearing around the top edge.

When the fondant is made up – and colour with harmless vegetable colouring if you so wish – cover it with a damp cloth (it dries out fast and this is when it can crack), and brush the top of the cake thoroughly with sieved apricot jam or melted redcurrant jelly.

Then roll out a generous third of the fondant over a cold surface which you have dusted with sifted cornflower very carefully.

When fondant is about ⅛in in thickness, slap the jammy top of the cake onto the smoothly-rolled upper surface and run a knife around the edge – all round.

Restore the cake to its proper way up and set aside the fondant trimmings. Now brush the cake's sides all round with chosen jam or jelly.

Next roll out a strip to precise circumference of the cake and from fondant top to table base. Then all you do is simply pick up the cake with the top and bottom half flatly by the palm of each hand and trundle it along until the fondant edges meet.

Gather up the trimmings, re-roll them and from them stamp out a number of the little fancy shapes with any available small or cocktail cutter.

Set these immediately around the top edge where the join shows and thus mask it. Thereafter, you can elaborate, if you wish by using fancy scraps of crystalised fruits to decorate.

Finally, if you are up with the dreary dard type of cake can holders, you can make your own in fondant.

For ours stamp out *fleurs de lys* with one cutter. Sometimes stamp little stars on and scatter the cake top. Place candles in tiny circles around the fondant and decorate the top with glace closed petals, making the candles in holders the centre of each 'flower' and cut fine strips of angelica for the flower stems and slender tapering spike leaves.

Your cake, if made with the given quantities, will weigh between 4¼ lb and 4½ lb, and you will need for the icing the quantities given in the Fondant recipe.

This is a cake which is far too good for one of those nasty paper frills around the sides, if using the suggested fondant icing, would be too elaborate with decorated sides.

The Cake
Ingredients:

7oz three-times sifted flour;
3¼oz cornflour;
9½oz floured, rough-cut glace cherries;
8oz rough-cut glace pineapple;
7½oz unsalted butter;
8oz sifted icing sugar;
4 standard eggs;
4oz mixed, diced peel;
8oz sultanas;

2oz rough-cut walnuts;
2oz rough-cut pecan nuts;
2oz diced angelica;
2 fl oz brandy;
The grated rind of 1 fine-skinned orange;
1 teaspoon orange flower water;
1 teaspoon rosewater;
The strained juice of 1 small orange

Method: Mix sifted flour and cornflower together. Mix in a separate bowl the prepared cherries, pineapple, peel, sultanas, walnuts, pecan nuts and angelica.

Mix together, in a third container, the brandy, orange juice, rosewater and orange flower water. Separate the egg whites from the yolks and beat the yolks with the brandy mixture.

Cream the butter with the orange rind – ideally by hand, but an electric mixer will do. Beat butter until it is pale and very loose. Then beat in the sugar very thoroughly, this most emphatically by hand.

Add the mixed flour in handfuls of the mixed fruits and nuts and little splashes of the brandy mixture.

Beat well after each addition until all ingredients are absorbed. Whip the egg whites very stiffly and draw the firm foam down in to the mixture with a wooden spoon. Turn into a buttered and floured paper-lined 10in-diameter sliding-based cake tin.

Set tin on 4 folds of brown paper on a baking sheet and bake at 325°F (gas 3) one shelf below centre until the mixture stops 'singing' or until a fine skewer or kitchen needle comes out cleanly after being driven into the centre of the cake.

Cool on a rack in its papers. When cold, wrap in wax papers and store in a tin with a really well-fitting lid. As an added precaution, we seal the lid edge with adhesive tape and store on a very dry shelf.

The Fondant

Ingredients:

2 lb sifted icing sugar;	*2 separated, not too-fresh, egg*
4oz liquid glucose (from chemist);	*whites (using standard eggs)*

Method: Place sifted sugar in a roomy bowl. Make a well in the centre. Soften glucose over hot water until it is runny. Pour into well, add the unbeaten egg whites and work up with a wooden spoon until mixture becomes smooth and achieves a thick, soft, rolling paste consistency.

Note: If you should by chance be using egg whites which are slightly deficient in albumen and the mixture becomes too thick just add a drop or two of extra egg white and all will be well. Finally: orange flower water or rosewater for culinary use are sold by most good chemists. Do not try to use orange flower or rosewater hand lotions – your icing will be indescribably nasty!

11 December 1976
BOTTLE UP A SEASONAL WELCOME
Johnnie Cradock

As our theme for Christmas is traditional but informal, it is likely that friends and neighbours will be dropping in unexpectedly. Equally, if you are Scots or a Northerner, the New Year will bring first footers – uninvited – on what is almost certain to be a cold night.

To meet either case, I suggest you make up and bottle, ready for 'instant heating up', some of our ancestors' brews.

Either mulled wine or mulled ale can be so treated, and this has the dual virtue of getting the job done in advance, and also of ensuring that there is absolutely no waste. For, with mixed, humble ingredients – no one would mull a vintage wine – what has been heated once can be heated again after return to bottle and shelf.

If your callers appear mid-morning treat them to a true Victorian welcome, and provide a wedge of really moist Madeira cake and a glass of Madeira. Specifically, give them one of the two aperitif Madeiras; Verdelho or Sercial. Both are fairly reasonably priced at between £2.20 and £2.50 a bottle.

Moreover, glasses should be small ones, permitting you to serve 12 glasses from one bottle. Both should be served slightly chilled.

In the afternoon choose between the Verdelho or one of the two dessert Madeiras: Bual, about £2.40 or Malmsey, about £2.65. After six o'clock serve one of the mulls.

Another good standby for 'casuals' is Dubonnet, at around £2. Serve in a long glass with fizzy lemonade and a couple of ice-cubes.

There is a dry Dubonnet on the market now to meet the taste of those who consider the red one rather too sweet. This is just the thing, very well diluted with lemonade, for young fry who consider they are frightfully sophisticated but whom you do not intend to make tipsy.

There is also a wide range of Vermouths (£2) which can be served, again in tall glasses, with ice and either soda water or lemonade. If you are prepared to pay a little over the odds the indisputable best of this group is the Chambéry, at about £2.50 a bottle.

You might also like to experiment with that ideal between-meals wine, a Moselle. I have always maintained that to appreciate these German wines fully they should be so served without benefit of any kind of food, or, if you must include just a nibble, make this a plate of what the French call *Petits Fours Sec*, or those new-to-us biscuits, sold by the packet and called Gingerellas.

Because of my predilection for Moselles served like this I always keep some in mild domestic refrigeration. They need not be costly ones, for example a Piesporter Michelsberg Riesling '75 will be about £1.75 or a Zeltinger '73, about £1.85. Or you can look to the Rhine for a Niersteiner Gutes Domtal, £1.70.

22 November 1952
CHRISTMAS IN THE KITCHEN STARTS WITH 'STIR-UP' SUNDAY

Tomorrow, 'stir-up' Sunday is the traditional time to start the making of the Christmas puddings. Our ancestors, more knowledgeable than we are in the art of good living, chose this day to allow the pudding time to mature. Its quaint name comes from the collect for the day (Sunday next before Advent) which begins, 'Stir up, we beseech thee. O Lord…' This was taken by many country folk to refer to the beginning of the pudding stirring!

Make the pudding no later than the end of November. By giving it a long maturation the ill-effects of our rich Christmas fare can be avoided.

The following recipe is a traditional one from Gulval's Mead House: ½lb finely shredded suet, 2 to 3 eggs, 1 ripe russet apple, 5oz prunes (stoned and halved), 2½oz mixed peel cut in fine strips, 2oz almonds blanched, 6oz raisins, ½lb sultanas, 6oz currants, 3oz sifted flour, 6oz brown breadcrumbs, 1½ dessertspoonfuls lemon juice, rind of ½ lemon, chopped finely.

Also, ½ teaspoonful mixed spice, ½ teaspoonful nutmeg, pinch of cloves and bay (and if possible ½ teaspoonful ground angelica and ground tonquin leaves), 1 teaspoonful salt, ½ pint milk, 2 tablespoonful honey, 3oz sugar, 1 large wineglassful of either Madeira, port, sack mead, sack metheglin or sherry.

The whole should be stirred very thoroughly, starting with the dry ingredients: add eggs one at a time. Pudding basins should be smeared with margarine or butter, three-parts filled with the mixture, tied up with a cloth and boiled continuously for 8 hours.

An excellent sauce for the pudding, in keeping with traditional old English Christmas, can be made with Madeira sack mead, sack metheglin or sherry.

Put 2 yolks of eggs in a pan with 1oz sugar and 1 to 2 wine-glassfuls liquor and about ⅛ of the grated rind of a lemon. Stir until sauce coats spoon (it can then be strained through a cloth for the more fastidious but this is not necessary).

25 November 1971
OUR FAVOURITE MINCEMEAT

Now is the time to make your mincemeat. If you have not done so already; the whole conglomeration needs time and both rum and orange juice to get it to the requisite state of maturity. This is the recipe for Our Favourite Mincemeat.

Ingredients:
1 lb currants;
1 lb rough-chopped, seeded raisins;
1½ lb finely-minced beef suet;
1 lb darkest pieces (soft brown) sugar;
1oz mixed spices;
1 lb (peeled weight) cored, minced apples with their juice;
The grated rind of 2 lemons and 3 oranges;
1 lb sultanas;
7 fl oz rum;
7 fl oz brandy

Method: Just mix them all together very thoroughly, pack into one large stone or earthenware jar in preference to a lot of small ones and tie down first with a piece of greaseproof passed through a spoonful of extra brandy in a saucer, laid over the top of the mincemeat, then with a piece of transparent polythene laid over (just split a polythene freezer bag) and finally with a doubled outer covering of heavy-duty aluminium foil.

20 December 1924
FOWL RECIPES
Elsie Wetherell

Select your turkey very carefully, passing over any that look at all of a purple colour. Choose the whitest one you can get. Male birds are considered best for roasting, as they are usually finer and plumper. A hen is very good for boiling or braising. See there is a certain amount of fat about the sides of the wings, and that the legs are short.

Braised Turkey
Prepare the turkey as for roasting, using whichever stuffing is liked. Arrange a bed of mixed cut-up vegetables in a large saucepan, and cover them with some nice stock. Place the turkey on top of them and cover with greased paper, then put on saucepan lid and cook slowly from three to four hours. Just before serving put the turkey in a hot oven to get a nice brown. This is a very good way to cook an old bird.

Roast turkey
Choose a male turkey and let it hang for a few days. Use whichever stuffing is preferred, or two kinds may be used, one in the neck and the other in the body. Chestnut and sausage-meat stuffing go well together, and are generally liked. Truss the bird for roasting, making it as plump as possible. Cook in a moderate oven from 1½ to 2½ hours, according to size. A small bird of 8 lb to 9 lb will take 1½ hours, one of 10 lb to 12 lb 2 hours, and one of 12 lb and 14 lb 2½ hours. Baste if possible with bacon fat or good dripping. A few slices of fat bacon laid on the breast is a good plan, and the basting must be very thoroughly done, as otherwise the bird will be dry. If it is inclined to get too brown cover it with paper. Serve with good brown gravy and bread sauce. Rolled bacon, small fried sausages, or boiled ham, are usual accompaniments, with cranberry sauce or jelly.

For Brown Gravy
Prepare the giblets from the turkey or goose, put them into the pan, and cover with cold water, and simmer for 1½ to 2 hours. Put 1oz butter and

1oz flour into a pan and mix well, strain on to it 1 pint of the stock from the giblets, and stir until thickened. When the turkey or goose is dished up pour off all fat from the baking-tin very carefully leaving the brown goodness from the bird. Pour the thickened stock on to it, strain, and put into the sauceboat, seasoning with salt and pepper to taste.

Roast Goose

1 goose, 4 large onions, 2 teaspoonfuls powdered sage, ½ lb breadcrumbs, salt and pepper, 1 egg.

Remove any soft fat from inside of goose and truss for roasting. Peel onions and cut into slices, and put into pan and cover with hot salted water. Bring to boil and cook slowly for ½ hour. Then drain as dry as possible and chop finely and put into basin with crumbs, sage, and salt and pepper to taste. 1½oz butter may be used instead of the egg; melt it before adding to dry solid. Put this stuffing into the body of the bird at the tail end, sew up the opening, cover bird with greased paper, and cook in a good oven for 1½ to 2½ hours, basting, as it is so fat in itself. Serve with good brown gravy and apple or cranberry sauce.

Boiled Turkey

For those who cannot eat roast turkey a boiled one is acceptable. A small hen bird should be chosen, and may be stuffed or not as preferred. It should be well rubbed with lemon juice and wrapped in greased paper, put into a pan of boiling water or light stock. Add a little salt and a few sticks of celery and cook gently, allowing fifteen minutes to the pound and fifteen minutes over. Serve with celery, egg, parsley, oyster or béchamel sauce, and garnish with cut lemon and rolled bacon. Boiled ham or tongue is usually served as well. Some sauce should be used to mask the bird. A fowl can be cooked in exactly the same way, and would take about 1½ hours.

14 December 1976
TURNING HISTORY UPSIDE DOWN
FOR FESTIVE TREATS OF THE PAST
Bon Viveur

Let us stay with the past by serving Tipsy Cake instead of Trifle; Topsyturvey Mincemeat, or mincemeat turnovers, and an Angelica Tart trellised with twists of almond paste which the celebrated cookery books extolled in the 17th century.

The Tipsy Cake can have its basic sponge made and baked now, then just be wrapped in foil and finished when required. If you possess a rabbit, hedgehog or tall Savoy mould, the mixture should be baked in this. If not, bake in an ordinary 6in diameter sliding-based cake tin with a high wall lining around the top.

Mincemeat turnovers require floured baking sheets and the paste should be rolled out to a scant ⅛in thickness and cut into 6in circles. These can be cut and brushed free of any flour, laid over greaseproof layers in a plastic box and frozen until required, or they can be filled, pinched together and frozen ready to thaw, filled with mincemeat. You then cook freshly as needed.

Make Angelica Tart in either one or more Victoria Sponge tins, or glass flan dishes, thus avoiding any pastry doorsteps and making it possible to bring the filling right to the pastry edges.

20 December 1981
THOUGHT FOR FOOD:
A CHRISTMAS FEAST
Denis Curtis

A year or two ago I was a touch enthusiastic with my invitations, which resulted in 26 friends and relations sitting down to Christmas dinner. But the stuffing for the turkey had been completed the night before (my three favourites of mushroom, pheasant and chestnut); the goose had been filled the French way (1 lb black pudding pounded with 1 crushed clove of garlic and the bird's liver, then blended with 2 grated large dessert apples, seasoned and bound with 3 fl oz port); and there were hands of pork with a fruit stuffing, which gained its flavour from mixed dry fruits and grated orange peel. On the morning the house guests found kedgeree awaiting them on the hot plate, with hot croissants and coffee, and were then packed off to church or on an appetite-provoking walk.

The well-trained ones (by me, over the years) were dragooned into helping in the kitchen. Marie took the rind off the bacon and secured it with orange sticks into rolls for grilling (half the quantity having cooked and stoned prunes at the centre). Uncle Harri concentrated on prising open 5 dozen oysters (they keep fresh for up to a week if covered with a damp sack). Paul scooped cod's roe from its skin, pounded it with lemon juice and pepper and then parcelled it in smoked salmon for those to whom oysters were anathema. Potatoes were parboiled, ready to be roasted (some around the goose and the rest for 40 or so minutes in beef dripping).

Dinner was served in the barn, converted by my graphic-designer friend Douglas into a baronial hall, with clever use of giant rolls of photographers' coloured background paper upon which had been sprayed a gallery of ancestors' portraits. Three braziers provided a good heat. After hot pea soup, the amplified sound of *Carmina Burana* heralded the entrance of my main course. The turkey (bedecked with bacon rolls and chipolatas) and the goose (on a bed of pureed apples and trailing streamers of apple peel) were paraded round the room. Platters of vegetables were placed with military precision down the centre of the white-clothed table (trestles borrowed from the village hall); tiny sprouts (boiled for 5 minutes, shaken in hot butter, then some combined with fried almonds and some with fried mushrooms); pureed parsnips studded with pine nuts; broad beans saturated with crisply fried diced bacon and its sizzling fat; and a version of *gratin dauphinois* as an alternative to roast potatoes (slices of Desiree layered in a garlic-rubbed dish, flecked with butter, pepper and salt, then covered with cream and baked for 40 minutes until fondant). Afterwards there were crackers and mince pies (3in rounds of puff pastry sandwiching mincemeat enriched with a slug of whisky).

The Grandmama's pudding made a flaming entrance with orange-flavoured brandy butter, followed by a whole ripe Stilton, Taylor's port, nuts, chocolates and crystallised fruits. Finally there was coffee and cognac Delamain. Champagne corks popped later to revive us for a snack of Bradenham ham to fortify the departing guests. Supper at the end of the day was eaten around a fire blazing with apple tree logs (saved for the occasion).

Auld Lang Dine

22 March 1979
CHANGING TASTES IN FOOD
Paula Davies

Watching Italian shopkeepers, complete with berets, moustaches and expansive gestures ordering food from Italian importers at Olympia for English customers seemed a little unusual.

But this was the first international food exhibition to be held in England and one was driven to the conclusion that the food scene in the country has changed to an enormous extent. Among the new foods, designed not only to whet our appetites but also to be trouble-free, is a lasagne pack imported by United Preservers which includes both the béchamel and bolognese sauces and takes only minutes to prepare. Expected to sell at around £1 it tastes extraordinarily like the real thing, although I would want to add more meat to it.

There was a time when the only vinegar the English knew was malt vinegar. The wine version is now positively commonplace and there are two new ones being imported by Costa, one with green peppercorns suspended *en branche* and one with lemon peel, which is superb in a mayonnaise.

Carob bars are no longer that much more expensive than chocolate. For non health food addicts, these confectionery bars are made from the carob bean instead of the cocoa bean, contain no caffeine nor refined sugar, and were on show at the exhibition. Called Kalibu bars, they are both delicious and filling with a curious, honey-like aftertaste. Stockists include most health food shops of any size and the bars, weighing 80 grammes, come in four varieties – plain and mint, selling at about 34p, and hazelnut and nut and raisin, at about 37p.

31 December 1956
YEAR OF SUPERMARKETS BEFORE US
Egon Ronay

The encouraging improvements in the quality and variety of our food in the past year will continue in 1957 and the whole food world, from supermarkets to mass caterer, is full of ideas to serve our convenience and compete for our customs.

Supermarkets which have supplied the basic foods will now add a few frills. In 1957 cups of coffee from a slot machine – black or white, with or without sugar, light or strong – will be available in plastic cups, to be thrown away after use. Tea and sandwiches from automatic snack bars will revive us after the fatigue of label-gazing. Gramophone records, knitting wool, lingerie and cosmetics will all be machine served and, as a final anachronism, at a dairy chain's supermarkets, there will be canned beer, too.

I hope our refrigerator manufacturers will increase our frozen-food compartments. Deep-freezing will cover new fields from January. Frozen blueberries will be a welcome change from blackcurrants. They are less sweet and have more character. I have even discovered a term new in this country. A large Swedish firm will bring separate 'chicken thighs' to our table, the meaty – and to me the best – bit, usually attached to the drumstick. Wings will be packed separately, too; wonderful for risottos and soups.

Frozen peas had the final acknowledgment a few weeks ago; they found their way into the cost-of-living index. I predict that, because of Swedish competition, they will be cheaper next year.

Experts say, to my regret, that half of the meat we shall eat in 1957 will be frozen in packets in spite of its high price. It is easier and cleaner to carry, more standardised (mother will not be faced with the problem of to whom to give the smallest chop), competition between packers is a guarantee to better quality. But personally I still prefer fresh meat. The frozen joint loses the vital juices after de-frosting, unless it is in its skin, e.g., a leg of lamb.

Mr W. Moore, typically English expert of Smithfield, warmed my continental heart with his prediction: continental cuts, introduced by a Knightsbridge store, were so successful that he can foresee their spreading rapidly next year. So we will be able to ask for topside (*noix*) of veal to ensure that we get the right meat for our escalopes and we shall have no waste when buying fillets of pork for pork Wellington.

Good news for the grill-minded: the quality of home-killed meat will improve further because of artificial insemination and better breeding methods, without an increase in present, reasonable prices.

Good news for the stew-minded: Argentine beef, though not of English and Scottish quality, will be in ample supply and its price is expected to be lower.

The news is less cheerful in the fruit world. Mr Schorno, an old hand in Covent Garden, fears an increase in the price of oranges because of the Middle East situation. We shall have to forgo for a time the unsurpassable Hungarian peaches. But melons will be plentiful. They will not only be the easy way out of first-course difficulties in restaurants harassed by staff troubles, but they are bound to be cheaper and to figure more often on the ordinary household table. Potatoes will be cheaper, too, be of inferior quality, not like the waxier ones of this year which were so good for *pommes soufflés*. In 1957 one would have to buy them from Aberdeenshire, where I have discovered the waxy salad potatoes, new in England.

The big-time caterers, who have made luxury and finesse available to scooter pockets with limousine tastes this year, will continue their competition to our benefit. The Pronto, the first kitchenless restaurant in Richmond, is to be duplicated ten times at London's busiest spots. Its backer, Mr Garfield Weston, the biscuit king, is convinced that there is plenty of room for improvement in London's catering.

Mr Charles Forte, just back from States, will put some American ideas to use in his new restaurant to be opened in Coventry Street. A conveyor belt will take cutlery and china almost from our hands at the snack-counter to the kitchen for washing up.

Fashion, Food and Decoration
Ideas for New Year's Eve

If you are going to a party wear some really glamorous gloves. A novelty is a long-stemmed rose caught to a pasted-toned evening glove.

If you are giving a party a gay idea for the buffet table is to use Irish linen roller towelling as a cloth.

Egon Ronay suggests the following recipes:

Teenagers' Punch – There is a kick in this party drink, without the extra strong punch the grown-ups like on New Year's Eve. Make 4 pints China tea, add 12oz lump sugar (rubbed one by one against orange peel), the juice of 6 oranges, ⅓ bottle of brandy and 2–3 sherry glasses of maraschino.

My tip for a short drink – 4 parts brown vermouth, one part brandy, a few drops of pure lemon juice and a tiny piece of scratched lemon peel.

Small-hours snack – If your party is still going strong in the small hours and your guests feel hungry again, try this quick-to-make snack: For about 12 people place 1½ lb luncheon meat-slices cut in half, or whole slices of continental knackwurst on a dish, mixed with 2–3 thinly sliced onions. Make a dressing of 1 part vinegar, ½ part water and 1 part salad oil. Pour over meat. Serve with iced lager.

13 November 1988
FOLLOWERS OF FOOD FASHION
Teresa Waugh

Marco Polo is believed to have discovered spaghetti in the Orient and to have introduced it into Italy at the end of the 13th century. Half-way through the following century a glutton in one of the stories of the

Decameron is described by Boccaccio as dreaming about mountains of spaghetti with tomato sauce running down it in rivulets. *Plus ça change* ... one is tempted to think.

It is now more than 600 years since Boccaccio's death and still the thought of spaghetti *al pomodoro* is intimately connected with Italy in most people's minds. Yet in other parts of Europe and, no doubt, in some respects of Italy, too, fashions in food have changed as dramatically as fashions in dress.

A mouth-wateringly beautiful book dealing with this very subject has just been published. *Food in Vogue* is edited by Barbara Tims with an introduction by Arabella Boxer and, as the subtitle – *From Boulestin to Boxer* –suggests, it covers a period of 60 years, dating from the time when Marcel Boulestin became the first food writer on *Vogue*, until the present day. Drawings, photographs and recipes are all reproduced as they first appeared in *Vogue*.

There can be few people who are not aware of the changing fashions in food, of how *nouvelle cuisine* took France by storm in the seventies and travelled like a hurricane across the Channel. We were no longer presented with an enormous helping of meat and vegetables, more a delicate painting of a flower.

What would Louis XIV have thought had he been offered a little arrangement of kiwi fruit and grated carrot? He who was 'feeling so ill one evening in June 1708 that all he could manage was a few *croutes*, a pigeon soup and three roast chickens, out of which he has four wings, the breasts and one leg'.

A most enjoyable pastime with *Food in Vogue* is to read the recipes and then try to guess their date. I found it difficult, although I might have supposed that in war-time Britain people could have been tempted by apple soup and I know, too, that any mention of a blender rather than a sieve must suggest more modern times.

I was quite near the mark, though, in guessing that the recipe for Eggs in Aspic – hard-boiled, halved, scooped out and filled with a mixture of yolks and *pâté de foie gras* before being stuck together again as invisibly as possible and set in aspic – was from between the wars.

Salads are, perhaps, something especially associated with today's health-conscious eating habits and yet the most amazing recipes were printed in 1944. Green walnuts and cress – and as for cowslips, which are probably by now a protected species: 'As soon as (they) appear in the fields, send the children to pick them ... good for a sandwich filling, too. Use only the petals of the freshly gathered flowers, removing them carefully from the calyx. Drop them lightly on to the hearts of lettuce and serve with mayonnaise.'

I was a child during the war and I have no memory of eating cowslips, which I am sure are delicious but it would break my heart to do so now.

Kenneth Tynan is quoted as saying that eating is the only thing that one can happily do three times a day every day of one's life without ever being bored. I am not sure that I agree with that, partly because the fashion in food has changed so much that many people who were probably brought up on eggs for breakfast now eat nothing until lunchtime.

In the twenties, we are told, a dinner party would usually consist of a thick and a clear soup followed by seven courses, including a savoury. How would today's superwoman cope with coming home from a hard day at the office to produce all that?

When you come to think of it, fashion in food is as fascinating as fashion in anything else. It reflects the times in which we live, from the opulence of Louis XIV's Versailles to the lean years of the war, post-war recovery and our own preoccupation with health.

Food in Vogue is published by Pyramid, £16.95.

5 November 1978
TRYING A TASTY TREE...
David Brown

An official tasting panel has been set up by the Government to sample a new generation of artificial foods including mince from manure, steaks from trees and tasty delicacies derived from North Sea oil.

Scientists are experimenting with foods like these to fight world famines and produce cheaper alternatives in Britain to natural beef, lamb and pork.

The panel, consisting of Ministry of Food and Department of Health scientists, will taste the new concoctions, examine the processes by which they are made and tell the public whether they are made to eat. Every approved packet will carry a Government mark of safety.

Farmyard manure, grass, leaves from tree and oil waste are all sources of protein which scientists can process into food.

Micro-organisms are grown into a form which can be spun and textured into meat-like products, such as those already based on soya beans.

Known as 'novel foods' the new generation of meat substitutes are expected to develop into a big business for food manufacturers because the world population is rapidly out-stripping the capacity of farmers to feed it.

Companies already engaged in research are keeping their processes secret in an effort to keep competitors out of the market.

Mr Cyril Coffin, director general of the Food Manufacturers' Federation, said: 'We are just at the beginning of this technology and we will be co-operating with the Government panel.'

12 July 1981
GASTRONAUT
Anthea Hall

The idea of trying out the food that astronauts eat in spaceships has about as much appeal as an invitation to dress in the clothing they wear down the salt mines.

On the other hand, the details sounded intriguing. Just imagine economies of time, space and labour with portions weighing less than half an ounce (shrimps) or under two ounces for a main course (chicken stew) and requiring no greater cooking expertise than adding cold or hot tap water, or at the very most boiling a kettle, leaving one unworried and free to play the perfect hostess.

David Barnard ('I'm no gourmet') of Survival Specialties, the company which imports this freeze-dried 'as-used-by-astronauts' food from the United States, talked in terms of how well the food 'came back', thereby investing the whole operation with a kind of resurrectional quality. The French beans, he said, came back 'exceedingly well', though the strawberries were a bit mushy. He wasn't altogether keen on the Turkey Tetrazzini, which he said was 'only middle of the road tastewise'.

To give the food the benefit of the best sauce of all, hunger, I decided to forego my usual substantial breakfast. By lunchtime, or rather five minutes before, I had the kettle on the boil and the packets ready to open. Nobody was at home to spoil things with the usual family scepticism.

I opened everything and inspected my four samples: green beans, Gulf shrimps, tuna and chicken stew. My stomach seemed to sink slightly. The green beans and Gulf shrimp looked exquisite, like *papier mâché* replicas – good enough to eat, as they say. But the chicken stew looked like superior dried pet food and the tuna like wood chips. It suddenly seemed that nothing, short of grappling with the Eiger North Wall or starvation combined with a very stiff gin and tonic, would make me feel hungry.

I poured boiling water on to my four bowls and decided that the addition of freshly-ground black pepper would not constitute cheating. In any case, the shrimps were accompanied by the suggestions that they might be dipped in seasoned breading mixture (when re-hydrated, of course) and deep-fried. I expect that astronauts have got that kind of thing under control.

My verdicts were surprising. The unappetising-looking chicken stew was quite delicious and I even had a second helping. In appearance and texture the beans and shrimps had, indeed, come back exceedingly well, though I found the beans improved with three minutes' extra simmering instead of just soaking in boiling water. The tuna was quite adequate, and the shrimps and the tuna made an excellent risotto later.

Where freeze-dried food, which is packed in nitrogen atmosphere, scores so heavily over all other storage food is, of course, its longevity. So far, tests have not detected any signs of deterioration over 12 years – one can visualise buying a portfolio of dried goods and reaping the benefits of eating at 1969 prices. It may disappoint Mr Barnard that their best customers so far are not mountaineers or yachtsmen but those stocking up fall-out shelters. One customer has spent more than £3,000 on a year's supply. Compared with tinned food it is expensive, but in terms of reduced weight (22oz of tuna reduces to 5oz) there is no comparison.

The normal pack sizes are 750cc or three litres, but Survival Specialties are offering three smaller sample packs. Send a stamped addressed envelope to Old School, Herd St, Marlborough, Wiltshire.

22 February 1967
THE MISSING INGREDIENT IN ENGLISH MEALS: IMAGINATION

People's eating habits often arouse comment. A recent article on school food and what mothers feed their school-age children provoked the following replies:

'If, as the article said, many children are not being fed properly, why are schools not teaching the mothers of tomorrow about nutritional needs?' asks Mrs H. M. Lawson, of Sevenoaks, Kent. 'My daughter has reached beyond the school leaving age without being taught cookery or dietetics. This is in a State grammar school.'

And Mrs Gwen Davies, of Purley, Surrey, asks: 'What is the point of 20 or 30 little girls solemnly sitting down to learn by heart the portions of fat to flour for various kinds of pastry when, in their own homes, they need only turn to their cookery books?

'Surely it is more practical to show the rising generation how to make use of modern developments – how long food can be stored in the fridge, how best to shop, how to prepare meals in advance, how to make package products taste less mass-produced?'

Still on the subject of food Prudence Duncan, of Holt, Norfolk, writes: 'Let's face it – cooking is a chore if three meals a day have to be produced, but one food meal in the evening, when all the family are home, is fun to prepare.

'I think Englishwomen just lack cooking imagination.'

24 April 1972
NOT JUST A LOT OF BOOJUM
THAT £34M APPETITE
Richard Walker

Shark soup and boojum bread as the boom markets of tomorrow? Just maybe. Food futurologists have much to chew over following a report that pictures spectacular rises in the sales of the exotic.

After trailing the progress of canned snail and lobster tail and such through the nation, new product research specialist System Three estimates that total sales of what it classifies as 'unusual, exotic or premium quality foods' are now worth about £34 million a year and this should almost double within five years – it projects, at today's prices and at very least, £64 million in 1977.

The whole thing has advanced far beyond specialist shop. Supermarkets and the bigger self-service stores now take 60 per cent of these sales, the delicatessen only 13 per cent. Safeway and Waitrose are the most advanced in stocking the odd, followed by Tesco, possibly because its policy of decentralised responsibility allows small local groupings to buy products not stocked throughout the system.

True, progress is a little lop-sided, the London area probably accounting for about half of all sales, while Scotland manages 2 per cent, but the message is that when Marks and Spencer begins to sell its own *boeuf Bourguignon* and *coq au vin* (as it has) then it is time for general action.

No sector is increasing by less than 10 per cent a year and some, like cottage cheese (a £2 million market), are galloping along at up to 50 per cent. French paté, at about £3 million, is managing 30 per cent, herbs, spices, canned pasta, prepared salads, all 20 per cent.

Fresh fruit and vegetables have particularly ripe potential. Imports of pineapples, avocados, peppers, mangoes and guavas have risen dramatically, in many cases doubling in a year. Peter Mitton of System Three points to sweet peppers which, with less than half the outlets, has twice the sales of premium quality marmalades and suggests that the appetite's there if more retailers can be brought in.

The researchers' principal practical tip for entrepreneurial explorers: markets undoubtedly now exist for the most uncompromisingly non-British products, but the real winners will be products presented as exotic variations of the things comfortably normal: game soup is a good example, while *chilli con carne* might do wonders for someone if presented as stewed meat with peppers. Twinings, they suggested, has already discovered this with its latest campaign pushing exotically imaged teas.

Missed by the report, which avoids what it considered to be the specifically ethnic, is the case of kosher foods. Here one old-established manufacturer, Rakusen's, is making for the mass market in a purposeful sort of way and has stirred into its tradition-orientated, largely Jewish sales force, new salesmen of the Procter and Gamble breed as shock troops to tackle the multiples at head office level. Ad agency Compton Partners was recently signed up too.

With some of its products like vegetable cooking oil already achieving a general appeal, the push is now on sweet and sour pickles. But the crunch comes with the matzo, a cracker with a built-in seasonal problem, since it is eaten mostly in the three months before Passover.

The matzo market features a private little battle between Rakusen's and Bonn's (which as a part of Carr's Biscuits is in the Cavenham empire).

Bonn's, which is credited with observing all the kosher regulations, such as stopping the production line when the rabbi calls to inspect. Rakusen's, which keeps the line flowing and turns a blind eye whenever tradition tampers with economics, claims sales of about £300,000 to Bonn's £60,000.

Now they are out to make matzo eaters of us all and so build up year-round sales. First problem: how do you design a pack of wide appeal yet traditional and old fashioned enough to hand on to your basic market?

29 December 1955
RING IN NEW IDEAS AT YOUR PARTY
Egon Ronay

The success of a party depends on many unforeseen elements. There is no fool-proof plan for it. But at least your New Year's Eve party is likely to be talked about if the food and drinks are different. Here are some of the things I have found successful which may be new to you.

Olives with aperitifs or at a cocktail party are banned from my home. They are so boring. A dish of rolled-up anchovies speared by cocktail sticks, crisp radishes and ⅛inch thick raw carrot slices with red pepper on them, is far more imaginative.

Unusual and always welcome start to a cold buffet supper (serve an hour before midnight at your New Year's Eve party) is a hot cup of consommé. Make it from richly selected vegetables and an inexpensive cut of rather fat beef.

Stuffed eggs are decorative and easy to do. Mix the hard-boiled yolks with mustard and butter, season, pipe into halved whites and cover with mayonnaise.

My favourite cold meat is a well-larded fillet of beef, bound before roasting to ensure round slices. It must be underdone and thinly sliced. Paper-thin salami-cornets, filled with grated raw horseradish, are colourful and thirst-making additions to the cold meat dish.

Gervais-filled celery-boats are a good finish. Better still is the Hungarian version of cream cheese. Mix thoroughly a fair quantity of ordinary cream cheese (about 1½ lb for 12 people) with enough paprika to turn it rusty-red, finely chopped onions, pepper, salt, caraway seeds and mustard.

Now we come to the drinks. Build up your guests' interest gradually. I like to receive my guests towards 10 p.m. with sherry or a dry Madeira – not forgetting whisky for the habit-bound. Then with a cold buffet such as I have suggested, most people would prefer lager, but some would like a dry white Mâcon or even a Beaujolais.

All this builds up to the pièce de résistance, a party drink with the widest appeal: the sentimentally mellow Bowle (pronounced Bowlé). It was popular at Court balls at Schönbrunn. The one-eyed English butler of the fabulous Count Nicky Eszterhazy out-shone his master in preparing it.

The first glass quenches the thirst, the second gives enjoyment, the third creates romance. The effects of the fourth are not recorded.

It is well worth the trouble of mixing it in advance. For 20–24 glasses, slice 6 peeled oranges and 1 peeled lemon into a large bowl standing on crushed ice. Cover with 5–6oz icing sugar. Leave for ½ hour. Add 1 bottle of Riesling or Niersteiner, 1 bottle Beaujolais, 2 measures of brandy and

2 measures of Curaçao (or Triple Sec or maraschino). Leave this mixture to stand and just before serving add a bottle of sparkling white wine or, indeed, a bottle of champagne for toasting the New Year.

I have never been to a party where the sparkle of the Bowle did not evoke the sparkle of gaiety.

Party drinks without solid tit-bits to eat amount almost to cruelty. But I would prefer even this fate to eternal sausage rolls. Try something new, marble-sized meatballs, made of finely minced, well-seasoned pork and veal (half and half), bound with egg and fried in oil.

These look attractive with cocktail sticks, arranged around a glass dish of mustard in which to dip them.

Surprisingly tasty are small cheese biscuits with Hungarian cream cheese spread thickly on them.

Whom Shall I Marry?

It was a New Year's Eve dumpling game that foretold my marriage. The bachelors of the party at my future in-laws' house in Budapest wrote their names on pieces of paper. These were rolled into individual dumpling-doughs and placed in boiling water. (It was – and still is – the sign of a great success to end a party in the kitchen.)

The girls fished out the cooked dumplings as they came to the surface one by one. Mine was fished out by my future wife. Her mother had mixed the dough and I have never stopped wondering...

Lead Shapes

Collect lead bottle-tops of an old piece of piping. Melt it quickly in a ladle over the fire. Each person in turn drops a little into a bowl of cold water. It solidifies into the weirdest shapes.

It is then up to the surrounding company to decide what the shapes indicate for your future. Some come out money-shaped, some like a house, others look like hearts.

OUR PET HATES OF 1971
Bon Viveur

Looking back on 1971 it seems that the spate of maddening, frustrating and sometimes frightening infliction upon housewives is increasing far too rapidly.

Do we agree that…

We are all sick and tired of struggling with Cellophane over-wrappings, or bending or breaking our nails trying to gain access to anything from biscuits, sweets and gift labels to chemists' medicaments?

We are thoroughly rebellious over biscuits and sweet packets which appear to be uniform half-pound size, but under their multifarious wrappings can contain as little as 5½oz.

Mrs Susan Vaux raises the questions: 'Do you not think it a kind of cheating to have different weights in packets which look identically sized?'

Concerning those empty milk bottles outside our doors: Susan and we maintain these have become weapons for vandals, besides being furiously time-wasting. 'Why can milk not be delivered in disposable boxes as on the Continent?' asks Susan. 'Then there would be no washing and putting out. We could just burn them.'

While we are about it, she and we want cream and cream cheese in proper cartons with replaceable lids, so that a portion can be scooped out easily and the lid replaced thereafter.

We are all absolutely fed-up with those cardboard cartons of cream which you have to scissor open, spread out on a working surface and scrape at with a knife in order to get the remaining cream off those terribly pleated cardboard walls! The waste of time, labour and cream is appalling.

Who else is infuriated besides us by the misuse of the English language and the contradictions in terms of that frightful phrase 'Fresh Frozen'? 'Fresh' is one thing 'Frozen' is another; both can be very good, but like male and female, they cannot be the same.

Why are we sold rabbit in pieces, bereft of heads, livers and kidneys? We need these items and our dishes lack flavour without them.

What has happened to pig's fry? That inexpensive but delicious English dish has, seemingly, vanished from the butchers' shops.

Wouldn't you, too, like to know what the skins of pork sausages are made of nowadays? We have tried chewing them, which is suspiciously like trying to eat your way through part of a pair of plastic baby-pants!

Best of all, can we go back to old-fashioned sausage skins please?

19 December 1976
WHAT'S COOKING IN THE BRITISH KITCHEN?
Marika Hanbury-Tenison

There is a popular belief, both among foreigners and ourselves, that we British are a conservative nation. Yet consider how our tastes in food and our eating habits have changed over the last hundred years.

Our kitchens reflect this change. A few years ago, when everyone was clamouring for food that could be prepared within the minimum of time and effort and when 'instant' on a packet made the product saleable, kitchens were as stark and streamlined as an operating theatre. Now there is a swing away from all that. Kitchens are becoming family rooms again, with stripped pine furniture and herbs hanging from the ceiling. Children do their homework at a scrubbed table while their mother cooks.

The pattern that emerges seems to be anything but conservative. We appear to have shown an almost chameleon-like capacity for accepting new trends, fashions and innovations; from being hearty John Bull trenchermen we seem to have turned into a nation of snack eaters, deep-frozen food fanatics and cosmopolitan gourmets.

This morning, for instance, you probably breakfasted off one of a selection of garishly packaged cereals, with a glass of orange juice, a cup of coffee perhaps, just because it is Sunday, an egg.

Things would have been very different in the 1870s. Breakfast for a middle-class family was a big meal with porridge, a selection of succulent dishes like kedgeree, grilled kidneys and mushrooms, bacon, devilled chicken bones, pickled salmon and a cold cut or two of game, with a ham and collared beef thrown in for good measure.

Then, and later, we were a nation of tea drinkers and proud of it. Tea filled the gap on every occasion. We drank it, well mashed, from thick mugs decorated with transfers of the Royal Family; we served it from elegant teapots with a choice of China or Indian, milk or lemon, one lump or two; in cups belonging to a fine bone tea set splattered with roses, and water was boiled in a silver kettle over a spirit lamp.

Are we in danger of becoming a nation of serious drinkers instead of tea addicts? Our consumption of spirits has doubled in the last 10 years, we drink nine million more gallons of beer annually than we did in 1966 and we are becoming fond of a glass of wine as any Continental. We start drinking younger and we go on drinking for longer than we used to. We are not yet up to the level of an ancestor of mine who, 200 years ago, drank, with a little help from four friends, 28 bottles of port in one sitting; and the consumption of gin in those days was horrific; but we certainly seem to be heading back that way.

In the 1870s the basic diet of the working people, for all meals, was bread and butter with only an occasional piece of bacon, an egg or a joint of pork, served with Yorkshire pudding, on Sundays. Take-away meals were already popular, thanks to pie, fish-and-chips and faggot-and-pea corner shops: what has radically changed over the years is the kind of food served. Now there are more than 17,000 takeaway shops in England. It is hard to find any of them serving food that could in any way be considered English.

Even our fish and chips these days are often cooked by Chinese; take-away chicken chow mein is eaten with a knife and fork, Kentucky Fried Chicken with the fingers, kebabs and doner kebabs are wrapped in Greek bread, taramasalata is sold by the tub, Italian pizzas are shovelled out by the hundred and German frankfurters, with or without onion and mustard, are ever popular. The man in the street is developing a confusing taste for food from all over the world.

In the 1970s the frozen food revolution suddenly took off in a big way. Freezer supermarkets sprouted overnight and home freezers became as essential a part of household furniture as a television or washing machine. Strawberries out of season were no longer the food of the rich, but became available to everyone all the year round, hamburgers could be bought by the dozen, peas could be served with any meal and even chips to go with everything were peeled, cooked, mashed and reconstituted to make for swifter cooking.

Patterns in food, like patterns in clothing, were already changing fast at the turn of the century when restaurants and public eating places began to make a great breakthrough. Escoffier in 1899 produced the first à la carte menu at the Carlton hotel. The Trocadero had already opened and for the first time it became acceptable for ladies to dine out and even to entertain. Lyons opened its first great Corner House, followed by a rash of tea shops where women, for the first time could go alone; and, indeed, Lyons became so popular that they were even employed to cater for parties at Buckingham Palace.

Now the Corner Houses of Piccadilly and Marble Arch have disappeared, but the popularity of restaurants goes from strength to strength. In the 1950s it was coffee bars and small bistros, then came the great infiltration of the Italian scene, followed by the Chinese restaurant, the kebab house and the Indian establishment. The only kind you don't see is an English restaurant, and the only place where an average working man can get anything approaching an English meal these days is in a pub, where hot and cold quick meals are becoming more and more popular.

Langan's Brasserie in Stratton Street is hitting the top of the restaurant bill at the moment. There, in an enormous room studded with parlour palms the trendsetters meet for lunch and dinner. Tables are so closely packed that waiters often have to serve across rather than around them. The air is thick with cigarette smoke and clients table-hop between courses. Clogs and cloth caps are in, diamonds and mink are out. Little is left of the Coq d'Or which the brasserie replaces. The cutlery and the champagne buckets are the same but the dark red plush has gone.

Peter Langan, an Irishman who probably knows more about the London restaurant scene than anyone else at the moment, opened Odine's restaurant, a small, cosy establishment much patronised by artists, 10 years ago. This was transferred to a larger restaurant next door with a more luxurious atmosphere, and followed by a bistro on the original site. The food is mainly Continental, the service is slow, but the ambience is just, it seems, what the younger swinging set want today.

'These days,' Peter Langan says, 'if they are going to eat out people want the best of all possible worlds. Bored with all their convenience foods at home they want to eat well for as little as they can. We cater for every culinary kook.

'I give them the best but with overheads soaring it isn't easy.' Restaurant food he feels, 'has improved beyond all measure since the 1960s but service has declined.

'Restaurants have improved because the British have become more aware of good food, they know what it is and they demand a higher standard. They will never reach the all-over standard of restaurants in France because the British are just not interested enough in good food. In France eating out is an extension of home life. In England the restaurateur tends to be the amateur rather than a professional.'

Perhaps the Second World War played the largest part of all in changing our tastes over the last hundred years. Suddenly, our eating habits levelled off at a stroke. From the Royal Family down, everyone had the same rations and although they may have seemed meagre at the time the nations' health flourished; rickets and obesity disappeared and there is no doubt that the restricted diet did us good. Being British we never took to eating horse as the French did but, urged on by the liquid voice of Lord Woolton, the Minister for Food, we nibbled at whale steads, dug for Britain and made amazingly *recherché* dishes from a few potatoes and a tin of corned beef.

Yes, but what about the good roast beef of old England? Has that gone forever? Sadly it seems as if it could be priced out of the market in the future. Roast chicken is beginning to take over, with one in every five families having it instead of the Sunday joint

Who leads the change in food patterns? Although trimmed down a little in the number of courses and dishes, a recent banquet at Buckingham Palace wasn't much different from one that would have been served 100 years ago in Queen Victoria's day: consommé, salmon, roast lamb with three vegetables, salad and a *Bombe Glacée Royale*, all heavily-disguised under French names.

Personally I believe it is the women who set the pattern. The kitchen is one place where they can really assert themselves, the temptations of the supermarkets are there to lure them, cookery writers bombard them with advice and encouragement and the television assures them that if they don't stuff their turkey they are not doing justice to their families.

Fashions of all kinds tend to go in cycles. It will be interesting to see, during the next five years, whether the economic crisis of today will lead us to experiment yet further into the instant, convenience food of the seventies or whether we will, as so many people predict, turn back to the simpler country style of our forefathers and the austere but nourishing food of wartime rationing.

25 September 1983
COOKERY QUIZ
Josceline Dimbleby

This competition, which entertained and educated our family while I was devising it, has been just as much fun to mark.

Where it transpired that there was more than one answer or a different view, I have taken it into consideration during the marking. Unfortunately, there was also a misprint in question 25(a) which, as a result, I didn't mark. For 'maple' you should have read 'apple', and therefore the answer would have been Germany.

The Answers
1. (a) Onions; (b) The Prince de Soubise, Marshal of France.
2. The American Indians.
3. Both are stuffed cabbage, one from Bulgaria, the other from Poland.
4. 1–b, 2–c, 3–e, 4–f, 5–a, 6–d.
5. The Medlar; all the rest are tropical.
6. Brillat-Savarin.
7. It is carried out at the beginning of the cooking, not at the end.
8. (b) Grilled with butter and parsley.
9. Samuel Johnson on cucumber.
10. (a) The Durian; (b) Because of its terrible smell.
11. (a) A wheel for cutting pastry; (b) Two earthenware pans which fit together; (c) A frying pan with two handles used in Spain for cooking rice.
12. Decorative radish flowers.
13. Clarified – the other three are ways of cooking eggs.
14. (a) Mexico; (b) Mole; (c) Spain and Italy.

15. 6,000.
16. (a) 16–18; (b) 1½–2 months; (c) Sturgeons' eggs.
17. (a) After the Resurrection, to Jesus in Jerusalem (Luke, 24, 42); (b) Aaron and his sons, Eleazar and Ithamar (Leviticus, 10, 14-19); (c) Her son (Kings, 11, 29).
18. (a) Aubergine; (b) Allspice; (c) Cape Gooseberry; (d) Courgette; (e) Banana; (f) Peanut oil; (g) Pawpaw.
19. Celery, Marmite, oysters, asparagus.
20. he name of a village near Naples, where the flour for true Pizza dough comes from; also a word for pie.
21. The avocado.
22. (a) Marinate it in fresh lime or lemon juice; (b) Ceviche; (c) South America.
23. a) Add vinegar to the water; (b) Smear it with lemon juice; (c) Prick them with a pin first; (d) Add a bay leaf or a piece of stale bread to the water; (e) Add a spot of oil to the cooking water.
24. (a) Marcel Proust; (b) Arnold Bennett; (c) Henry I; (d) The demoiselles Tatin; (e) Dame Nellie Melba; (f) Rossini; (g) Bisarck.
25. (a) Germany; (b) South India; (c) Balearic Islands; (d) Indonesia; (e) Spain; (f) Yugoslavia.

Acknowledgements

I would like to thank Gavin Fuller, Cerys Hughes and the library staff at the *Telegraph* for their kindness, support and help with my research – Gavin especially for his countless treks to the archive, fielding my many questions and letting me loose on the microfilm machine.

To all the editors, writers and contributors to the newspaper's food pages over the past 160 years: without you, none of this would be possible.

Thank you also to my editors, Fiona Hardcastle and Liz Hunt, for giving me the time and encouragement to pursue this project; and the team at Aurum – particularly the brilliant Melissa Smith – for making it such an enjoyable process.

To my parents, Philip and Susan, thank you for always being there for your endless words of wisdom and for bringing me up to have such a hearty appetite.

Finally, thank you to Michael, my wonderful husband-to-be, for inspiring me, putting up with me and letting me be in your team. I owe you a lifetime of cricket weekends.